A Foundation Course for Graphic Designers
Working in Print, Moving Image and Digital Media

# GRAPHICDESIGNSCHOOL

SIXTH EDITION

A Foundation Course for Graphic Designers
Working in Print, Moving Image and Digital Media

# GRAPHICDESIGNSCHOOL

DAVID DABNER / SANDRA STEWART / ERIC ZEMPOL / ABBIE VICKRESS

First published in the United Kingdom in 2017 by
Thames & Hudson Ltd, 181A High Holborn,
London WC1V 7QX

British Library Cataloguing-in-Publication Data
A catalogue record for this book is available from the
British Library

ISBN: 978-0-500-29285-3

Printed and bound in China

To find out about all our publications, please visit
www.thamesandhudson.com. There you can subscribe to
our e-newsletter, browse or download our current
catalogue, and buy any titles that are in print.

# Contents

# Introduction

This book is written with the intent of providing an introduction to the underlying principles of good graphic design, whether it is print-based, digital or environmental. The content has been constructed to mirror, in part, how the subject is taught in college design programmes, and the visuals, which are a mixture of student projects and professional design work, have been carefully chosen to illuminate specific teaching points. Many of the sections contain step-by-step exercises and assignments, offer practical advice and point towards further resources.

The first part of the book, Principles, supports the idea that a thorough understanding of design principles should support the process of creating design works in response to specific briefs and problems, while allowing room for self-authored experimentation and visual freedom. As you are introduced to the basics of research, typography, colour, photography and composition, you will learn to become visually aware and able to articulate these design principles into your future works. You will also come to understand that these principles cross disciplines and are the vocabulary of visual literacy.

In the second part of the book, Practice, you will be introduced to invaluable practical skills that are important support systems to the skill sets of research and creative process that you will have read about in Part One. They do not replace them, but serve as methods and practices for developing critical problem-solving skills and learning to manage complex projects. Designers need the whole range of skills to be truly successful, and expertise will come with continued study and practice in both areas. Unless you learn the practical skills and technology of design production, including how to manage images, create digital files for specific media, and design, build and structure a website, you will be unable to bring your brilliant concepts to life.

None of these visual skills can be viewed in isolation from the context in which design happens and its larger role in society and the world. Designers are visual communicators, often giving visual voice to new and provocative ideas. They create images that can inform, persuade and entertain millions of people. This comes with great responsibility, and it is necessary to be aware of the role of design in shaping the world we live in, and changes in the discipline that transcend trends or the latest software. While any kind of comprehensive account of these topics stands outside the scope

of this book, becoming visually literate and technically skilled should go hand in hand with an understanding of such issues as global audiences, communication theories, systems theory, sustainable issues in design and the changing role of technology.

Finally, design education is a lifelong experience that can bring great personal satisfaction and reward. Technologies, styles and demands change rapidly in this industry and, as a result, graphic design is a subject to be taken on with independence and an expectation of lifelong learning and commitment. With this book as a gateway, a new way of seeing the world may lead you to a career path that will be a constant source of surprise and delight.

# Principles

The first part of this book is concerned with design principles, the building blocks that connect the basics of all good design. Every discipline has its own set of rules, methods, technical requirements and specialised technologies. Each one is rooted in the interactions of its history, theory and practice, but unlike learning law or biology, the language of design is visual. It involves the need for a highly developed awareness of visual relationships, proportion, the perceptions of visual principles, and of the modern world and its complex events and practices. A good designer can filter this information and create relevant, engaging, visually eloquent design that responds to multiple problems, needs and contexts. While a design student needs to develop the research, concept-development, compositional and organisational skills associated

with design, he or she also needs to be engaged with the world, and interested, aware and sensitive to the changing contexts in which design plays a part.

Chapter 1 introduces the primary and secondary research skills needed by designers, followed by an introduction to theories of image, the importance of audience, and of organising your work and time. In Chapter 2, the idea of form is spotlighted. Form involves composition of the fundamentals of design (text, image, proportion, space, colour, scale) and requires an understanding of the visual dynamics created by combining them with intent. Understanding form comes from the ability to see intrinsic and subtle qualities in the various design elements, and the observation of, and sensitivity to, the changing relationships between them. Chapter 3 introduces typography, a core skill for all designers that is layered with complexity, and cannot be understated for its beauty, history, versatility and ability to influence an audience. Developing a deep understanding of typography is of critical importance. Chapter 4 introduces colour as one of the primary tools in the language of design, including theory, terminology, associations, issues of legibility and emotional response. Managing colour and understanding its ability to communicate are skills that also evolve with greater understanding of its influences. Whatever design discipline you ultimately pursue, from editorial art direction to web and motion graphics, these basic principles will give you a solid foundation and serve as the groundwork for further exploration and understanding of design and the role of the designer.

PART 1

# 1

# Research
and Concepts

The first step towards becoming
interesting is to be interested. The
best creatives of all kinds – painters,
designers, writers, sculptors, musicians,
playwrights – make the world their
inspiration, and draw ideas and content
from both experience and research.
They make it a priority to stay aware
of what is happening, not only within the
world of design, but in the world in
general, and this level of engagement
enriches their work.

" What you see and hear depends
a good deal on where you are
standing; it also depends on what
kind of a person you are "

*C. S. Lewis*

### ➔ Observe and collect
Research should be specific to
each project, but the process of
observation and recording your
impressions should be ongoing,
and should become a part of your
daily routine. When something
catches your eye, document it;
capture an image and put it into
your notebook/sketchbook/device
for reference later. Everything you
come in contact with can inform
your work, so make sure you have
a great collection of objects and
impressions for inspiration.

**Modern media demands an increasing amount of
visual information to illustrate its content in print, packaging
and motion graphics, in the built environment or online. Graphic
designers are the conduits for all types of communications from
multiple sources to specific audiences, and to be successful
they must be well-informed, accomplished researchers with
inquisitive natures.**

### Broaden your outlook
Designers who seek information from the greatest range
of references are those who successfully communicate
with people of all ages, professions and lifestyles, and
who properly contextualise their design work.

• Read about events from multiple sources. Compare
  stories, noting how information about the same
  events changes, how the language is used to target
  various audiences, and what type of imagery is used
  to support the text. Never rely solely on editable web
  postings or crowd-sourced information for accuracy
  if you are researching facts.
• You can never read enough books, but don't limit
  yourself to the kind you usually read. Reading only

about graphic design can be particularly dangerous: although extremely useful for information and guidance, this may turn you into an armchair expert; you want to be an original practitioner. Expand your reading to include novels and plays, and books on sculpture, architecture, art history, cooking, sports, archaeology, travel and maths – it really doesn't matter, as long as they provide you with a broad spectrum of knowledge.

- Be open to new experiences. Visit galleries, clubs, retail environments, archives and museums you've never been to, listen to music you've not heard before, and eat food you've never tried before. Travel whenever you can, and learn about global issues and cultural treasures.

- Share ideas and listen to people. Create surveys and facilitate interviews, have conversations with real people. Whatever language they use, there is always a way to establish communication, if you try. Pay attention to what inspires them, and learn from others while also sharing your insights.

- Online research can be quick and provide extensive results, but also an un-unique solution. Try other forms of research to avoid duplicating the obvious ideas.

⬆ **Experimentation reveals possibilities** The journey from a posted process board to a final design is always different, but the research and process itself is the teaching tool of design. In these images, you can follow the evolution of the designer's process and see how variation leads to discovery.

⬇ **Look closely at details** Through the simplification of the forms, the enlargement of the dot screen pattern and the placement of layers, the enlarged and cropped letterforms become fluid, artistic subjects that are vibrant with colour.

## RESEARCH TECHNIQUES

| Primary sources/<br>Factual research | Secondary sources/<br>Factual research |
|---|---|
| • Previous knowledge/opinion/<br>  memory<br>• Observation<br>• Conversation<br>• Analysis<br>• Role-play<br>• Interviews: in person or by email,<br>  online chat or phone<br>• Questionnaires<br>• Focus groups<br>• Commissioned video/written diaries<br>  (first hand)<br>• Ethnographic research ('deep<br>  hanging out') | • Museums, archives, collections<br>• Newspapers, magazines, journal<br>  articles<br>• Published interviews<br>• Films, TV broadcasts, theatre<br>• Transcripts/recordings of film,<br>  TV, radio<br>• Books<br>• Music<br>• Internet: blogs, websites, forums,<br>  magazines<br>• Surveys<br>• Statistics<br>• Organisations, agencies,<br>  gatekeepers<br>• Lectures, public debates,<br>  conferences |
| **Primary sources/<br>Visual research** | **Secondary sources/<br>Visual research** |
| • Photography<br>• Drawing/sketching<br>• Media experimentation: 2D and 3D<br>• Rubbings/casts<br>• Typographic experimentation<br>• Compositional experimentation<br>• Image manipulation<br>• Photocopying<br>• Video recording<br>• Audio recording<br>• Writing | • Exhibitions<br>• Images/photographs from<br>  magazines, books, leaflets, Internet,<br>  billboards<br>• Work by other designers/artists<br>• Printed maps/diagrams<br>• Ephemera (e.g. tickets, receipts,<br>  packaging)<br>• Found or bought photographs,<br>  postcards, posters, drawings<br>• Imagery taken from films, video,<br>  performances<br>• Architecture |

**Other general work practices/approaches**
• Put your own point of view into the subject
• Work in groups and respond to feedback from others
• Develop ideas by generating a number of visuals in response to one idea
• Explore the full capacity of your visual language

### Record it all

Constant, direct observation is one of the most important tools a designer uses, and learning to look at anything as a designer requires attention to minute detail, and the inclusion of all things that surround the object of your focus. Consider your way of seeing as a kind of inner zoom lens that draws you in and away from a point of observation. As you learn to see with a designer's eye, ordinary things you may have seen before can become amazing sources of inspiration. It can be as simple as a pattern of lace juxtaposed against flat, wide stripes, or as unexpected as the geometry revealed by light and shadow in an architectural setting. Textures, patterns, colours and visual relationships will begin to have a profound effect on the way you think about your design process.

With this in mind, every practising designer should carry some form of recording device, such as a sketchbook, camera, smartphone, video camera, or whatever works best for you. Make time for observation and research, taking it seriously as an integral part of your work. Designers, artists, writers and illustrators all frequently keep scrapbooks/sketchbooks/collections of material that interests them. These bits of inspiration need not have a clear purpose when collected, but the material will become an archive of ideas and inspiration from which to draw on at a later date.

If something commands your attention, sketch it, write about it, photograph it, upload it, or file it away immediately. Collect ideas and build upon initial thoughts by writing, drawing or sketching. Not only will your drawing and research skills improve by doing this consistently, but over time you will have built yourself a 'catalogue of inspiration' that can be drawn upon at any point in your career, and will become especially useful when you are short of ideas. This kind of practised research helps you to begin defining your own outlook, and to develop a distinctive visual voice.

**Multiply the possibilities** Collect multiple images
of every subject, and vary your techniques as you photograph.
Each of these pictures captures a slightly different sensibility
in light, colour, shadow and composition. When they are
combined with deconstructed typography that echoes the
abstract forms revealed in the photos, the results are striking.

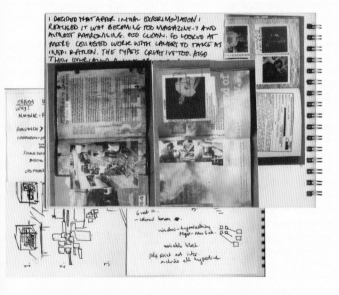

**Ideas are organic** They can grow from a single phrase,
the sum of a series of images, or a combination of both.
Record the evolution of your thinking process in whatever
manner is meaningful for you. When you reference
the sequence of your observations, they can become
visualised as layers in a composition or simply lead you
to the most relevant point in image or text.

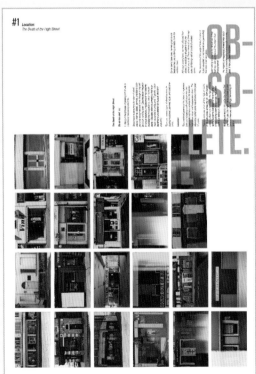

| PART 1 | PRINCIPLES |
|---|---|
| CHAPTER 1 | RESEARCH AND CONCEPTS |
| MODULE 2 | **Linear reasoning/lateral thinking** |

**In the initial stages of concept development, the two main ways to approach a design brief are to use linear reasoning and lateral thinking. These are virtually opposites – the first focused and methodical, the second diffuse and expansive – but both are equally useful as research and development tools.**

Linear reasoning implies a strategic thought process, using step-by-step logic, and follows a specific trajectory. This kind of reasoning frequently involves a pre-determined idea or concept that is then worked towards in stages. Generally, this will involve splitting the idea up into manageable components, considering colour, type, composition and scale, and working each through to finalise the form to fit the concept.

Lateral thinking involves indirect exploration, generating ideas that are less readily available by linear reasoning (or hidden by the linear process, so that less obvious associations aren't readily seen or generated). The emphasis is on indirect, creative forms of research. Edward de Bono coined the term in 1967.

Brainstorming, or sketching in a non-linear diagrammatic way, approaches problems by exploring each component in as much depth and breadth as possible, finding connections and associations that work to strengthen the concept. This process aims to push achievable boundaries. Think of it as if it were a walk through a city. You may set out knowing exactly where you are going, focused on the end goal: reaching your destination. Alternatively, you could just stroll along the streets without any predetermined destination in mind. Each will provide very different experiences; in the non-predetermined form, you may notice things along the way that are not obvious if your sights are set only on reaching your destination.

You might consider beginning with a lateral thinking session – where you brainstorm as many ideas as possible – in order to generate your initial ideas, then move on to a more linear process at a later stage. The two are not necessarily mutually exclusive, but often complementary ways of researching a design problem.

**GLOSSARY**

**Lateral thinking:** A form of research where the emphasis is on indirect, creative forms of inquiry and thinking.

**Linear reasoning:** A form of thinking that implies strategic thought process, one in which step-by-step logic is employed.

⊕ **SEE ALSO:** BASICS OF RESEARCH, P10

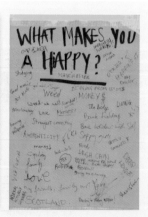

## EXAMPLE – GETTING STARTED

Your first brainstorming sessions can be intimidating, so it will help, initially, to work with familiar tools and to combine linear and lateral thinking. Until you are able to think in pictures, begin with words. Make a list of absolutely everything that comes to mind when you consider your brief. Then, make a secondary list of things associated with each item on your first list.

**Brief**
Design a logo for the Folklore Museum. It should be elegant, lighthearted and whimsical enough to attract families, but sophisticated enough to appeal to researchers and scholars of folklore.

**1** Once you have determined the usage of the logo and the type of audience the client would like to reach, you can begin your descriptive lists, drilling down to as many levels as you need to bring images to mind. Discard nothing at this stage; just allow your mind to make associations freely. There's no such thing as a bad idea in the creative process; there are only some that are more appropriate than others.

**2** When your lists are lengthy enough to allow you to visualise individual items from your columns, you can combine two or more thoughts from different columns into one image, and you are ready to begin sketching. One idea will always lead to another, so never settle for just one, and save all of your ideas as you work through the process. You may find the seed of something brilliant hidden in an idea you nearly discarded.

**Folklore**
*magic* ➡ *wand, sorcerer*
*prince/princess* ➡ *crown, castle*
*good/evil* ➡ *light/dark*
*homespun* ➡ *cottage*
*nature* ➡
  *animals* ➡ *frogs, goats, birds*
  *plants* ➡ *lilypads*

**Museum**
*display* ➡ *exhibits signage*
*Information sources* ➡ *books, objects, antiquities*
*objects* ➡ *natural, invented*

⬆ **Thematic variation** All three of these logos are drawn from the associations recorded first in words, and everything about the design work is influenced by those ideas, from the choice of image to the selection of the typeface.

⬅ **Lateral or linear?**
Whether your process unfolds in an orderly sequence or a random scatter of thoughts, the process of discovery and the sequential development of an idea are exciting parts of the design process. Relax, examine your recorded research and let the ideas flow. The more experience you have using these methods, the faster you will generate ideas.

| PART 1 | PRINCIPLES |
| --- | --- |
| CHAPTER 1 | RESEARCH AND CONCEPTS |
| MODULE 3 | **Exploratory drawing** |

Exploratory drawing is a means of translating the outside world and of giving concrete form to abstract ideas. Sketching and drawing engage you in a constant process of observation, and help you understand the world around you. Whereas computer technology is another tool for the development of ideas, you should treat drawing as the basis of expression that underpins your design decisions.

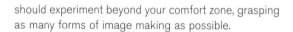

Representational, or observational, drawing (drawing used to document) allows you to see the subject as a shape or a series of shapes, and colour as tones and hues. It teaches you to understand and manipulate perspective, to understand how an object exists in space, and to create the illusion of space and depth, and shows you how to convey texture and density. Non-representational, or non-observational, drawing, where your expression is freed from the need to represent what is seen and the result is a gestural abstraction, can generate valuable expressive drawn responses, and is widely used.

In representational drawing, train your eye to see diverse subject matter in detail. Studies of still life and life drawing train your eye to observe static objects in detail from a series of points of view, and evaluate the relationship of the surrounding space to the objects of study. These alternate views and perspectives will stimulate a variety of moving and static subject matter, which in turn changes how you draw. You can work directly in a sketchbook, or photograph your subjects for reference for more finished drawings at a later date. It is important to familiarise yourself with as many diverse aspects of form as possible.

You can always develop your drawing, regardless of how good you feel you already are. Continual practice is the key, and drawing should be a lifelong activity. You should experiment beyond your comfort zone, grasping as many forms of image making as possible.

**Understanding tools**

Experiment with a variety of media, to determine and affect your created image. Whether charcoal or pencil, crayon or brush, each tool you use requires some understanding of its specific effects and mark-making qualities. For example, pencils allow tonal control, detailed modelling and a strong line, whereas ink and brush will generate an entirely different mark. Try not to limit yourself to conventional media; other implements, such as a toothbrush for a spatter effect, a piece of string, or even a sewing machine, can create interesting images. The aim is not merely to interpret the objects pictorially (representing them as they look) but to interpret the image in your own way. All forms of drawing have their value and purpose, and should be treated as equally valid.

**Understanding form**

There are no lines around an object. It consists of its own solid form, defined by the light and shadow that illuminate and surround it. Creating black-and-white drawings, or studies, is the best way to begin to understand form. As you render your study from real life, you are translating the language of colour into a tonal

**Abstraction:** An aesthetic concept describing something that is drawn from the real, but has been 'distilled' to its barest minimum form, colour or tone, often removed from its original context.

**Documentation:** The recording in written, visual or aural form of what is of interest.

**Representation:** Something that looks like, resembles or stands for something else. In drawing, this is also known as figurative, since it deliberately attempts to mimic the thing drawn.

**Thinking in pictures** Tight contour line drawings are used to explore the relationships between new and supplied elements in these studies for elaborate Nike packaging. Each study is carefully composed to fit within a particular space on the package and on the product before the colour is assigned. See also the finished artwork on page 55.

greyscale, substituting monochromatic values for the spectrum in the existing object.

Be as direct and spontaneous as is possible. For immediacy, do several studies in a short space of time. Use materials to describe form and mass as areas of colour, replacing a monochromatic scheme, while using an outline only as a guide to subsequent layers. Concentrate not on an end product, but on the process of a rich description of forms.

Figurative drawing from observation can produce beautiful studies, but it is also the tool that will sharpen your sketching abilities, and will eventually help generate ideas as you work through a design problem. As you draw, you will notice that what you choose to include and what you choose to exclude are equally important. As an object exists in space, so your drawing lives within the finite boundary of a page, and the relationship of the study to the page is part of the image.

When you complete a study, consider recreating the same subject with different media, eliminating all but the most necessary of descriptive marks. A gradual abstraction of the figurative image will help you to discover more about structure, form and spatial relationships as you work.

**Options** Multiple studies are roughed in and considered during the creative process. Promotional material for the band Runaway Dorothy is shown in stages of development. The position the display typography might occupy is considered as a shape in the composition before any style selections are made, and changes in perspective and scale are incorporated in the final illustration of the dog.

Early sketches for second study show the development of the concept and the changes in viewpoint that made it more moody in the final illustration.

| PART 1 | PRINCIPLES |
| CHAPTER 1 | RESEARCH AND CONCEPTS |
| MODULE 4 | **Visualising ideas** |

**Visualise and organise**
Your first sketches can be loose and expressive. Try variations, and do as many thumbnails as you can think of before you begin to finalise the idea.

**All designers need to develop the skill of putting ideas down on paper. This involves preparing rough visuals/design sketches – thumbnails, scamps or roughs. Students often tend to bypass this process and set about producing ideas directly on screen. This practice can inhibit the development of ideas, because you may restrict yourself to only those images you are capable of producing with the available technology. It's better to think freely at first, and to produce as many ideas as you can sketch.**

Initial ideas are generated more quickly and prolifically if you do a bit of brainstorming, recording your thoughts rapidly using various diagrammatic methods or other ways to structure information.

Start with your word lists, and as you begin to think in pictures, move on to sketching directly. In this process, co-ordination between brain, eye and hand can be amazingly fast, and by working quickly you can generate many diverse (and sometimes unexpected) ideas, concepts and associations. Your mind starts flowing and loosening up, and becomes open to the diverse aspects of the project, swiftly moving the thought process forwards. Literal and non-literal, lateral and non-lateral forms of thinking are used to maximum effect in these early sketches.

**Roughs and thumbnails**
There is no predetermined size for rough drawings. Thumbnails are, as the term suggests, small. Designers usually begin with thumbnails, a series of rapidly drawn,

**Putting it all together** Looking spontaneous takes time. Finished artwork may be the result of experiments in various media and techniques, and it may be the sum of many successful combinations. Once you have the concept and the general proportions in mind, consider the best way to execute the style you want to communicate. Then, determine the right tool for the right job, and use as many as you need to get the right visual language for your message. For this poster promoting an exhibition of rock 'n' roll music posters, the artist wanted an image that expressed the concept of 'art at 1000 decibels', a part of the copy line on the poster.

First, a sans-serif typeface was selected and type treatments were designed on computer in several variations, then printed in black and white. The result felt too static.

The printed type was placed on a copy machine and the paper copy was moved during the copying process to blur the image. Several versions were scanned back into the computer, and the best were combined and cropped. The balloon form was added.

The bird was hand drawn with pen and ink, and the hands were drawn separately.

stamp-sized compositions that block out the general structure and content of a design. Thumbnails should be spontaneous and prolific; they are the recorded thought process of developing ideas and should move as rapidly as you can think. Obviously, this can leave no time for the inclusion of any detail or refinement. These will be considered in the final stages of design development. Thumbnails that have the most interesting potential are selected and a rough, larger, loose drawing, with more detail but as yet still unfinished, is created that further develops the composition and placement on the page.

### Drawing by hand

Although roughs require a certain degree of drawing skill, these will be learned easily for this kind of work, where the generation of ideas is the focus, not drawing as an end in itself. This is unlike observational drawing, or drawing as documentation, which needs to be precise. Hand-drawn ideas can be vague and leave a lot to the imagination, which can be a good thing. Excluding detail from the sketch will allow you to leave your options open for more deliberate decisions at a later point in concept development. Remember, the 'big idea' is the most important part of the process at this stage.

Once you have a number of ideas sketched out, you can step back and make judgments regarding their value, and potential for development, without having committed to any design in detail. This allows maximum flexibility and fluidity in the design process.

An important advantage of developing the ability to produce quick, effective roughs is that when presenting ideas to clients, alternatives can be quickly sketched out, keeping your approach fresh and relatively unrestricted. This, in turn, gives clients confidence in your willingness to be flexible and open-minded, while also showing your design abilities.

### Computers and visualisation

Roughs are usually generated on a sketchpad. When generated on a computer, roughs tend to look too fixed and polished, and students can be reluctant to change or refine them. Wait until you have a sketch that excites you, then scan it and look at it on screen.

Once you have chosen an idea or shortlist of ideas that you feel may have potential, computers come into their own, because they enable you to produce as many alternate versions of your ideas as you wish, changing colours, typefaces, line weights and images. Typefaces and grid measurements become fluid decisions when you are working digitally, and you don't need to commit immediately. In fact, it may be better not to. It's fast and easy to change these on screen.

**GLOSSARY**

**Brainstorming:** A visual aid to thinking laterally and exploring a problem, usually by stating the problem in the centre of a page and radiating outward spokes for components of the problem. Each component can then be considered separately with its own spokes, so that each point, thought or comment is recorded.

**Roughs:** Loosely drawn compositions from thumbnail drawings.

**Thumbnail:** Small, rough visual representation of the bigger picture or final outcome of a design.

⊕ **SEE ALSO:** LINEAR REASONING/LATERAL THINKING, P14

The artist added a washy ink texture to the background, and added a bit more onto the top of the artwork by taping it to the top. All the elements were scanned into the computer and assembled electronically.

When all of the additional typography was complete, the artist explored several colour variations (above) until they were pleased. Two different colour versions were printed: the magenta one (right) and a predominantly cyan version (not pictured).

| PART 1 | PRINCIPLES |
| --- | --- |
| CHAPTER 1 | RESEARCH AND CONCEPTS |
| MODULE 5 | **Theories of image and text** |

The success of visual communication depends on the ability to reach a targeted audience and elicit a desired response. Sometimes the response is an immediate call to action and a clear, concise message with little open to interpretation. Most often, visual imagery is used to evoke an emotional state that will put the viewer in the appropriately receptive frame of mind to receive the message targeted at them.

Designers influence the message through the development of provocative imagery that may persuade, shock, entertain and provoke with purpose. In order for designers to speak clearly and visually say exactly what they mean, they need to develop a clear and strong visual language.

### Rhetoric

With its origins attributed to ancient public speaking in Greece and Rome, rhetoric is a skill of persuasion most often associated with politics and public speaking. To construct a strong rhetorical speech, ancient philosophers used something kindred to contemporary design thinking to define and refine the categories of invention, arrangement, style, memory and delivery within a compelling dialogue. If we examine these subjects as design vocabulary, the same can be said for the construction of a successful and equally compelling visual. In visual communication, the concept of visual rhetoric usually describes the visual tone of voice chosen for a given communication task.

⤊ **Make an impression** Each of these approaches to package design has a distinct message. The chocolates packages are as rich in colour as they are in content. With luxurious metallics, deep saturated colour and intricate graphics, they invite elegant indulgence with every design decision. The clean simplicity of the die-cut labels on the bottles allows the actual ingredients to become the vibrant colour in the artwork, promising freshness and the visual implication of 'nothing added'.

⤢ **Didactics** Information graphics should be beautiful in addition to delivering a body of information in a clear and immediate way. Economical use of space and carefully considered typography are essential for clear communication.

→ **Universal messages**
The pictograms used in the 1972 Munich Olympics set the standard for subsequent Olympic designs. Each sporting event is clearly represented through an economy of line and shape, yet each symbol is visually strong enough for signage and promotional use at any size.

↑ **Dependable artwork** International symbols transcend language and communicate instantly. The appearance of a symbol can vary greatly in style through line weights and positive/negative balance, as long as the symbol is easily understood. Symbols like these in public places play a part in public safely.

## Semiotics, signs and symbols

Ferdinand de Saussure is generally acknowledged as the father of semiotics. His theory divides signs, or all things that represent meaning, into two categories: the signifier and the signified. The signifier is the symbol that represents something from which meaning can be extracted; the signified is the actual object or meaning it represents. For example, the universal symbol, or signifier, for a male or female public toilet has instant recognition that transcends languages, and the signified is the actual toilet. This type of non-verbal vocabulary of signs has increasing relevance in the global reach of contemporary communications and, when designed well, can command instant recognition.

## Didactics

The term 'didactics' refers to clear, pragmatically delivered information and instruction with unambiguous meaning. Airport signage, road signs and warnings are prime examples of didactic information. It is important to note that nuance can be added to most visuals, even in the strictest definition of category: didactic panels in museum exhibitions must deliver clear information, but can be associated with the subject matter in inventive visual ways.

## Symbol style

Signs can be simple or complex, depending on the accompanying message. A denotative sign denotes exactly what it pictures and should be visually direct, but can convey secondary information through the use of a particular style. A connotative sign will be single-minded and may convey a range of associated messages that are to be interpreted by the viewer. Symbols and signs can have rich layers of associated meaning.

The Olympic symbols are prime examples of design defining attitude. The symbol for swimming usually doesn't change much in content, but the designer may also assign an element of playfulness, structure and discipline, or reference other time periods through the use of line weight, drawing style or colour. The five interlocking rings of the Olympic symbol itself represent the five continents or major geographical areas of the world that participate in the games. Exposure to the Olympic symbol, over time, has elevated it to iconic stature and it may now evoke an emotional response in some through its association with the actual events.

## Symbol families

Complex systems and extended families of symbols usually share common essential criteria. They have clarity and are easily recognisable with a simple message. All symbols in the system share a look, with similar treatment in line, style, weight and scale. They are easy to reproduce in any size and will retain clarity, and are flexible enough to be combined with other elements, and will still remain distinctive.

↑ **Identity to icon** The first Apple Computer, Inc. logo was designed by Ron Wayne, a co-founder of Apple Computer. The original was illustrative and included a full image of Sir Isaac Newton sitting under an apple tree with type in a traditional banner arrangement as an integrated border. That logo was replaced in 1977 by graphic designer Rob Janoff, with an image of a rainbow-striped apple with a bite taken out of it. The bite was added for scale, so that the image would not be mistakenly identified as a cherry. This monochrome version was adapted in 1999.

↑ **Abstract icon** The Nike 'Swoosh' was designed in 1971 by Carolyn Davidson. Originally, it appeared with the word NIKE above it. As the brand's recognition grew, the trademark was gradually streamlined.

### Metaphors

Signs and symbols are primary sources in the design and development of logos and trademarks, and are essential in the development of the visual metaphor, an image that will trigger associations to other meanings or signifiers, and is connotative in nature. A visual metaphor might be as obvious as a lightbulb to signify an idea, a heart to signify love, or a book to represent learning. Logos become metaphors for the business, goods or service they represent through association, and some become so memorable that they need no words to explain them.

Carolyn Davidson designed the Nike 'Swoosh' in 1971. Originally, it appeared accompanied by the word 'NIKE'. As the brand grew, the trademark was streamlined to the positive tick/wing of the current version.

### Poetics

Some of the most involving design work can deliberately engage the viewer for much longer periods of time. With current media, the attention span of a target audience is shortened by the number of competing stimuli encountered daily, and by the availability of viewing options, handheld and environmental. They can pull your audience in too many directions to concentrate on your message. If you can engage your audience members, they are more likely to remember what you have told them or to associate your message with a visual style that can be revisited.

Poetic forms of work have much less immediately accessible meaning, and the message is deliberately left open to interpretation. Graphic designers make

↑ **Connotations** This book cover illustration uses visual connotations of industry to allude to inventiveness and power. The combination of these themes and the dark, unsettling colour palette hints at the violent and peculiar civilisations featured in the series of short stories.

↑ **Colour** The use of striking shapes and the combination of textures in this bold illustration convey simultaneous messages of adventure, encounters and friendship. The colourful narrative is alluded to through the use of line, colour and composition.

↑ **Concept** Without resorting to clichés of space, robots and time travel, the illustrator has used composition and subtle photographic and block-colour collage to portray the book's themes of technology, theology, intelligence and human nature.

conscious decisions to leave the work open to provoke thoughtful responses, to stir controversy, or to tease. Ad campaigns, posters, and book and publication design are examples of media that can support more complex visual allegory, and the illustrative and graphic works that support them are often produced though a range of media and stand as works of art in their own right. Poetic work can be seen as the polar opposite of didactic, but all graphic design is visual communication, and the decision to use one or the other is part of the designer's problem-solving process.

**Didactic:** A pragmatic and unambiguous method of giving clear information.

**Metaphor:** Word or image that sets up associations; for example, a 'piece of cake' is a metaphor for easy.

**Poetic:** A style that is less clear, but more artistic, more open to interpretation.

**Rhetoric:** A style of arguing, persuading or engaging in dialogue. For a designer, it is a way of engaging the targeted audience.

**Semiotics:** A system that links objects, words and images to meanings through signs and signifiers.

**Symbolism:** A way of representing an object or word through an image, sound or another word; for example, a crossed knife and fork on a road sign means a café is ahead.

⊕ **SEE ALSO:** AUDIENCES, MARKETS AND CONCEPTS, P24

STEREOTELESCOPE
8:00 PM TT THE BEAR'S FRIDAY 4.8 CAMBRIDGE

ANIMAL
COLLECTIVE

FRIDAY MARCH 23 - 7PM
First Unitarian Church
2125 Chestnut Street Philadelphia, PA

◀ **Poetic ambiguity**
These poetic images use colour and composition to imply and suggest, but leave conclusions to the viewer. The suggestion of telescoping movement is accomplished through a series of colour blocks carefully placed to move the eye around the graphic, and maximises the placement of complementary colours.

◀ **Softer suggestion**
A painterly loose wash of colour in a cascade design might express animal markings, the bars of a cage, or liquid, or simply set a mood, depending on how the viewer interprets the imagery. These images are deliberately ambiguous, and invite a longer examination.

⬇ **Plan ahead** Try to keep track of your process hours and plan ahead to ensure that you meet your deadlines.

| Job ref | |
|---|---|
| Client | |
| Job description | |

| | |
|---|---|
| *April 1* | Research completed |
| *April 15* | Sketches/concept development<br>*Materials considered*<br>*Samples ordered* |
| *April 20* | Presentation sketches/roughs |
| *April 22* | Client meeting |
| *April 30* | Refined comprehensive concepts (comps) |
| *May 5* | Revisions |
| *May 8* | Client meeting |
| *May 15* | Finished files |

⬆ **Development** After some comprehensive research, it is important to get your ideas down on paper. In this example for Green Structural Engineering, the designer has experimented with sketches and comps to incorporate the feeling of structure. This can be seen in the diagrammatic construction of various elements of the drawings.

⬆ **Refinement** When the concept is developed and sketches have advanced your ideas, start to digitise your strongest visuals to aid discussions with the client. Use grid systems and a range of colour palettes to experiment with the visual balance of the designs.

⬆ ➡ **Presentation and production** Comprehensive designs that simulate the finished product are presented for approval before the artwork is sent into production. At this stage it is important to consider the output for your visuals. This logo, for example, needs to work in print on small business cards, on a digital platform such as a website, and on a large scale for onsite boards.

---

🛈 **Remember**
• Write everything down. Don't rely on memory.
• Without a relevant concept, your visualisation has no meaning.
• Try creating a flowchart/spider diagram with routes for different ideas.
• Look for professional criticism and use it constructively.
• Talk about your work. Learn to be articulate, and explain your intentions, influences and solutions.

Over longer jobs there may be only one deadline per week (for example, interim presentations to the client); on shorter jobs this may be two deadlines per day (for example, multiple proof stages). One way to organise ideas into sequence is to write everything down on self-adhesive reminder notes and put them in a logical order. Job jackets, envelopes with deadline lists, approvals, and everything else related to the job, help keep track of multiple projects.

If you'd rather do it all electronically, software programs such as Excel and applications such as Evernote can be invaluable in plotting job progress and in maintaining an overview. Organise your digital files logically, making sure everyone working on the project knows the system, and back up your files regularly. You can create a timetable with each checkpoint assigned a date (see above). Include all of the subcategories you need to cover until they become second nature.

Many good designers miss the importance of time management and organisation, and their work and client relationships suffer as a result. Get into the habit of good time management, now!

### Comps (comprehensive sketches)

Comps are the most finished approximation of an actual product and often look exactly like the real thing. They will evidence all design considerations, including final colours, tints and halftones, all typographic considerations, textures, and paper finishes and weights. If a project has many parts, comps for the extended system may be produced at different stages. After a client approves the comps, an artworker can take over the job, if needed, and match all aspects of the production to the designer's choices.

### Page plans/flatplans

There has to be a logical visual (and conceptual) sequence in any design project. Magazines and books

**Storyboards** Motion graphics or film and video can be expensive to produce, especially if animation and effects are involved, so be clear about your intentions. Storyboards clarify the concept by showing the progression of the idea and the transitions from scene to scene. An expert storyboard may even serve as a shooting guide on the set.

are normally laid out in miniature on a page plan several times before full-size layouts are started. The page plan may consist of no more than the article title, but can be much more specific, including a list of all the page elements or a thumbnail drawing of the layout with text blocks and artwork sketched in. The page plan is intended to clarify logical sequence, distribution of colour, change of pace and so on.

## Storyboards

Storyboards give the client or production person enough information to allow them to begin to design their assigned spreads or pages of the final product. As well as in multimedia design, storyboards are commonly employed in films, comic strips, animation and TV commercials. The storyboard contains a sketch of the visual aspect of the screen, information that will be present, descriptions of animations, interactions (for example, dialogue boxes), sounds and any other media.

Although storyboards were originally linear (for film), non-linear elements are incorporated. Web design uses a similar approach through wireframes. Wireframes are used to plan individual pages or sequences before engaging a web designer.

These website flowcharts show how pages link up in a logical order (see page 158). The organisation of a website reflects the actual body for which the site is designed. It is important to get the structure right before designing the look of the pages.

### ⓘ Timescale

Research can be very time-consuming, so bear in mind that there has to be a cut-off point at which you have to start generating your visual concepts. 'Design' is a verb as much as it is a noun: it's about doing things, so jump right in. One idea will always lead to the next.

(see page 158)

### GLOSSARY

**Comps:** Comprehensive sketch, a close approximation of the printed product.

**Page plan/flatplan:** A document with a series of numbered thumbnails set out in an ordered grid that represents each page in a book.

**Storyboard:** A document similar to a flatplan, but with a sequence of thumbnails that specifically lays out the narrative for a comic strip or film.

# **CHAPTER 1:** ASSIGNMENTS

## ● RESEARCH: OBSERVE AND RECORD

Take a walking tour of your neighbourhood or walk to a location that provides you with an interesting route, or even one you might take every day. Consider what materials you might need to document the route (e.g. sketchbook, camera, dictaphone, tape measure, decibel meter, Geiger counter, metal detector, etc.). Consider the visual, historical, observational, social and political aspects of the route itself. As you walk, really look carefully at your surroundings and record your observations using photography, sound recordings, handwritten notes, sketches and collected ephemera. You should try to see things differently and be very sensitive to light, shadow, textures, patterns and the random relationships of objects and colours. Zooming in on the pavement, a wall, or a streetlight can reveal subtle textures and colour variants you may have missed, so crop your images creatively. Shoot some images from several points of view and at different exposures. Record your own impressions of what you see, and transcribe any chance conversations you have along the way. Primary and secondary research for a particular project can take weeks, and the process is an important influence on the final outcome.

## ● APPLY YOUR OBSERVATIONS: YOUR JOURNEY AS IMAGE

**1** Once you have gathered your first batch of primary research, start to analyse your findings and observations. What was it about the journey that intrigued you most? What part of the journey do you want to share with others and why? Continue to build up your research by adding secondary sources.

• Consult library archives for historic images and information of the same locations
• Read histories of the neighbourhood
• Interview residents and shop owners

**2** When you feel you've researched to a high level, begin to edit and curate the information to the most important elements. Think about who

might be most interested in your research, or who it is most appropriate to engage with it. Decide how you would best catch their attention, and how your story should unfold. Brainstorm possible outputs for this information: what format could they take; what audience could they speak to?

**3** Using your edited and refined research, create several sketches for a series of posters to be placed along the route of your journey. The emphasis of this assignment is on the creative process, not on the final project, so use your skills in observation and research as expansively as possible, and consider all of the possible interpretations of your research before you commit to a single idea. It is always worth doing some research into the format written in your brief, in this case research poster design and creating narratives with sequential images. Create a storyboard or a spider diagram to organise your thinking, then generate as many thumbnail drawings as you physically can. Use words, images and collage materials you may have collected. When you have a series of five thumbnails you really like, enlarge them, either by drawing them again or by using a copier, and clarify your intentions by writing a short descriptive paragraph on each one.

## ● LATERAL THINKING

Start by very quickly drawing a self-portrait and put it to one side. In a sketchbook, start to brainstorm your physical traits, your character, your likes, your dislikes, what is it that makes you unique. This short task aims to develop your problem-solving and creative insight, finding ways to approach a brief that will result in original, creative and memorable work. What happens to your outcome if you scrap the first 30 ideas? Or if you ban Google images as a point of reference? Try bouncing ideas off your peers and begin to avoid the obvious. Once you've exercised your brain, draw another self-portrait. This time take a little longer to decide what it is you want to communicate about yourself. Sketch a few thumbnails before you start your final image. Once finished, compare with your portraits: which do you think is more engaging?

## ● DRAWING: OBJECTIFY AND ABSTRACT

**1** Take a sketchbook or a piece of paper and grid up a series of small squares – no smaller than 2 x 2cm (¾ x ¾in) – in a six-by-six grid. In each square you are going to draw a sphere. Whether this be a ball, a marble or a bead, the object you choose should be spherical. Each line of squares will have a theme for your drawing.

Title the first line of six 'perspective'. What happens to the shadows and the shapes if you move your point of view or the point at which the light hits the surface? In one square draw the sphere straight on, in another to the side, and another at bird's-eye view, and one angled from below. Continue with a variety of angles until you have filled your six squares.

Title the second line 'materials'. Select three conventional mark-making tools (pencil, pen, paint, etc.) and three non-conventional (a stick dipped in ink, watered-down mud from the garden, oil from a bicycle chain, etc.). Draw the sphere using a different tool for each square.

Title the third line 'music'. Select six different genres of music and play one as you sketch a sphere inside each square. Try to generate a variety of sounds, from classical to heavy metal; the more varied, the better the exercise.

For the next three lines come up with your own rules or limitations.

How do perspectives, materials and environment change the impact and meaning of the simple imagery you have generated?

**2** Choose a few favourites from the numerous drawings and enlarge them on a photocopier. Can you crop the images so they still describe the sphere in some way? Can you convey the essence of the object by just showing a portion of it?

## ANALYSE AND VISUALISE

**1** Find three different logos and analyse them in detail. On first impressions what do they connote? Determine whether they are didactic or poetic, and identify what techniques they use to communicate their meanings. Pay close attention to the point of view the mark expresses. Is it steadfast and reliable or lighthearted and fun? Does it look elegant or casual? Is it easy to understand or does it require a second, more careful examination? Analysis of existing work is an important step in learning about effective graphic communication. It will help you learn to deconstruct and improve your own work.

**2** Record your critique, then choose one of the logos you think might benefit from a new design. If your logo is quite complex, can you simplify it? If your logo is a simple vector shape or pictogram, how can you make it more complex? Share your observations with another design student, another designer or someone with an appreciation of design.

## AUDIENCE RESEARCH

Choose a logo from the previous exercise or a piece of design you are fond of. Can you decipher its audience? What clues point you in this direction? Imagine someone is creating a poster for you, how would you go about describing yourself as an audience? Write up a quick summary of your thoughts and discuss with a tutor, peer or someone interested in design.

## MARKET RESEARCH

Conduct your own market research on the company whose logo you redesigned in a previous assignment. Write up your findings in a report you might present to the client at one of your preliminary meetings. Make a ten-page PDF presentation summarising your ideas.

- Learn everything you can about the company.
- Determine who the competition is and look at their communication tools. Evaluate them. Are they working, if so why? If they are not working, why not?

- Create a survey to speak to current customers, and to non-customers, about how they perceive the company.
- Use the product/service yourself for personal insights.
- Look at the target market, researching who they are, what they do and how they spend their time. Is the product/service researching them?
- Read market reports online or in the library.
- Determine the usage of the logo. Will it be in print, on the side of a lorry, on a website, animated for TV, or all of the above? Will it be consistent or change based upon variables?

## CONCEPT DEVELOPMENT

Based on the target audience you want to reach, and using the findings of the research report from the previous assignment, determine if the new logo should be pictorial (using a representational drawing), typographic or abstract, and explain your decision.

**1** Begin the brainstorming process by associating as many words as you can with the ideas, values, services and/or products your company represents.

**2** Set up a spider chart or flowchart to record your word process, and connect ideas that help you generate images.

**3** Generate thumbnails, eliminating any visual clichés or derivative ideas, and allow the ideas to flow very freely. Discard the ones with limited potential and choose the best three. Think about how the message they communicate might be enhanced through a particular drawing style, line weight or colour treatment.

**4** Begin working on the details and develop your thumbnails into clean comps. Consider how the finished product will work in various applications, such as corporate identity components (business cards, letterheads, folders and so on), direct mail, websites and animations.

## BUILD A SCHEDULE

Organisation and planning are esse
of graphic design: arranging meetings, wo
out schedules, commissioning and booking photography and illustration, keeping to print deadlines, arranging workflow, and organising budgets and finances, as are visualising, explaining and making complex ideas accessible. Using the following questions as a starting point, design and produce a visual plan of your life. The plan should begin today, and can stop where you think necessary, whether that be in ten years or tomorrow.

Begin by considering the following:
- Why am I studying graphic design?
- What is the role of graphic design in the modern world?
- What kind of work do I want to do, and who do I want to work for?
- Should I be self-employed/in a large company/ small team?
- Where do I want to be geographically/socially?
- Where will I be in one/two/ten years professionally/personally?
- What systems govern my life, and how important is organisation to me?
- What technological/political/social changes will occur in the future?
- What am I looking forward to/do I fear in the future?
- What are my strengths and weaknesses?
- What do I want to achieve today/this year?

**Further Reading:**

Lucienne Roberts and Rebecca Wright, *Design Diaries: Creative Process in Graphic Design*, Laurence King Publishing, 2010
Steven Heller and Lita Talarico, *Graphic: Inside the Sketchbooks of the World's Great Graphic Designers*, Thames & Hudson, 2010
Meredith Davis, *Graphic Design Theory*, Thames & Hudson, 2012
Steven Heller and Veronique Vienne, *100 Ideas That Changed Graphic Design*, Laurence King Publishing, 2012
Ellen Lupton, *Graphic Design Thinking: Beyond Brainstorming*, Princeton Architectural Press, 2011

# Fundamentals
# of Composition

Good composition is an essential element of all art forms, graphic or otherwise, and should be considered the foundation of visual communication. Successful graphic designers are masters of the fundamentals that underlie all aspects of design. Elements on a page or on the web, in motion or in three dimensions, should always be led by concern for spacing, visual organisation, style, and the size and format of the finished work.

Graphic design projects use text and image in concert, with consideration for the relationships established between each of the elements. These compositions should also establish a visual hierarchy that directs the viewer's eye through a deliberate visual sequence.

" Visual literacy also is an ability to view any image as an abstraction, to understand what is happening in purely visual terms as well as knowing and understanding visual terminology. It involves training the eyes to see minute detail and being sensitive to colour, shape, form, and line. It has little or nothing to do with content or style "

*Rob Roy Kelly*

PART 1 | PRINCIPLES

CHAPTER 2 | FUNDAMENTALS OF COMPOSITION

MODULE 1 | **Basics of composition**

**Composition refers to the visual structure and organisation of elements within a design. It concerns the process of combining distinct parts or elements to form a whole. Composition involves seeing the whole as greater than its parts, and is just as important as the individual elements that make up a design.**

Designers organise images and text – each with their own shapes, sizes, colours and textures – in many different media and in a wide range of formats; from two- and three-dimensional black-and-white design through full-colour work to web-based and time-based (moving) imagery. A practical understanding and exploration of composition is crucial for effective visual communication: it is the most significant tool in guiding the viewer through the complexity of visuals to the intended message. To create effective design work, no matter which medium you are working in, you must understand the principles of good composition.

### ⊙ Building a composition

In this series, horizontal and vertical lines gradually translate into lines of typography to illustrate a concept. The same principles of placement and relationship apply to the placement of body text and headline, and the hierarchy should be examined carefully to ensure typography is read in the proper sequence.

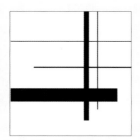

Carefully placed vertical lines of varying weights show a gradually imposed order as they begin to form a grid.

The substitution of typography for lines, using the word 'structure', reinforces the concept and identifies the relationship between typographic point sizes and line weights.

The structure of the series continues to build with layers of typographic lines working in concert to suggest heavier masses of line.

The final composition adds closely locked forms of typographic lines to create an architectural composition where each weighted area is visually supported.

**↑ Negative space** Placement on the page is critical. In the first composition, the shapes appear to be aggressively competing for space. When the objects are reduced in size and placed in the lower corner of the page, they appear to be racing to exit the image.

**↑ Organised chaos** In the initial composition, the placement of the circles creates tension though asymmetry and cropped edges. As the second and third compositions develop, the same principles are in play, using texture to create mass, and repetition and variation in placement.

### ⊙ Shape and space

By using simple forms like dots and lines or geometric forms, you can control the dynamics of the composition through the placement of each object. The relationship between positive and negative space, the strength of horizontal or vertical forms, the dominance of variations in scale and value, and the space between the objects will all work together to attract and direct the viewers' attention.

### Theories of composition

Throughout the history of the visual arts, different theories of composition have been advanced. Vitruvius, the Roman architect and engineer, devised a mathematical formula for the division of space within a picture. His solution, known as the golden section, the golden mean, or golden rectangle, was based on a set ratio between the longer and shorter sides of a rectangle. This principle profoundly affected theories in mathematics, architecture, painting, graphic design and industrial design regarding the use of spatial composition. The French painter Henri Matisse (1869–1954) put greater emphasis on inspiration, maintaining that composition is the art of arranging elements to express feelings.

Most contemporary theories have acknowledged the following elements as important considerations in composition: balance (the deliberate distribution of elements on a page); consistency or harmony (similarities in visual objects); contrast (obvious differences in visual elements); proximity (the relationships in the placement of the elements in play); repetition with variation; and white space (the deliberate open areas in a composition that give the viewer the ability to focus on everything else).

### Form and space

Positive space is a form or object that, to the eye, appears to exist. This can be a solid shape of any size, a line or simply a texture. Negative space is everything around or within an object, the 'empty' space that helps to define the borders of the positive image. It is important to learn to effectively control the relationship

The space around the rice-shaped white shape in the black box is repeated in the relationship of the typography in the square above it, and in the placement of the whole object on the page in the brochure.

**Expanded space** The perfect placement of a single white mark in a black square establishes the relationships for a greater extended system. Repetition with variation is demonstrated by the placement of the word treatment above the rice/box, reversing the angle of the rice by creating a triangle in the white space and enforcing the figure-ground reversal of the squares.

The packaging and display add texture in the choice of photography and in the use of the product itself.

The placement of the double box mark at the juncture of white space and image on the page echoes the packaging.

**Letters, dots and lines** Strong horizontal lines suggest blinds on a window when they are used as interruptions in this strong typographic treatment. The two black dots – the only circular forms on the page – placed asymmetrically in the composition draw the eye and suggest binoculars peering through the blinds. This typographic image supports and suggests the subject matter of the film it promotes.

**Make it new** Simple shapes, lines and circles suggest machines that defined an industrial society in this graphic illustration about the Modernist movement in arts and culture.

**Creative composition** These three images show how the relationship of composition in photography can translate to graphic images and, in this case, to the development of a logo.

between positive and negative space, and to explore this in basic compositional studies, before moving on to more complex designs. In general, negative space works to support the positive 'image' in any given area (also called the picture plane). To create a more considered and effective composition, control the relationship between positive and negative elements, and recognise the effect each has on the other.

White space can create tension or contrast, or can add the welcome open space needed to reflect on complex, visually active and textural images. You can easily see the effects of open space on the overall feel

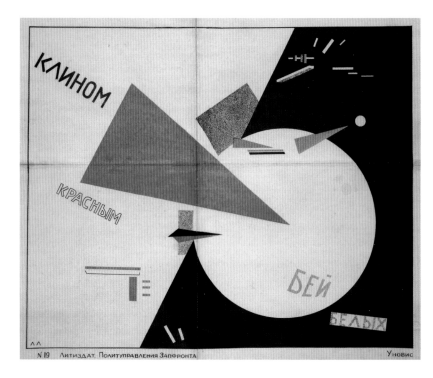

N 19   Литиздат. Политуправления Запфронта                      Уновис

**Symbolism** Dots, lines and shapes can be used as powerful symbols in the right context. Artist El Lissitzky combined geometric shapes and a bold red, white and black palette to create a strong political statement in *Beat the Whites with the Red Wedge*, 1919. The sharp red triangle of the Bolshevik army is invading and dividing the white circle in this graphic statement on the Russian Civil War.

**SEE ALSO:** FORM AND SPACE, P36

of a composition by altering the ratio of positive to negative. If you place a single dot in the centre of a relatively large square of white, far from disappearing, the dot becomes more important. This is because the expanse of white space highlights and focuses attention on the dot itself. You can also actively encourage ambiguity between picture elements and background. For example, a particular group of forms can come together to support each other and compete in such a way that the (normally negative) space is given form by the positive elements, as in figure-ground relationships (see page 36).

### Dots and lines

A dot exists as a mark, on its own, as a point in space, and it can also be the start of a line. Many points together start to set up a rhythm or a pattern that, depending on uniformity, repetitiveness, scale or quantity, can suggest regularity or variation, and can express tense or relaxed sensibilities.

A line is a pathway between any two points. It can be straight, curved, thick, thin, horizontal, diagonal, jagged, solid, gestural or broken. Soft, sensuous lines imply tranquillity and harmony, whereas sharp, zigzagged lines invoke discordance and tension. Two converging lines might imply a point disappearing in the distance, and can suggest the illusion of three dimensions in a two-dimensional space. Horizontal lines suggest open planes; vertical lines can suggest power and strength. Lines are elegant tools that imply motion, momentum, rhythm and upwards or downwards movement, and are primary aids in establishing visual hierarchies and closure. Simply put, closure is the ability of the human brain to observe an incomplete circle and to perceive it as complete in our imaginations.

Look at the expressive qualities of the artist Franz Kline's strong, emphatic painted line, or Cy Twombly's wandering, fragile drawn and painted lines. Examine Wolfgang Weingart's use of line in typography as a way to structure information or Russian Constructivist Alexander Rodchenko's powerful use of red and black line. El Lissitzky and Piet Zwart also used lines emphatically and expressively in their work.

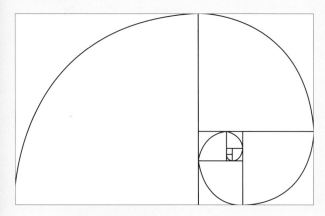

**↑ Fibonacci spiral**
Each time a square is taken from the section, a smaller rectangle remains with the same proportions as the original. The spiral (also known as the golden ratio) can be used to create a proportional and harmonious composition.

**↓ Tricks on the eye** Figure-ground relationships produce different effects that confuse the eye. For example, the Rubin vase (top left) relies upon a visual confusion between figure and ground, so that the eye sees either faces or a vase.

**In learning to create meaningful compositions, it is important to understand the role of visual perception (the way our eyes and brains make sense of what we see) and its role in visual communication.**

Whether consciously or not, our eyes are constantly supplying information to our brain, which processes and makes sense of that visual input. Being able to control that process and understand how it works is crucial. Good design thinking requires an understanding of how the relationship between visual elements affects the way we perceive them, as well as an understanding of how to control and exploit them.

**Figure and ground**

A form is always experienced in relation to the space it occupies and to other forms that may be present in the format. We call this the figure-ground relationship (where 'figure' refers to any object in a given space and 'ground' refers to the background, or space in which that object is seen). Another way to talk about this relationship is in terms of negative and positive space. Visual elements are always seen in relation to a visual field, background or frame. In other words, every form is seen in context and cannot be totally isolated.

Generally speaking, a form is considered to be positive and the space around it negative. The space within a format (the ground) is an important element of any design and not just something left over once a form is placed on it: it matters within the overall design, since the ground affects the form and vice versa. Usually, we tend to notice the form before we see the ground, or what is placed in a space before we see the space itself. However, a well-known example of where this relationship becomes confused is drawn from Gestalt psychology. 'Gestalt' is a German word meaning 'essence or shape of an entity's complete form'. Look at the Rubin vase (left), where the effect depends on whether we see the form as the white element, with the ground as the black, or see the black shapes as the form.

### The law of closure

Another phenomenon drawn from Gestalt psychology is the law of closure, which argues that we tend to 'close' or complete lines or objects that are not, in fact, closed. This can be a useful device in design, and is related to figure and ground, since it relies on our ability to collapse the space between foreground and background. It is also a primary tool in directing a viewer's eye through a composition in the designer's intended sequence.

### The rule of thirds

The rule of thirds says that most compositions become more dynamic when divided into thirds vertically and/or horizontally, with important elements placed within those thirds. Dividing a composition in half will halt the closure and keep the viewer's eye centred on the halfway point, especially if an object is placed at the exact centre point. The rule of thirds ensures movement on the page, and actively engages positive and negative space in the visual dialogue. The rule of thirds applies to graphic design for print, web and motion graphics and applies equally to framing for photography, film and video.

⬇ **Gestalt law of closure**

Examples of the law of closure demonstrate the ability of the brain to complete incomplete forms and, consequently, continue to move around the complete form. In page design, or any composition, it will keep the viewer's attention on the design in hand and move the eye around a page, package, poster or sign.

⬅ **Negative as positive**

Using principles of negative space and figure-ground reversal, typographer John Langdon's painting directs the viewer's eye to decode two words in one, 'you' and 'me'.

WOMEN
OF ART
AND ROCK

STEREO TELESCOPE
CASEY DESMOND
RHIANNA LAROCQUE
AMY LUNDSTROM
TOFUSQUIRREL

Live Music & Art
Sept. 12th, 7:30-11:30PM
@ afterHours
NU Student + 1 Guest FREE

⬆ **Thirds** Beautifully placed, simple geometrics and lines send a message of music in this dynamic example of the rule of thirds. The composition divides horizontally and vertically, with the placement of the most critical imagery right in the centre. Accent colour in the upper and lower thirds keeps the viewer moving between the two spots, lengthening the observation time.

| PART 1 | PRINCIPLES |
| --- | --- |
| CHAPTER 2 | FUNDAMENTALS OF COMPOSITION |
| MODULE 3 | **Symmetry/asymmetry** |

Symmetry in design refers to a spatial relationship between elements, and specifically to a situation where the elements in a layout are centred, having equal space to the left and right or above and below them, a mirror image on either side. The second meaning of symmetry is more general, and refers to a sense of harmony, or balance, which in turn is seen to reflect beauty. Symmetry carries associations of perfection, tradition, order, and rationality and peace.

### Designing without symmetry

In asymmetrical design (without symmetry), elements are not centred, but utilise the whole format, creating dynamic compositions that play with scale, contrast, space and tension between elements. Negative space is usually less passive in asymmetrical design, and becomes easily evident as a part of the design. Asymmetry is generally associated with fewer rules and limits, and more expressive possibilities. However, each kind of composition has its place, and the important thing is to learn how to identify when it is appropriate to use one or the other. While asymmetrical design may seem less rigid, it is crucial to spend time learning how asymmetry activates elements in a given space, and to

carefully control the effects you want to achieve rather than randomly placing elements in a design.

### Choosing symmetry or asymmetry

Similar questions arise in any design you undertake. How should the space be divided? How should the subject matter occupy the space? Each decision you make on placement will affect the emotion of the design. A symmetrical composition makes for a calmer, more peaceful work, while something more dynamic can be achieved if the elements are arranged asymmetrically. Symmetry tends towards balance, and lack of movement, while asymmetry injects movement and spatial tension into a design.

⬙ **In harmony** The ancient Chinese duality symbol for 'yin' (black) and 'yang' (white) is the perhaps the most famous example of perfect symmetry, each shape a reversed mirror of the other.

⬆ **Typographic symmetry** Beautifully mirrored hand-drawn letterforms produce this symmetrical ambigram, which reveals the word 'excellence' the exact same way when the book is turned upside down.

### Testing the theory

In these examples, various effects are achieved by simple variation of the position of the square within a stable frame.

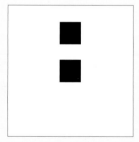

**1 Balance**
The centred square is stable or static, as the space around the square is equal on all sides.

**2 Movement to the left**
When a second square is introduced, visual forces develop. There is a sense that the squares are moving left.

**3 Movement to the right**
Changing the position of the two squares suggests movement to the right.

**4 Upwards movement**
The position of the two squares hints at movement upwards.

**Asymmetry:** A composition where elements are juxtaposed and do not mirror the other forms on the page.

**Symmetry:** A composition where elements are balanced or mirrored on a page.

### ⬅ Asymmetry

Placement of the image slightly to the right on the package is balanced nicely by the ghosted graphic on the lower left, providing balance and adding a bit of motion.

### ⬋ Symmetry

Perfect symmetry is in place on the smaller packages, with a nod towards the motion associated with asymmetry addressed in the placement of spot colour in the photos.

### ⬇ Different but equal

Equal weight is represented on opposite sides of this clean publication design composition. Both are aligned to the far edge of their respective sides, and the primary information on either side occupies about the same amount of space.

### ➡ Zang Tumb Tumb,

by F. T. Marinetti in 1919, uses creative asymmetrical typography to express the sounds of battle. In typography, 'onomatopeia' refers to the use of type to express sounds in a literal way.

### ⬅ Symmetry in asymmetry

Perfectly centred letterforms create symmetry within an active asymmetrical composition. The contrasts in placement and colour create visual rhythm in this dynamic composition.

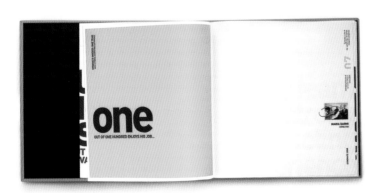

| PART 1 | PRINCIPLES |
|---|---|
| CHAPTER 2 | FUNDAMENTALS OF COMPOSITION |
| MODULE 4 | **Basic principles of design layout** |

The term 'layout' refers to the organisation of disparate material that makes up the content of a design. Well-designed visual communications present information in a logical, coherent way, and make the important elements stand out. Basic principles of good composition are of the upmost importance in the process, and a thoughtful approach to the delivery of the material is, as always, the designer's first consideration.

The use of a grid system and consistently styled design elements helps the reader to absorb information in a visually pleasing way, and enhances the communication of the content. Good composition in layout design is dependent on the grid, and there are many configurations to choose from.

### Practical factors

There are three basic stages in beginning any graphic design project. First, the designer receives a brief from the client, usually establishing what material should be included and the format for the project. This involves a combination of text or copy (main text, display copy [headings], boxes or sidebars, captions) and images (photographs, illustrations, maps, diagrams). The brief should also indicate the desired look or 'feel' of the work, which in turn will depend on the target audience. Should the layout look authoritative? Should it be densely packed with information? Does the message warrant a lean and structured design, with lots of white space? If the brief is vague, schedule time with your client to ask the right questions and help define the goals of the design.

Second, you will need to consider the format and budget. If there are many pictures and extensive copy for a small space, this will affect the look of the layout. Agreement should be reached on hierarchies within the copy; an editor may already have labelled their headings 'A', 'B', 'C', and so on, to indicate their relative importance. Such elements can be indicated typographically for emphasis, through differences in type size,

weight, form and choice of colour. Determine how many colours will be used. Beautiful design work can be created with a limited palette or with a full range of inks and effects. The number of colours used will affect a print production budget, so find out before you begin to conceptualise a project for press. If the project is hosted online, your palette is free, but certain colours are easier to read on screen than others. For website design, see pages 142–185.

### Grids

The third stage involves organisation. In print-based work and web design this means developing a grid system, in which various elements can be placed within a ready-made structure that underpins the entire design. The grid enables the layout of columns, margins, and areas for text and image. A well-designed grid allows for some flexibility of placement on individual pages, while providing an underlying system that gives visual coherence across a series of pages. This is obviously crucial in any kind of editorial work, including books and magazines, but certainly applies to well-designed website pages, where some elements stay the same and others change.

A grid system should never restrict creativity; working within a structured format will offer many excellent opportunities to break the rules, but it's best to learn them first. If you are having issues, turn the grid off, play with the composition and, when happy, turn the grid back on and align your design to it.

### ➔ Divide and conquer

Organising information on a page meaningfully is critical to the information transfer, especially when handling large amounts of text. There are many ways to divide the page and the choice should be a consideration of the type of design work, the format of the viewing platform, and the amount of information to be presented on each page or sub-division.

Individual units of equal size, separated by equal margins top and bottom, form a system perfect for compositions with many images. The units can be combined in any number for larger images or columns of text.

Three columns works well for mid-range amounts of text. The designer can use any given column in any system for added white space and can divide the page asymmetrically with text and image in this three-column system.

A four-column system begins to add more flexibility for variation in placement. The symmetrical division will add order, if desired, and added control in the overall system. A larger margin at the bottom of the page is particularly important in book and publication design as it makes the text more accessible/ easier to read.

CHECKLIST FOR
BEGINNING A LAYOUT

- Who is the target audience for
  the design?
- What different kinds of text will
  be included?
- Will there be photographs,
  illustrations, diagrams, or a
  combination of all three?
- How many colours can be used
  (the budget will affect this in print-
  based work)?
- What is the format and final size
  of the job (also related to budget)?
- What parts of the text need
  emphasising?
- Is the client looking for a particular
  style of layout?

⬆ **Flexibility** Many variations of the layout
can be explored as thumbnail sketches, before
committing. Here, you can see the kind of
flexibility a simple grid provides, giving indications
of structure without limiting creativity.

The top of the
x-height of text
blocks. No text
(except for running
heads/page
numbers) would
normally appear
above this line

➡ **Master grid** Margins,
columns and non-changing
typographic elements such
as page numbers and running
heads can all be placed
on the master grid, which
provides the design template.
The grids have been printed
over this module to show how
they structure the design.

Head
Fore edge
Back
Foot

The baseline grid
is based on the
size of type and
leading value
of the main
text used (the
body text), and
ensures that all
text starts and
ends at the same
horizontal point

Here you can
set the number
of columns per
page and the
space (gutter)
between each

Margins and Columns

Margins
Top: 14 mm          Inside: 14 mm
Bottom: 17.7 mr     Outside: 19 mm

Columns
Number: 10          Gutter: 5 mm

OK
Cancel
☑ Preview

What flowers are found in tropical rain forests?

**↑ Natural order** This tight, modular grid system shows the expressive freedom that comes with control. A wonderful range of shapes and sizes is available to showcase photography and text with this six-column format, and you can sustain the viewer's interest in larger publications.

## Margins, grids and structure

For any form of publication design you should begin by formatting a double-page spread that can then be applied to the entire publication. This is important because you need to see how the verso (left-hand page) relates to the recto (right-hand page) and judge how well they balance. Established practice in book design suggests that the back (inner margin) should be half the fore edge (outside margin), and the foot (bottom margin) greater than the head (top margin). These rules should ensure a balance, with the type area sitting comfortably in the format. Remember that the eye will need to move from one page to another, so the

gap, or gutter (the two back edges combined), should not be too large.

When establishing page margins, consider the material, the client and the reader. For example, paperbacks tend to have tight margins to keep page numbers – and therefore costs – down, whereas heavily illustrated publications have generous margins and use white space effectively. Economic considerations play a part: brochures and promotional materials tend to have bigger budgets, so even more white space is possible.

The grid shows the layout of columns, margins and areas for main text, captions and images; it also shows the position of repeating heads (running heads) and page

**↓ Variation** Spreads from the same publication showcase the system's flexibility, adding blocks of colour, half-page photography, translucent colour overlays and highlighted inserts, all while remaining faithful to the boundaries of the grid system.

numbers. These elements normally stay the same over a series of pages.

After drawing your double-page spread, you can prepare some layout roughs: these can be small thumbnails or half-sized visuals in which your first ideas are sketched out. This preliminary thinking time is key in the page-design process; it's where you make important decisions about the composition of pages and the organisation of material. Preliminary sketches can then be transferred to the computer and several variations quickly produced, based on the main grid. It takes less time to sketch ideas than to create designs directly on screen. Remember, the computer is simply a tool; it cannot think for you, nor can it generate ideas. With initial sketches, the imaginative designer can fully explore ideas and options before moving on to the production phase.

## Using a grid

The grid divides the available type area into proportioned units, providing an overall visual structure and helping to unite all visual elements. The most basic grid structure – used primarily for text-based material such as business reports or novels – is that of a single column. The width should relate to legibility, 8 to 10 words or 60 to 72 characters per line is usually considered optimum.

With complex layouts, in which text, images, diagrams and captions must be integrated, a more sophisticated horizontal and vertical grid is needed. Grid systems comprising between three and six columns enable you to use all kinds of elements. The more units used, the more flexibility you have to accommodate smaller pieces of copy such as captions, longer measures such as section openers, and displayed material. Never simply follow your computer's default settings for columns, but decide on your own.

Ideally, a grid should have some vertical controls, both for structure down the page and for order to the overall design. Give headings, subheadings, captions and page numbers set positions for continuity. Finally, be flexible. After two or three spreads the grid may seem too rigid, so adjust it. Grids should not be restrictive, but provide structure while giving rich compositional variations to spreads.

### ⬆ Form and function

Consider the format style and the user experience when you select a grid system. If the content information can be neatly divided into components, it may suggest the use of a particular fold that will help to display the information in a logical sequence. The tall, slender accordion fold on the brochure above adds elegant white space and repeats the form in the photo.

**⊕ SEE ALSO:** AUDIENCES, MARKETS AND CONCEPTS, P24

STYLES OF LAYOUT, P44

PACE AND CONTRAST, P46

SIZE AND FORMAT, P50

TYPOGRAPHIC EMPHASIS AND HIERARCHY, P78

| PART 1 | PRINCIPLES |
|---|---|
| CHAPTER 2 | FUNDAMENTALS OF COMPOSITION |
| MODULE 5 | **Styles of layout** |

In simple terms, page design, or layout, can be divided into two basic styles: symmetrical and asymmetrical. In broad terms, symmetrical style is a traditional approach in which design is structured around a central axis. This type of layout has its origins in the earliest printed books, which, in turn, borrowed their layout from handwritten manuscripts of the medieval era. Asymmetrical style is non-centred, dynamic, and associated with 20th-century modernism and contemporary design.

## Symmetrical style

Traditionally, symmetrical layouts are most commonly seen on title pages of books, where each line of type is centred above the others. Part of the tradition is also the use of serif typefaces, often set in letter-spaced capitals with, perhaps, the addition of an ornament or printer's flower.

Decorative borders and the addition of decorative elements became more popular in the 15th and 16th centuries, but until the 1920s most publications were designed with symmetrical formats. Achieving a balanced-looking composition within a symmetrical design is not as easy as it sounds. Type size must be carefully judged, and spacing between each line considered, since certain information belongs in the same typographic unit and should be grouped accordingly. Fine-tuning horizontal line space is critical. These judgments must be made while maintaining balance and beautiful composition. For superb examples of symmetrical typography, see the work of Aldus Manutius,

the Dolphin Press, and the Venetian printers from the late 15th century.

## The asymmetrical revolution

Asymmetrical layouts can be traced back to the 1920s and 1930s, in particular to the German school, the Bauhaus. Artists such as Kurt Schwitters and Theo van Doesburg experimented with layouts based on an off-centred axis, creating tension and dynamism. In this style, type is primarily ragged left; ragged-right setting is kept to a few lines, as Western cultures read left to right. Other predominant designers to note are Armin Hofmann, Herbert Bayer, Wim Crouwel, and the work of Josef Müller-Brockmann.

The modernist movement also rejected ornament, and sans-serif typefaces, with their clean lines and modernity, were the popular faces of the school. The work of the Bauhaus and their stylistic descendents, such as the Swiss typographers of the 1950s and 1960s, favours sans-serif faces and often completely

**↑ Asymmetrical page design** Justified blocks of text are important design elements of the modular grid system in this asymmetrical page design. The unusual division of the photographic image elevates the grid system itself to a central design element and, as the margins become lines, shows the influence of the Constructivist movement.

SOTTSASS ASSOCIATI

"Every color has a history. Red is the color of the Communist flag, the color that makes a surgeon move faster and the color of passion."

**← Balance** The symmetrical design system of these pages allows large display typography in different styles, both sans serif and serif, to divide the pages and play a central part as design elements in the compositions.

lowercase headlines. Rules, in a number of weights, are used as distinctive features in colour and in black and white, adding dynamic movement to the compositions.

Another amazing typographer, whose work over a long career shows both styles well, is Jan Tschichold. Early on he was heavily influenced by the modernist philosophy of the Bauhaus, and is considered a pioneer of the asymmetric revolution. He later changed direction, rejecting the hard-line approach advocated in his book *Asymmetric Typography*. Tschichold returned to the frequent use of centred, serif typography, but continued working in both styles.

### Integrating styles

Contemporary designers often integrate both theories of spatial arrangement and select the style to suit the project. Contemporary typographers, like Philippe Apeloig, also use both in their search for visual solutions. As a designer you need to understand both styles, and their historical precedents and contexts, so that your selections and design decisions are based on knowledge rather than guesswork. Read as much about graphic design history as you can, and follow the philosophy of Jan Tschichold: use both styles, but understand that mixing them needs to be undertaken with caution. Research and experimentation will be your best guides. Keep your options open, and be flexible and fearless in reaching appropriate solutions.

⊕ **SEE ALSO:** SYMMETRY/ASYMMETRY, P38

BASIC PRINCIPLES OF DESIGN LAYOUT, P40

SIZE AND FORMAT, P50

⬇ **Classically centred**
The *Hypnerotomachia Poliphili*, printed by Aldus Manutius's Dolphin Press, Venice, in 1499, is an example of the highest art of Renaissance printing. Its symmetrical typography harmonises with the wood-engraved illustrations.

**Combining styles**

Inserts, short pages and fold-outs create symmetrical and asymmetrical page designs and work in concert to evidence the decorative nature of pattern design in this book on the history of kimonos. The unusual combination is influenced by asymmetry in traditional Japanese art.

| PART 1 | PRINCIPLES |
|---|---|
| CHAPTER 2 | FUNDAMENTALS OF COMPOSITION |
| MODULE 6 | **Pace and contrast** |

Pace and contrast are vital qualities for catching and maintaining a reader's interest in graphic design: they provide variety, and set the rhythm and the mood. This is particularly evident in magazines and image-heavy books, where it is critical to be able to direct the eye to different pieces of information in a particular sequence. Think in cinematic terms: the audience should be given different experiences, have different reactions, and enjoy the complete experience from beginning to end. The digital age has created a world of multitasking citizens, and holding their attention over time can be a challenge.

In continuous text, the reader takes more time to cover information and is primed to read every word. In a highly integrated design – with panels, pictures, captions, and quotes, and so on – there is more competition for the reader's attention. An article may be skimmed over, some pages will be scanned for pictures, or the reader might be seeking only a specific piece of information.

The pace of a publication will be dictated by the content and space available. Contrast is closely linked to pace and is an excellent tool for controlling the pace

**Controlling the pace**
The same principles of design apply to any platform, whether it is web, print, motion or environmental. The system shown on-screen to the left maintains common elements in the titling and hierarchy, and varies the pace of the content pages with colourful full-bleed images and pages with smaller insets. The viewer has more options to zoom and link to new pages online than in print, so visuals should be planned out as a fully extended system.

**Momentum** The publication *Gateway 241* neatly divides spreads with a strong landscape/horizontal image and provides enough variety of form to keep it interesting. Pace is varied through contrast in scale, fine use of white space, large bleed photography, handsome display type and infographics that cross the gutters, and a landscape double-foldout image.

of an extended design system. You can create visual emphasis with large type and imagery, unusual cropping, sidebar information graphics and full bleeds of image or colour. Alternatively, you can create a quiet interval by having text-only spreads and open areas of white space.

### Planning for pace

In order to achieve good pacing, with contrast and visual rhythm over a succession of pages, an overall plan is needed. Too much visual complexity can be counterproductive, but a succession of similar-looking spreads will become boring and you may lose your audience. One technique is to construct a flatplan showing the total number of pages in the publication. The flatplan can be drawn small (thumbnail size) in double-page spreads. It should contain page numbers, titles and content. A quick survey of this plan gives you a broad overview of how your material will unfold (see page 28).

When you begin your design process, don't become too dependent on the images you create on screen. If the final result is meant to be in print, print out your document often during the process and view your pages at the actual size of the finished product. Type sizes and weights, image quality and scale, and the rhythm, pacing and transition from one spread to the next should be evaluated in the same format as the end user would see it. Check your pacing throughout the process and be flexible enough to initiate change where it is needed.

### Creating momentum and rhythm

At the beginning of an article, or section of a book, create momentum and rhythm and set the mood for a receptive reader using all the composition skills you have learned. You can use pictures as a frieze, in a narrow sequence of images running along the top of the spreads that moves the reader across the pages. You can create various mosaic arrangements on the grid, using one large picture and a series of smaller ones. You can break out of the grid at strategic points. Depending on picture content, you can create vertical movement with narrow vertical images. Conversely, with landscape-format pictures you can create a strong sense of horizontal movement.

You can control the pace by juxtaposing black-and-white images with bright spots of colour, or black-and-white with duotones, tritones and speciality inks. Variation between narrow and wide text measures will add pace to your pages, and using your grid system creatively is essential. Strong background colours or reversed-out type at specific points can also create a sense of movement to change the speed and vary the rhythm. Be deliberate in your decisions and interpret your subject matter thoughtfully. Keep it quiet if the material calls for introspection, or pick up the pace and build excitement if appropriate.

➔ **Publication pace** The designer of the Seventy-Five Familiar Faces publication has used monochrome to set the tone, and has placed text dispersed with images throughout to create pace and break up the text. As a result, tension is built throughout the story leading right up to the American football away game before the fatal accident.

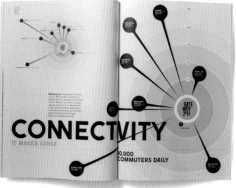

⊕ **SEE ALSO:** BASIC PRINCIPLES OF DESIGN LAYOUT, P40

### Printed publications

In publication design, pace and contrast are fundamental. There are more types of magazines – print or electronic – than any other category of design. They range from highbrow, political, economic or philosophical journals to sporting, arts, satirical, and leisure and lifestyle titles. Each publication will require different solutions to the pacing, depending on content and readership. Magazine readers differ from book readers because they view the product in unpredictable ways and in differing environments. Some will be led by the cover images to the contents page, where they will select their articles in an ordered way; others will dip in and out of any part of the magazine; while others will always read certain sections in a peculiarly personal order. Magazine readers may view the publication at home, in a relaxed environment with no distractions, or they may pick up an issue in a waiting room or a public place. Engaged, entertained readers become loyal subscribers, so the visual should work with the content to transport the reader, like any good book. For a design

⬆ **Flexibility** The layout of the Gloria Cortina Mexico brochure portrays the flexibility in composition available in one publication design. Through a series of dynamic spreads and interesting and unusual image placement and treatment, this flexibility adds rhythm and motion to the book and sophistication to each image.

to be memorable, visual interest should be present on every page and the editorial personality of the magazine should be evident at every turn. Designers use every tool, including pagination and wayfinding marks, to reinforce the style and mood of a publication. A true master of magazine layout is the American designer Alexey Brodovich, who worked primarily in the 1940s and 1950s. Bradbury Thompson also understood the importance of pace and contrast.

In illustrated books, change of pace is also required. Generally, readers behave in a relatively logical way, moving through the publication from start to finish. They, too, will dive in and out, but not to the same extent as magazine readers. In book design, economic factors also play a part. If plenty of pages are available, then you can introduce section openers and use lots of white space to create drama with headings and placement. Each book design should have a strong visual identity. If the spreads are too diverse, it can have a hazardous effect on the book and become confusing to the reader.

◀ **Breaking the rules**
This alternative London guide takes inspiration from fanzines, where the traditional rules of graphic design are broken in return for a fast, rough and dramatic aesthetic. It is important to understand the rules of layout and pace before you decide to break them.

## Digital publications

Digital magazines require different strategies; type and images interact much more immediately on screen. Imagery is much easier to manipulate and adapt to a variety of purposes and device formats. Some of the principles of print-based work may not apply directly to screen-based designs: one obvious difference is that, instead of turning pages, viewers scroll up and down for consecutive views of 'spreads'. Instead of using weight, style or position for emphasis, type might move or a static image may click through to a video presentation. Page structure and the placement of graphic elements must reflect the function of the site.

A new aesthetic continues to develop hand in hand with digital technology that ties form and function. Ultimately, though, basic issues of pace and contrast for print still apply, in part, for screen. The designer must still navigate the viewer through the maze of available information and present the appropriate markers for wayfinding. Due to the versatility and a different set of economic factors when designing digitally, it is important to challenge what can be done with digital publication design beyond what can be done in print. For example, most online newspapers are designed to the same space-saving specification and use flat information, which is rarely interactive, because their printed counterparts are used as templates. Digital publications offer a great opportunity to push what digital design could (and should) be.

Learning the basics of layout design from the model of print design is a stepping stone to the development of new ways of working in digital environments. The rules of good design should always be considered, regardless of format or media, and the designer should be able to apply them appropriately.

⬆ **Sophisticated wit** With humour and a touch of surrealism, Carin Goldberg's beautiful, iconic magazine covers for the *New York Times* and the typography magazine *U&lc* reflect contemporary culture through the designer's playful eye.

➡ **Complex systems** Digital publications have complex systems that offer multiple options and need to be considered in depth by the designer. Well-designed digital publications should have all the excitement and visual narrative skills of the printed page. *TLQ* magazine presents expert editorial art direction at every swipe, scroll or zoom, and provides the pacing and detail needed when the viewer can easily alter the pace.

**⬆ Purposeful shapes**
The inspiration for this project was an old-fashioned ice-cream van, and the die-cut cover conceals a traditionally shaped booklet inside.

| PART 1 | PRINCIPLES |
|---|---|
| CHAPTER 2 | FUNDAMENTALS OF COMPOSITION |
| MODULE 7 | **Size and format** |

Size and format are important considerations in any piece of design. They are affected by budget, practical restraints, the format in which they are to be produced, and by the needs of the job. The experience the end user has while interacting with the materials will affect the type of response the material evokes. Print is an intimate medium that's meant to be viewed close to the body. The tactile qualities of printed media are evidenced by weight, surface texture, binding, gloss, matt or metallic inks, foil stamps, and die-cut surfaces, all of which play a part in the personality of the product. Digital, on the other hand, is evidenced by user experience and depth of interactive engagement.

### Primary considerations

In deciding on format, the designer is often limited by external factors. Certain elements of a corporate identity package, such as letterheads, envelopes, forms and websites, are usually a standard size; other factors, however, may also have to be considered. Cost issues loom large: can the size selected for printing be cut economically from a bigger sheet of paper or will there be unnecessary expensive waste? Carefully evaluate the sheet size with the number of copies required. Will the finished work have to be mailed out? If so, weigh a mock-up to estimate postage costs: a larger format may prove to be too expensive to send by post if you are printing thousands of impressions. Can the job be folded economically in relation to the grain of the paper? Work with your printer to find the most economical and environmentally sound solution, and determine your size and scale before starting the design process.

### Content determines format

In book design, print or digital, format should be determined by purpose or nature, with the user in mind. Text-only books pose fewer problems than books with a heavy concentration of photographic or illustrative subjects. For continuous reading, a good point size on a readable, attractive font with adequate margins in play can help to determine the format as either portrait or landscape, and in paperbacks, which need to be both cheap and portable, point size is typically small. In illustrated books, the images should resonate the mood of the subject and a larger format book is appropriate – but check your size in a mock-up version before you begin, to ensure the book won't become unwieldy. Illustrations and photographs do not necessarily lose information value if they are smaller than at first anticipated, and there are benefits in making a product easier for the reader to handle. The largest

**⬆ Book art** Unusual formats can transform a simple design into conceptual art. An alternative binding can enhance the tactile user experience and reinforce the content in subtle ways.

**⬅ Dramatic landscapes**
The horizon line in the two-page bleed photographic image determined the typographic sight line on the preceding page, and adds drama to the page design.

**Vertical orientation**
Stacked vertical columns of text, supported by vertically oriented typographic illustrations, add height and drama in this text-as-image approach to page design.

**Nostalgic** The clever accordion fold was produced to celebrate and commemorate a community arts project run by artist Mark Storor in the seaside town of Jaywick. The concept design and format mimicked a vintage-style folded postcard.

**GLOSSARY**

**Concertina folds:** Folds in alternate directions.

**French folds:** Sheets of paper are folded in half, so that they are double thickness. The two folds are at right angles to each other and then bound on the edge.

**Gatefold:** A way of folding paper so that the outer quarters of a page are folded to meet in the centre. The result works like symmetrical doors that open onto an inner page.

**Paper grain:** The direction of wood fibres that make up a piece of paper.

**Perfect binding:** Method similar to paperback binding, where loose sheets are encased in a heavier paper cover, then glued to the book spine. Edges are trimmed to be flush with each other.

**Roll-over folds:** A way of folding a page so that successive folds turn in on themselves and the page is folded into a roll.

**Saddle stitching:** Binding method where sheets of paper are folded in the centre, stitched together along the fold, then glued into the cover spine.

formats are generally reserved for art and design subjects and museum catalogues, in which excellent-quality illustrations are central to the book's success. Digital publications are less of a concern as a user can zoom and navigate information slightly differently.

Whenever possible, content should determine format. Think about your subject matter and examine all available materials for inclusion before you determine the final format. If there are beautiful panoramic landscape views to be featured in the book, a horizontal or full-screen format may be your obvious choice.

Experiment in your initial layout sketches and determine the best way to showcase your materials to the greatest effect. If the subject matter calls for white space to be part of the design, be sure to anticipate the additional dimensions for your margins and gutters. Multilingual publications pose their own set of problems. It is probably best to try to accommodate two or three languages side by side to achieve a consistent flow of text and, if illustrated, to ensure that text references are on the same page or screen as pictures.

Although international standardisation in paper sizes helps keep prices down, the same old formats can become boring. There are some inventive solutions, but ensure they fit the design concept of the publication.

**Folds and binding**
With smaller publications and brochures, folds can play a big part in enticing the reader into the subject matter.

The aesthetically pleasing square format is simply achieved by folding the sheet in a different way. Organising copy to follow folds – whether rolling folds or concertina folds – creates a sense of fun and is an excellent way to entice the reader into the publication.

Simple binding ideas can also enhance the appeal of smaller publications and can be used inventively to add to the wayfinding of the content. You might consider trimming each spread a little shorter than the preceding one, giving the area at the end of the page a space for information graphics or subheads. An untrimmed fore edge makes for an attractively handcrafted feel, as does visible coloured thread for the stitching. These ideas are easy to implement; they don't necessarily cost a lot and can make your designs different and memorable. Make sure you consider all aspects of the project as part of your design process from the very beginning: changing one or two elements will affect your other decisions as well, and may cause you to back up the process and redesign certain elements. Part of the fun of design work is in the discovery of inventive solutions, new materials, new mediums and new combinations of tried-and-tested techniques.

Take the time to consider the importance of your choices and remember that if you can see something, your client can, too. Every aspect of the project should be evaluated with a designer's eye, right down to the smallest detail.

**SEE ALSO:** BASIC PRINCIPLES OF DESIGN LAYOUT, P40

STYLES OF LAYOUT, P44

PHOTOGRAPHY AND ILLUSTRATION, P56

| PART 1 | PRINCIPLES |
|---|---|
| CHAPTER 2 | FUNDAMENTALS OF COMPOSITION |
| MODULE 8 | **Identity and extended systems** |

**GLOSSARY**

**Identity:** A unified, identifiable look for a product or organisation.

**Patch:** The space on a bookshop's shelf occupied by spines of books from the same series.

Few things are designed to work as stand-alone pieces. Look at a successful branding: the logos and corporate identity, advertising campaigns, direct-mail campaigns, annual reports, websites and social-media presence all have common design elements, binding them together and identifying them as part of the same brand. Look at the total content of any magazine or newspaper: the information changes, yet the publication looks consistent, issue after issue, and at a glance, we can easily and immediately identify our favourites on the shelf.

This brand identity is achieved through a co-ordinated design and effective design strategy that is fluid enough to allow for variation and change, but is consistent throughout. With newspapers and magazines, this can be achieved with strict rules. For example, major headlines will be set in one font and ranged left; secondary headlines in another font and centred; body text in yet another font with fixed point size, leading and justification; feature articles in a bolder font with looser leading and alternate justification. These rules are never broken, but they should be comprehensive enough to allow for any situation while maintaining a consistent 'look'.

Authors may write more than one book, and publishers almost always use co-ordinated designs for their book covers. If a publisher is repackaging the back catalogue of a bestselling author, they will use a co-ordinated strategy for the covers that allows for changes of colour, image and titling, but also enables book buyers to identify the titles as part of a set, or brand. Perhaps the unchanging element is the type, set in the same face, at the same size and in the same position throughout. Or it could be the style of the photograph used – black and white, full colour, abstract – or that of the illustration, whether this is pen and ink,

🔽 **Rebranded** The identity of the Finnish baking company Backers has been redesigned with a concept inspired by research into the client's origin in the 17th century. In the resulting branding, the contemporary sans-serif font used for the company name contrasts well with the detailed B. The pennant shapes recall ancient banners from the times when Backers was originally founded.

In the tradition of folk art and woodcarving, the initial B has been detailed with baking and farming symbols that include a decorative wheat pattern.

In the packaging design, the wheat pattern is lifted from inside the B and repeated in a sunray around the dominant circular form.

The mark works equally when used small or greatly enlarged on the side of a lorry.

painting, digital, collage. A good designer ties together all the elements, creating a formula that not only makes each individual piece striking in its own right, but also ensures easy identification with its counterparts.

### Creating identifying characteristics

Well thought-out extended systems are the building blocks for all complex design projects. Corporate identity systems will partner clean, easy-to-decode logo designs with supportive graphics or photography that become an extension of the brand and can be used interchangeably on multiple applications. Most will also include a distinct colour palette and a particular typographic sensibility that support the content without diluting the brand's original message. These design assets keep the brand fresh and exciting, and enhance the presence of a product, something that motivates all manufacturers and organisations competing for attention in the marketplace whether the product is books, chocolate, a gallery or an online music service. The next

time you go out shopping, or attend a cultural event, look for this principle and you will notice that many of the products that have the most eye-catching and co-ordinated identity schemes belong to the most successful businesses and organisations. This is not a coincidence, and the designer who can successfully co-ordinate a brand or a company will always be in demand.

### Know the content

Getting to know your brand and your target audience is part of your preliminary research. To speak to your audience accurately, you must also understand the content. In package design the product is usually easy to recognise, sometimes visible through the packaging material, and positioned for attention in the marketplace. The architecture of the package and the details in the design system work together to create an image-aware brand that proclaims itself as expensive, healthy, fashionable or traditional by the very nature of the design system the artist creates and the materials used in the

**⊘ Understated elegance**
Simple shapes and large fields of colour define these elegant design systems by Carin Goldberg. The boxed set of books for New York's School of Visual Arts uses the rectangular form of the books and carefully placed dots to mark volumes one to four in the series, and extends the system of colour blocks and simplified and gestural shapes to the inside page designs. The system for the works of Kurt Vonnegut uses bars of colour that are reflected in the collective spines of the books.

packaging. It should also lead consumers through the functions of opening, dispensing and reclosing without making them work too hard to get to the product. In complex packaging, there may be enclosures, hang-tags and labels to design. The extended design system can enhance the product but should always remain true to the brand. In addition to housing and protecting the product, package design is advertising at the place where the consumer actually makes their purchase, sometimes in large displays that become part of the retail experience. To be really successful, it must communicate the correct message at a glance if singular, or work together in big displays of multiples, if it is to compete with other goods.

### Interpretation and detail

In editorial design, the content must be carefully considered for its message and the author's point of view. A book jacket is, in effect, a piece of packaging that advertises both product and publisher. It should be approached in the same way as an advertising campaign, but the imagery can sometimes deliver its message in a more thought-provoking, poetic way.

First, each book must compete with all the others on display, leaping out from the shelf before informing potential buyers as to what the book might be about and why they should buy it. In bookshops with limited space, only the spines will be visible, so how these detailed areas work as small-space designs is

**⊙ Restaurant identity**

Handsome use of elegant white space and interesting repetition of diagonal lines mark this strong restaurant identity system. Beautiful detail derived from the system is noted in the circular hardware at the top of the menu, a perfect complement to the circles containing icons.

The repetition and variation of the linework, the exchange of positive and negative colour, and the use of the diagonal in dividing space crosses over from the printed system to the website design.

⬆ **Type as image** Typography is a system of simple shapes that can be used to make complex patterns when they are combined in a dynamic composition. These beautifully positioned letterforms create an innovative and playful solution without the use of traditional imagery.

➡ **Background check** Plan your composition, photographic subjects and text before you photograph your finished subject. Clean, textural slate in neutral grey serves as the perfect backdrop for richly coloured images and decorative display type on these menus. Repetition in the composition and variation in type and subject keeps the series inventive.

## TIPS AND CHECKLIST FOR SELECTING IMAGES

- **Image, style and theme** Determine the look before you commit. It's fine to be inspired by images you see in your research, but be sure to resolve the concept before you make a purchase or hire a freelancer.
- **Be contrary** Consider the opposite of what is expected: this will either give you a new angle or help to consolidate your original thoughts.
- **Budget and schedule** Check that your solution is affordable and feasible in the time you have available.
- **Age/gender/socio-economics of the target audience** Who will see it? The visuals for the horoscope page of a teenage magazine, for example, could certainly be more quirky and abstract than the imagery for a financial company report and accounts.
- **Shelf life** The images in a weekly magazine can be transient, whereas those in an expensive book with a selling potential of ten years or more need to have more lasting resonance.
- **Clarity of information** The images for an editorial design might be deliberately obscure, whereas those for a technical manual must be clear and didactic.
- **Perceived value** This is tricky to pinpoint, since often something that is inexpensive is marketed as valuable through its image, and something that is really expensive can seek to appeal to a mass market through a casual, trendy approach.
- **Design criteria and usage** Do you want a dynamic cut-out shape or a square image bled off the page? Will you use it in black and white or colour?
- **DIY** Can you create this image yourself? Graphic designers with image generation skills are more likely to be hired than those without.

# CHAPTER 2: ASSIGNMENTS

## ○ BASIC COMPOSITION

This exercise can be done electronically or by hand; however, it is highly recommended that you develop your craft skills and work with traditional media. You can use cut paper, or draw each of the elements with pencil and fill them with black paint, but be precise.

Prepare three white 20-cm (8-in) squares. Using only five black squares positioned within the larger white ones, express the concepts of harmony, chaos and structure. The black squares can be any size, and you can position them however it feels meaningful to you. Begin by creating 20 thumbnail sketches for each of the three concepts, then select the best one for each final version.

Pay attention to the negative space that is created when you crop squares off the edge of the page or overlap them, and remember that negative space is part of the composition. Think about the effects of symmetry and asymmetry, closure and field ground as you work.

## ○ SYMMETRY

A B C D E F G H I J K L M N
O P Q R S T U V W X Y Z

Separate the letters from the Latin alphabet according to which ones are symmetrical into three groups: the letters that are vertically symmetrical (like the letter A); those that are horizontally symmetrical (like the letter D); and those with both vertical and horizontal symmetry (like the letter O). Can you do the same for a collection of logos? Why do you think they are successful? Apply this thinking by taking the first letter of your name and using symmetry in an interesting way to sketch up a few examples of logos.

## ○ UNDERSTANDING GRIDS

Choose a magazine that you find attractive or compelling and select three different spreads – both right- and left-hand pages. These should include feature editorial spreads and spreads that contain a mixture of multiple images and text.

**1** Remove the spreads carefully from the magazine and mount them on boards. Cover each spread with a sheet of tracing paper that will reach from edge to edge.

**2** Using a pencil and measuring carefully, identify and trace the grid lines on each of the page designs. Note the column widths and the margins at the top, sides, bottom, and to the left and right of each column. Look carefully for the edges of all the elements placed on the page, some of which may reach over two or three columns, so your lines may cross right through an element on the page. Look carefully before you draw.

**3** When you have finished, identify the system on each page. Is your selection based on a two-column, six-column or a modular system?

**4** Write a brief summary of your findings, and explain why you were attracted to the pages you selected and how you think the grid system supports the design work.

**5** Carry out this task again on novels, newspapers and websites. Can you determine any patterns? Why do you think this is?

## ○ PAGE DESIGN

Bring a news article to life in an expressive visual way using typography.

**1** Select your article, examine the text and decide how it should be divided, identifying which text should head the article and be the clearest, which text takes secondary importance, and so on. What are the most important parts within the text? Perhaps there are certain areas of the text you want to draw particular attention to. Identify the tone and subject matter of the article. Is it urgent, serious, lively, good-humoured, sombre? These things should help inform your typographic approach. Think about scale, tension and visual drama, and think about telling the story.

**2** Using InDesign, set up a considered and appropriate grid for your planned visual expression (this will become clear through sketching). Think about margins, gutters and the general impact a grid system can give a spread.

**3** Select one typeface, either serif or sans serif, and determine a point size, weight and leading.

**4** Using the same typeface and type presets each time, develop six different dynamic compositions utilising the same grid system. Remember how symmetry and asymmetry affect composition. Think about placement on the page and test the flexibility of the grid system you have chosen.

**5** Repeat the exercise with a more complex grid system and add a photographic subject to each of the compositions.

## ○ DECONSTRUCTING PACE AND CONTRAST

Publication design requires the co-ordination of carefully placed text and imagery to lend variety, anticipation and drama, whether the publication is printed or appears online.

Select a printed magazine, brochure or book. Identify the design strategies used to vary the pace. How is the white space used? Are there variations in the grid system? Does the placement of type and image vary in size and scale? Is there smart use of contrast and scale? Are certain pages making you pause for a lengthier examination? If so, why?

Now examine an online publication and note the differences and similarities used to set the visual pace as you click through. Can you follow the flow of information? Is there enough variety to keep you interested? Make special note of any tools that might be unique to the online experience. Write your findings up and layout this information in ways you have just analysed. Using the same content, try an approach to speed the pace, and one to slow it right down.

## ○ EXTENDED SYSTEMS

**1a** Identify a favourite brand and examine it closely. Find three examples of the brand used in different applications – for example, printed page, web page, packaging. Make a list of every element that is repeated and elements that are added to the composition or varied in any way. Design an additional application of this brand, perhaps a vinyl on a bus or a billboard, using what you've discovered about extended system patterns to apply this thinking to another format.

**1b** Select a famous person, fictitious or real, living or dead, and develop a vector logo for them that reflects their personality. It can be any type of logo you think is appropriate – pictorial, letterform or abstract. Make sure your logo design can be reduced and enlarged without losing legibility.

**2** Design a letterhead and business card that uses the logo in a controlled system. Make sure the design of the letterhead and card continue to reflect the overall personality of your subject.

**3** Add a third element and extend your system. It could be the design of a website, or you might imagine your famous personality has developed a signature product line – for example, clothing, perfume, jewellery, sports equipment. To do this, look carefully at the work you have just completed on the logo, letterhead and business card. Identify three characteristics that make your system constant on all three designs. Now begin sketching ideas for your third element, using at least two of the three elements, and adding one or more variations.

## ○ PHOTOGRAPHY AND ILLUSTRATION

**1** Select a classic novel that you have read and are fairly familiar with. Consider the storyline, the message and the overall tone of the writing. Make a list of the most influential elements in the novel – for example, characters, circumstances, defining events, time periods. Define the target audience for the novel. Select a key theme for an image that represents this novel, draw it, stage a photograph of it, research archival images, come up with as many creative means to visually represent this theme.

**2** Sketch three to five ideas from your extensive list that best illustrate your concept for the book's cover. When you have selected the best sketch, begin your final versions by tightening up the composition and clarity of the concept.

**3** Develop a more refined version using traditional media – paint, pencil, collage – to determine coloration and value. Consider whether photography or illustration would best suit the concept, or if a combination of both would be most effective.

**Further Reading:**

Phillip Meggs and Alston W. Purvis, *Meggs' History of Graphic Design*, Wiley, 2016

Steven Heller and Louise Fili, *Stylepedia*, Chronicle Books, 2006

Richard Hollis, *Swiss Design*, Yale, 2006

Timothy Samara, *Making and Breaking the Grid*, Rockport, 2005

Gavin Ambrose and Paul Harris, *Basic Design 07: Grids*, AVA, 2012

Milton Glaser, *Art is Work*, The Elephant's Eye, 2008

Horst Moser, *Surprise Me: Editorial Design*, BATTY, 2003

Josef Müller-Brockmann, *Grid Systems in Graphic Design*, Verlag Niggli, 1999

Beth Tondreau, *Layout Essentials: 100 Design Principles for Using Grids*, Rockport, 2011

Francesco Franchi, *Designing News: Changing the World of Editorial Design and Information Graphics*, Die Gestalten Verlag, 2013

# Fundamentals of typography

Typography is the process of arranging letters, words and text for almost any context imaginable, and it is among the most important tools a designer masters for effective visual communication. Graphic designers learn the nuances of typography in order to use it creatively, with imagination and a sense of exploration, while maintaining respect for its rules and traditions.

In design, typography is the visual manifestation of language, utilising all its expressive and practical qualities, and occupies a unique place where art, science and communications connect. You need only look at work presented by concrete poets, or to various art movements such as Futurism and Dada, to see typography's significance as an aesthetic medium. It also involves the design and selection of type for both legibility and communication of information, and, in some instances, aesthetic experimentation takes a backseat to pragmatic concerns.

Expressive typography and hand-drawn letterforms are a calligraphic art form in their own right. With so many interpretative typographic choices, sketching and hands-on experimenting with layouts will help you learn to evaluate the readability and nuance of the message before working onscreen, essential stages that help in learning about the subtleties of type.

**New vintage**
Hand-drawn letterforms evoke the decorative typography of another century in this beautiful logotype by Tom Lane. The configuration of the letterforms, the overall shape created by the type design and the selective use of ruled lines for depth and underscoring keep the composition unified. The overall effect is one of tradition and craftsmanship.

| PART 1 | PRINCIPLES |
|---|---|
| CHAPTER 3 | FUNDAMENTALS OF TYPOGRAPHY |
| MODULE 1 | **Typography and meaning** |

**By definition, a typographic message, aside from an intrinsic beauty, must convey a meaning. Meaning, and its expression, is at the core of typographic activity, at the level of both individual words and entire passages of text. This is called linguistic meaning, since it resides in language.**

Letters and words have an abstract beauty, seen and appreciated through experiments in type anatomy, which isolate the forms and separate elements of individual letters, and frequently reveal them as shapes, rather than meaningful linguistic objects. However, the instant words materialise on page or on screen, they begin to express ideas and possess this elusive quality we call meaning. Linguistic meaning, an essential element of typography, can be expressed, controlled and amplified through such typographic variables as size, weight, typeface (or font), placement on the page and letterspacing.

Sometimes, as in the pages of a book, the visual aspects of typography must take a backseat to the process of understanding. However, designers use such visual techniques all the time, to communicate messages effectively; building confidence in working with text in this way is important, so that linking typographic form to linguistic meaning becomes second nature.

## Meaning

But what is 'meaning'? An alternative term is 'semantics', an important subtopic within all aspects of design, which is worth exploring in more detail. Semantics is the study of meaning and applies to both images and language. 'Syntax' (or grammar) refers to the rules that govern the organisation of elements of a sentence or paragraph, so that meaning is conveyed. If the syntax is wrong, then language becomes nonsense, or meaningless. In a general sense, to say that something has a meaning (a semantic value) relies upon its ability to present its idea in a form that can be communicated and shared. In linguistic meaning (the language-based meaning that typography participates in), this communicability is based on sets of symbols in the given language, which include letters and words, and also on the space between words, punctuation and placement of the characters.

Typographers such as Wolfgang Weingart, Willem Sandberg and H. N. Werkmann pushed the expression of meaning in typography to its very limit and, in so doing, expanded its visual vocabulary and expressive potential by working at the boundary between language and meaning.

Dada and Futurist artists such as Kurt Schwitters and Tristan Tzara, Marinetti and Wyndham Lewis experimented with the relationship between language and meaning. These historical practitioners are worth studying closely, as are their inspirational typographic experiments. Look at the works of the concrete poets e.e. cummings and Apollinaire, and contemporary designers such as Robert Massin, Johanna Drucker and Erik Spiekermann. Look at the experimental work of David Carson, who used type as texture in *Ray Gun* magazine, and at Paula Scher's graphic type solutions in poster design and environmental graphics.

"When you look at a city, it's like reading the hopes, aspirations and pride of everyone who built it."
—Hugh Newell Jacobsen

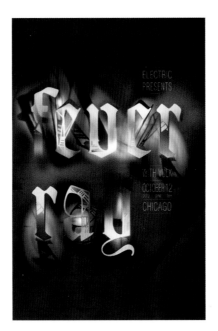

↑ **Word as object** Expressive typography can be used as an image, and the meaning of the words can be linked to the image. Here, the vision of the city is visually expressed by the adjectives that describe it.

◀ **Constructed letterforms** Dimensional letterforms die-cut with lacy patterns are illuminated to create graphic shadows in the composition. The positive and negative shapes are defined by light and shadow in the delicately half-toned photographic image used in the final poster.

◀ **Abstract composition** Here, oversized and carefully cropped letters create dynamic abstract forms in a strong composition. Depth is added though variation in scale and texture, and bold colour adds to the strong declarative voice.

## GLOSSARY

**Font:** One size, weight and width of a typeface: Garamond Roman 12pt is a font.

**Linguistic:** Of, or relating to, language.

**Semantics:** The study of meaning in language and elsewhere.

**Syntax:** The study of the rules for the formation of grammatically correct sentences.

**Typeface:** The set of visual attributes (design or style) of a particular group of letters: Garamond is a typeface.

| PART 1 | PRINCIPLES |
|---|---|
| CHAPTER 3 | FUNDAMENTALS OF TYPOGRAPHY |
| MODULE 2 | **The anatomy of type** |

Familiarity with the basic structure of letterforms, the anatomy of type, is essential to understanding how typefaces differ and what characteristics they share, and allows the designer to make decisions about selecting and using the multitude of typefaces now available. The most basic element of typography is the letterform, and each typeface has its own unique characteristics, while sharing a basic language that describes its parts.

← **Typeface** A block of letterpress type, showing the face of the letter, whose surface is inked and printed, giving us the term 'typeface'. **a** face, **b** body or shank, **c** point size, **d** shoulder, **e** nick, **f** groove, **g** foot.

Oblique, angled stress, associated with old-style typefaces

Semi-oblique stress, associated with transitional typefaces

Vertical stress, associated with modern and sans-serif typefaces

↑ **Language of letterforms** Each distinct part of a letter has its own name, forming a 'language of letterforms'.

↓ **Identifying characteristics** The different stresses of typefaces are essential information in identifying their place within the classification systems, and to locating them within an historical timeline.

Common terminology of typefaces includes the size of the x-height, counterform, serif (or sans-) style and stress of the letter (vertical/oblique). The ability to compare these characteristics between typefaces establishes essential knowledge about the suitability of a particular typeface. By providing valuable information, or 'earmarks', about how typefaces relate to classification systems, such as old-style, transitional, humanist, modern and serif/sans serif, knowledge of type anatomy helps graphic designers to identify and select appropriate typefaces for different purposes.

Technology has accelerated the creation of new faces and produced digital versions of classics. There are so many choices available that selecting an appropriate typeface can be daunting. There are some digital fonts on the market that are of limited use, often downloadable for free. Many don't have much to offer in versatility and lack a timeless quality. An argument can be made that that they do appear different or somewhat experimental, and novelty has its uses in certain circumstances. For general use, especially where readability is a key concern, however, it is better to select classical fonts. Criteria for selection should normally be based on a careful evaluation of the media, the readership and the design objective.

**Key terms**

There are over 25 anatomical terms applicable to letterforms. For general typography it's not necessary to know all of them, but some are essential to making visual judgments that aid typeface selection for different situations, and you should be able to describe

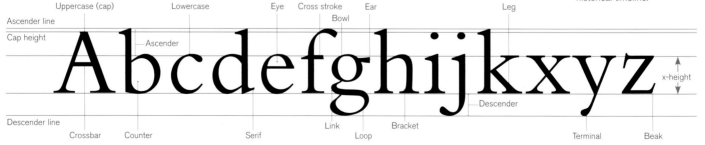

Uppercase (cap)     Lowercase     Eye    Cross stroke    Ear     Leg

Ascender line

Cap height    Ascender     Bowl

x-height

Descender line     Descender

Crossbar    Counter     Serif    Link    Loop    Bracket     Terminal    Beak

Times New Roman    Bodoni Book    Times New Roman    Bodoni Book

those differences in a technically correct way. For example, you may want to argue for the use of the beautiful 18th-century typeface Bodoni in a particular design. You should be able to state that its characteristics include a vertical stress and a high degree of contrast between thick and thin strokes, and that the humanist quality of the font is appropriate to the readership and message.

Information about the difference between x-heights of typefaces is very helpful, since this allows the designer to choose typefaces that are more or less readable at smaller sizes. The x-height is the size of a lowercase 'x' in a given typeface, and the ratio between x-height and the ascenders and descenders of the lowercase letters, such as 'g' and 'h', define the overall appearance of a font. As with all design decisions, the space around the design elements, type or image, is part of the picture and should be considered. Typefaces that have a large x-height may need more space between the lines (leading), so that they don't appear visually heavy on the page.

Typefaces of the same point size can appear larger or smaller. Futura has a small x-height, and long ascenders/ descenders, whereas most sans-serif typefaces, such as Helvetica, typically have large x-heights. Although a general understanding of the terminology of typefaces is adequate for most designers, if you become interested in designing typefaces you will need to develop an intimate knowledge of type anatomy, in all its nuances, and have an excellent understanding of typeface history and development.

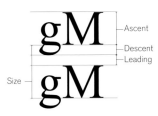

### Measuring
The point size of type is measured from the baseline of one line of type to the baseline of another. Leading is the vertical space between lines of type, and affects the readability of text.

### Impact of x-height
The x-height is the height of a lowercase x and determines the visual size of type. The x-height size varies from typeface to typeface: some, like Bodoni, have a small x-height, whereas Times New Roman has a large x-height. However, each type has the same body size. Type with large x-heights tend to have small ascenders and descenders, whereas type with small x-heights have large ones.

### Small x-heights
In typefaces with small x-heights, such as Caslon and Futura, there is more white space above and below the lowercase letters. Such type is easier to read, because the eye can travel back and forth along lines without difficulty. Use less leading in these typefaces, or even set them without any additional leading ('solid'), and set them in a larger point size.

### Large x-heights
In typefaces with large x-heights, such as Bookman or Helvetica, the lack of white space above and below the lowercase letters, and the larger white spaces within the letters, requires more space between lines. Increase the leading so that the text is easier to read, and the overall 'colour' (another term for density or texture of the type) on the page is less heavy.

**Baseline:** The line on which the lowercase letters sit and below which the descenders fall.

**Earmark:** Identifying or distinguishing marks or characteristics of a typeface.

**Point size/pica:** The relative size of a font. There are 72 points in an inch.

**Stress/axis:** The angle of the curved stroke weight change in a typeface. Seen clearly in letters such as 'o'.

**Type anatomy:** The language used to describe the various parts of letterforms.

**x-height:** The height of a lowercase 'x' in any typeface.

**SEE ALSO:** UNDERSTANDING AND SELECTING TYPEFACES, P66

1234567890

1234567890

### Numerals
Aligning (above, set in Palatino) and non-aligning (or old-style) numbers (below, set in Bembo Expert).

Helvetica          Futura          Bembo

Typefaces of | the same size | look different sizes | because they | have varying | x-heights |

Bodoni          Bernhard Modern          Times New Roman

| PART 1 | PRINCIPLES |
| --- | --- |
| CHAPTER 3 | FUNDAMENTALS OF TYPOGRAPHY |
| MODULE 3 | **Understanding and selecting typefaces** |

Since the introduction of digital typefaces, the number of fonts available has increased exponentially; it is virtually impossible to know them all, or be able to reference all of their attributes. However, it is always advantageous to know a typeface's historical background, since this can help in relating its characteristics to the content of the text. Selecting and understanding typefaces is a complicated business, but one that becomes easier with practice.

For example, a sans-serif typeface such as Univers references modernity in a way that a serif font such as Garamond does not. Bodoni, designed in the late 1700s, has certain formal characteristics that, in their own era, were considered modern, including its use of perfectly vertical stress and sharp contrast between thick and thin lines, departing from 'old-style' typefaces based on pen-drawn forms. In a modern setting this font is associated with classicism and history. Although it can be used in a contemporary way, it's important to understand Bodoni's history and associations, and to take these into account when considering its use.

Understanding a typeface's historical origins and references, and its associated formal (visual) characteristics, is crucial when it comes to matters of selection. Broadly, contemporary typefaces such as Futura and Univers tend to work in modern contexts, whereas traditional type such as Garamond might be more apt for a literary classic. Of course, all these conventions are there to be played with and broken, but only when you have a full understanding of their significance. Research and read books on graphic design history, since our design past is always influencing the present.

**⊙ Newspaper fonts**
Sans-serif fonts were first seen in 1786. Shown above is an early use of a sans serif working with serif fonts, in a French newspaper, from 1898. Until this time, all newspaper text and headings were set in serif fonts, and to this day, text setting is usually in serif.

---

## SERIF

### oAad
Bembo regular

#### Humanist Old-Style

Typefaces of the 15th and 16th centuries are based on hand-drawn calligraphic letterforms. They are characterised by having slanted (oblique or diagonal) stress, bracketed serifs and low contrast between thick and thin strokes. Sabon, designed by Jan Tschichold in 1966, is a contemporary example, based on the 16th- century typeface Garamond.

### oAad
Baskerville regular

#### Transitional

A more vertical axis is visible in these 18th-century typefaces. The sharp contrast between thick and thin strokes was considered controversial at the time. Serifs are still bracketed, but they are moving away from the calligraphic influence. Baskerville is an example of a transitional typeface.

### oAad
Bodoni Book

#### Modern

In the late 18th and early 19th centuries, typefaces became significantly more abstract. Bodoni shows a highly exaggerated contrast between thick and thin strokes, a perfectly vertical stress and serifs that are no longer bracketed, but straight lines.

### oAad
Rockwell regular

#### Egyptian and Slab Serif

In the early 19th century, in response to the Industrial Revolution, many new typefaces were designed for use in advertising. Their bold, robust, decorative forms grew from this context. Egyptian typefaces are typical of this period, with their heavy, slab serifs and 'industrial' quality.

## SANS SERIF

### oAad
Gill sans book

#### Humanist Sans Serif

Sans-serif typefaces originated in the early 19th century but became dominant in the 20th century. Gill Sans, designed in 1928, combined the characteristics of both old-style serif and sans-serif fonts, with its calligraphic qualities but lack of serifs.

### oAad
Helvetica regular

#### Anonymous Sans Serif

Sans-serif fonts were first produced by Caslon in 1816 (in capitals only), and William Thorowgood in 1832 (with lowercase), and they were known as Grotesques, since they were thought to be ugly. Helvetica was designed in 1957 by Max Miedinger, and is one of the best known sans serifs.

### oAad
Futura book

#### Geometric Sans Serif

Typefaces such as Futura (designed by Paul Renner in 1927) are extensions of earlier sans serifs, but have a more geometric design, based on monolines (lines of one thickness, with no variation of thick and thin as in old-styles), perfect circles and triangular shapes. Such typefaces are associated with Modernism in the early part of the 20th century, but continue to be popular.

## Type classification

Before you examine the various factors involved in selecting type, it is worth considering the broad categories into which typefaces can be placed: type classification systems. Categorising type is never an exact process, and there are many layers to the classification process, but a rough guide can help in distinguishing the characteristics of typefaces and learning the appropriate uses for the various type families. A clear initial division is sometimes made between text and display type, each of which has its own criteria for selection, but there are also faces that function well in both roles.

## Text type: old style, transitional and modern

Primarily, text types are meant to be read in continuous form or at least with few interruptions.

• Old-style serif typefaces, such as Bembo, Garamond and Caslon, are ideal for this purpose. They are regarded as 'classic' fonts because they have stood the test of time and still command respect. These Roman fonts have been in use since the origins of printing in the 15th century, and are considered humanist, because the original designs referenced the hand-drawn characteristics of manuscripts. Much later, during the 1930s, a number of new 'Romans' were introduced to coincide with the new monotype hot-metal typesetting system and many of the classics were also re-cut for the same purpose. Times New Roman and Imprint are good examples of this group, known as 20th-century Romans. Later the German type designers Hermann Zapf and Jan Tschichold added, respectively, Palatino and Sabon to this group. Contemporary Romans, such as Minion, have now been designed using digital tools.

• Transitional Roman fonts have a vertical stress, sharp and bracketed serifs, and in most cases a medium to high contrast between thick and thin letter-strokes. Baskerville and Century Schoolbook are prime examples. The term captures a movement away from the old-style group, influenced by pen-drawn forms, towards modern faces rooted in geometry rather than the traditional pen stroke.

• Modern serif faces also have a vertical stress, but an abrupt contrast between the thick and thin letter-strokes, fine horizontal serifs and a narrow set width (in most cases). Bodoni is one of the earliest and best-known examples; Walbaum is a slightly more contemporary version of a 'modern' typeface.

There are many fonts in these three groups, which cover pretty much all kinds of book work. They can also be found in brochures and magazines, but other groups are more often used for this kind of publication.

**Classifying differences** Type classification charts are useful guides to the various characteristics (sometimes known as 'earmarks') of different typefaces. They allow you to place typefaces within their historical contexts and to see how their basic visual attributes are shared across different, but related, fonts. For example, Romans always have serifs, while sans-serif humanist typefaces such as Gill Sans share properties associated with both old-style Roman and sans-serif typefaces.

Correct fonts

*Italic* **Bold** SMALL CAPS Condensed Expanded

Pseudo fonts

*Italic* **Bold** SMALL CAPS Condensed Expanded

Unless you choose a real italic from the font menu, a computer will only slant Roman letterforms

Pseudo bold is simply thickened digitally rather than being the true, carefully crafted font

Small caps are used within lowercase text when smaller, non-dominant capital letters are required. They are used for emphasis within traditional typesetting

Artificially condensed or expanded letterforms should be avoided, since the computer distorts them by applying a percentage reduction or expansion. Always use a 'true' condensed or expanded typeface

**Old-style serif faces**

ABCabc
Bembo

ABCabc
Garamond

ABCabc
Caslon

ABCabc
Times new roman

ABCabc
Imprint

ABCabc
Palatino

ABCabc
Sabon

ABCabc
Minion

**Traditional roman fonts**

ABCabc
Baskerville

ABCabc
Century schoolbook

**Modern serif faces**

ABCabc
Walbaum

ABCabc
Bodoni

### Display type

Major social changes in the 19th century brought about the need for display type. The Industrial Revolution brought the masses into the cities, increasing the production and consumption of goods and services, which led to the need to communicate to a wider audience. Existing fonts were used primarily for books, then limited to an elite sector. Printers found the available typefaces inadequate for the new billboards, posters and pamphlets produced, especially since there were many more messages being displayed in public spaces, all vying for attention. Bolder, stronger faces were needed to suit this new context, and to meet demand.

The sans-serif typeface was bolder and more 'industrial' in its look, along with slab serifs and thickened modern letters known as fat faces. The Victorians were innovative; their typefaces are full of vigour and still fascinate today. John Lewis' book *Printed Ephemera* has excellent examples of Victorian display fonts used on posters and playbills.

### Sans-serif and script typefaces

The 20th century saw the extensive development of the sans serif, notably by the Bauhaus school in the 1920s and 1930s. Their philosophy was to sweep away the traditional forms characterised by excessive ornament, employing the principle of 'form equals function'. Simple typographic structures called for clean, functional typefaces, hence the interest in the sans serif with its mono weight and functional forms. Futura was introduced in 1927, and two years later Gill Sans was unveiled. In the decades that followed, well-known fonts such as Helvetica and Optima in Europe, and Franklin Gothic and Avant Garde in the USA, kept the sans serif among the most popular of type styles.

A significant advantage of the sans serif is the large number of potential variants within one typeface. In 1957 Adrian Frutiger introduced a complete family of different weights and forms when he conceived the design of Univers, which comprises 21 variants ranging from light condensed to bold expanded.

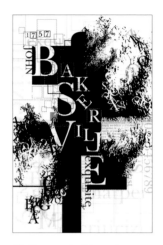

⬆ **New again** This poster design uses Baskerville in a contemporary way, eliminating the formality of the original design and creating texture and depth using the descriptive words that define the Old Style font (see page 67).

# Stone Sans Semibold
## Stone Sans Medium

**This intro type is set in Stone Serif Semibold, this intro type is set in Stone Serif Semibold**

This body type is set in Stone Serif Medium. Designed in 1987, the Stone family consists of three types of font – a serif, a sans-serif and an informal style – all designed to work together. The styles are legible, modern and dynamic, combining the old with the new. The Stone fonts integrate perfectly with each other, giving the typeface a wide range of design applications.

⬅ **Perfect harmony** Type designers have recently produced serif and sans-serif versions of the same typeface – for example, Officina and Stone. The advantage is that you can use a serif for the text setting and a sans for the display, and they will harmonise perfectly because they have been specifically designed to work together.

⬆ **Elegant letterforms** In this example, beautifully formed mixed serif and sans-serif letters are centred on each page composition in this promotion for *U&lc* magazine.

**Experimental type** *Emigre* magazine was published between 1984 and 2005. Only 69 issues were produced, but the impact of the experimental design and innovative use of typography are still impacting contemporary design. *Emigre* was among the first to champion digital typography and was one of the first publications to recognise the impact of the personal computer on the discipline of graphic design.

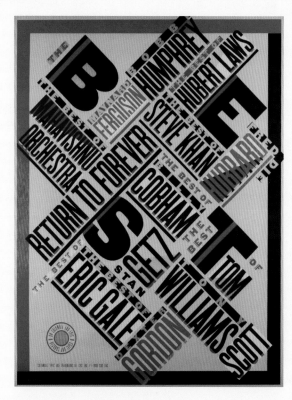

**Inspiration before and after** Iconic graphic designer Paula Scher's Best of Jazz poster for CBS Records in 1979 shows the influence of constructivism and the beginnings of her own influence on the contemporary use of type as image. Recommended reading: *Make it Bigger* by Paula Scher (2002).

**Custom typography**
Master typographer John Langdon styled this custom lettering for a heavy-metal band. The designer cited the influence of Century for its classic formality. Designing custom letterforms requires an excellent knowledge of typefaces and letterform construction. Work your way up to it, and reference existing fonts when you begin.

**Hand made** Logo and type-design legend Gerard Huerta handcrafted custom letterforms that connect with elaborate swashes and cartouches, creating a beautifully decorative emblem for the *Cigar Collector's Guide & Journal*.

## Selecting fonts

The content of the material and the purpose of the design are the main factors in deciding your choice of font. Design clarity is essential in information dissemination, and it is telling that sans-serif types such as Interstate, with their simple mono-weight structures, are designed to maximise readability for highway signage. Sans serif is also ideal for small notation in diagrams, captions and maps. The font Futura is one of the most widely used for onscreen and web, and arrives pre-installed in most computers.

- Font choice can be influenced by subject matter, and knowledge of the font origins might help in the final decision; for example, Caslon and Baskerville are classical English, Garamond is French, Goudy American, Bodoni Italian, and so on.
- Publication design can be more adventurous, because magazine readers tend to jump in and out of the text rather than reading from cover to cover. With small segments of copy, unusual fonts can sometimes bring freshness to the overall feeling of the design. However, it's wise not to mix too many fonts together in one design.
- Display types offer much more variety than text types because their purpose is expression rather than readability, so you can engage in playful experimentation in your headline design.
- Sans-serif and slab-serif faces are seen as more authoritative and bolder than typefaces that are designed for reading over long periods. If you are reversing out type or printing tints in small sizes, sans serifs are a good bet. For elegance, serifs have the advantage of tradition.
- Not all fonts are web-friendly. When designing an outcome that runs across online and offline mediums it is important that you research compatibility before you start.

➕ **SEE ALSO:** THE ANATOMY OF TYPE, P64

➡ **Opposites attract**
Design Bridge used contrasting fonts to reflect the subject content in their self-promotion book *25 Stories*.

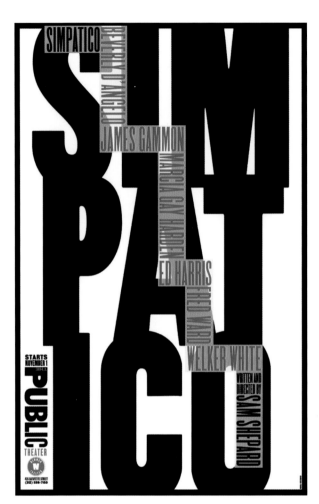

⬅ **Simplicity rules**
The development of the logo for New York's Public Theater, and the sophisticated simplicity of the sans-serif type on the theatre's promotional materials, show the influence of old wood type in different weights. Designer Paula Scher developed a typographic style that defined the theatre for years to come. For Sam Shepard's play *Simpatico*, 1994, a staircase of condensed letterforms easily brings the eye up and down through the composition.

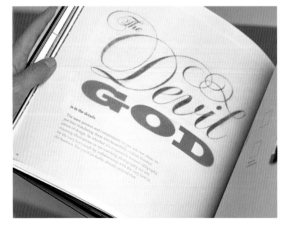

**Sans serif:** Without serif. Typefaces such as Univers, Helvetica, Aksidenz Grotesque and Futura, characterised by their lack of serifs. Predominantly associated with the 19th/20th centuries.

**Serif:** Structural details at the ends of some strokes in old-style capital and lowercase letters.

| 45 Light | 45 Light italic | 47 Condensed light | 47 Condensed light italic | 55 Regular | 55 Regular italic |

| 57 Condensed | 57 Condensed italic | 65 Bold | 65 Bold italic | 67 Condensed bold | 67 Condensed bold italic |

| 75 Black | 75 Black italic | Extended | Extended italic | Ultra condensed | Bold extended |

| Bold extended italic | Extra black | Extra black extended | Extra black extended italic |

**Univers** Designed by Adrian Frutiger in 1957, Univers is a modular system, with 21 numbered typefaces in various weights, widths and oblique versions. This flexibility makes the font ideal for incorporating many differing levels of information within a design. It's interesting to compare the slight but important differences with other sans-serif typefaces such as Helvetica. You should learn to observe the fine distinctions when choosing between one sans serif and another.

**Clarity** Well-chosen fonts for the body text can support the message it delivers. Here, a rigid column of justified, sans-serif text offers descriptive support to the direct and unblinking works of Gilbert and George.

**Fluid** Serif type in long columns of uneven lengths seems to drift down the page with hazy watercolour-hued images in an article about filmmaker David Lynch, titled *Down the Rabbit Hole.*

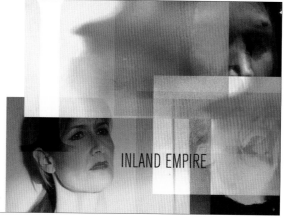

DAVID LYNCH

DOWN THE RABBIT HOLE...

INLAND EMPIRE

| PART 1 | PRINCIPLES |
|---|---|
| CHAPTER 3 | FUNDAMENTALS OF TYPOGRAPHY |
| MODULE 4 | **Spacing** |

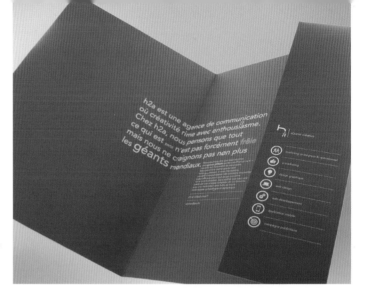

**Understanding how to deal with space in typography is essential. Proper spacing affects legibility, and space is also an integral and powerful part of any composition, whether symmetrical or asymmetrical. Develop an eye for detail, and consider the role of space in both legibility and meaning as you progress at every stage of the design development.**

In most cases, the designs you produce will consist of a mixture of images and copy in the form of either headings (display type) or body copy (text). Display type ranges in size from 14pt and upwards, whereas the main text (also referred to as body copy or body text) generally falls between 8 and 14pt. It is advisable to avoid the default setting of 12pt where you can, because it is industry default and suggests you have not made a design decision to change it. As you design, important choices will need to be made regarding typefaces, sizes and measure (width of line). You will also need to decide on spacing (letter, word and line) and, later, adjustments will need to be made by eye, even if the tool is a computer. There is no automated function on any computer that can replace the keen eye of an experienced designer.

### Letterspacing

When you keystroke or import text from a file, a computer sets the type at default space settings, both between individual letters (letterspace) and between lines of type (leading). The computer doesn't make the fine-tuning decisions that a designer must. If your type is too close together, with the letters almost touching, the letterspacing needs to be adjusted (called kerning). If they are too far apart, individual word shapes break down and legibility is compromised. One of the most common mistakes that new designers make is to set their text either too closely or too widely, or to accept the computer's spacing decisions. Designers need to learn as much as possible about the ways in which

leading affects readability and impacts on the overall texture, sometimes called 'tone', of the text on the page. There are many programs to help you understand readability, and the website type.method.ac is a particularly useful reference.

Extra or negative letterspace can be inserted to customise and reinforce a particular idea, but these are the exceptions and need to be carefully considered. Hyphenation is often used to allow for more text on a page, but it is notorious for disrupting reading flow. Bear these factors in mind when deciding how to lay out your text. Type designers for software programs are careful to produce settings for good visual spacing between letters at different sizes. However, never take this for granted. For instance, condensed typefaces

**⬆ Delicate balance**
Dramatic display and body text keeps the correct visual balance in letterspacing, even when there are dramatic changes in scale. Note the carefully managed spacing within the display text where the point sizes change, and look closely for the beautiful h2a agency letterform logo.

**⬇ Kern your caps** Kerning is the process of optically adjusting the space between (mostly capital) letters, so that they appear evenly spaced.

Reduce space   Add Space

These upright letters appear much tighter visually than the rounded letters below

Rounded shapes give the illusion of more space between each letterform

The word 'AVID' has been set with InDesign metrics auto kerning; the same word below has been adjusted by eye to visually even out the letterspacing should always be treated cautiously, as should those set in justified measures: in these cases, small additions or subtractions can improve the evenness of spacing, or allow a word to be taken into a line to avoid widows or orphans (single words from the end of a paragraph left at the end or beginning of a column of text).

## Design objectives

The main aim in display and text type is to try to achieve visual evenness throughout a series of characters. Consistency is important, because readers interpret shapes of words rather than individual letters. If there is unevenness in letterspacing, the eye can be distracted by the space rather than seeing the words.

You can test the importance of even letterspacing by setting text with different spacing, including altering it within the same line. As type size increases the unevenness can worsen, requiring the designer to make optical adjustments. This problem is prevalent with capital letters, because they fit together in complicated ways as a result of their inherent forms. Characters with straight stems such as 'I', 'J', 'E' and 'F', when placed together, require more space between individual letters than those with rounded shapes, like 'O' and 'Q', or those with diagonal strokes, such as 'A', 'V', 'Y' and 'W'. Letters in certain words may need adjusted spacing to compensate for the reduced space between characters, such as 'A' and 'V'. This is because the letters occupy different amounts of space, having varied widths.

Kerning allows for individual reductions or incremental increases to the letterspacing, whereas tracking increases or reduces space between words. Always trust your eyes.

## Word spacing

In display type, one way to gauge the amount of space to leave between words is the width of a lowercase 'i', but it will depend on the design sensibility. In some fonts, more than an 'i' space will exacerbate difficulties in reading.

⬆ **Type in motion** Paula Scher's 1996 iconic poster design for New York City's Public Theater is a masterful example of text management that redefined designing with type for a generation of graphic designers. The movement of the dancer is embodied in the placement of the letterforms, creating enormous energy while managing a huge amount of information at the same time. Note the use of a controlled palette to assist the hierarchy.

➕ **SEE ALSO:** THE ANATOMY OF TYPE, P64

READABILITY AND LEGIBILITY, P76

## GLOSSARY

**Alignment:** The setting of text relative to a column or page.

**Centred:** Text that is aligned neither to the left nor to the right: symmetrical, with an even gap at the end of each line.

**Hyphenation:** The point at which a word is broken at the end of a line in continuous text and a hyphen is inserted.

**Justified:** Text that is aligned on both the left and right margins of a column (lines are equal in length).

**Kerning:** Adjustments to the spaces between two letters (used extensively for capitals).

**Leading:** The horizontal space between lines of type. Related to the historical use of strips of lead in letterpress.

**Ligatures:** Two or more letterforms joined to create a single character.

**Optical adjustment:** Making adjustments to letterspacing by eye, not mechanically.

**Orphan:** A single word or line of text that overruns into the top of the next column, breaking how the text is read.

**Ragging:** When text is aligned left, some words at the end of the lines might jut out further than the rest and cause uneven-looking paragraphs.

**Ranged (or Ragged) left/right:** Text that is aligned to a column, either left or right.

**Tracking:** The space between words, which can be adjusted.

**Widow:** A single word on its own at the beginning of a line. It should be typeset to sit at the end of the previous line.

# The lowercase i is a good guide

Word spacing is traditionally based upon a space equivalent to the body width of a lowercase 'i'.

Word spacing in text type also needs careful scrutiny, and typesetting style plays an important part. There are two basic setting styles for continuous reading: justified and ranged (or ragged) left. With justified setting, word spacing will vary because words are pushed out to fill the requirements of the measure. Space between words can become excessive, particularly if the chosen measure is too small or the typeface too large. Hyphenation (word breaks) can be adjusted to even out word spacing as far as possible, but justified setting is always tricky unless type size in relation to set measure is carefully considered. Setting justified text on a short measure with many long words is especially difficult, since fewer words end up on a line. This often occurs in newspapers.

With ranged-left setting, you have the advantage of being able to space words consistently. Many designers prefer this style for obvious reasons, although problems of legibility can still arise and ragging text (lines that jut out further than others causing unevenness) becomes a major issue. Type style also plays an important part in word spacing. Percentage adjustments can be made within the hyphenation and justification (H and J) settings of electronic page-layout programs, to accommodate closer or wider word spacing depending on the

width of character of the typeface. In general, ranged-left setting should not be hyphenated, except sometimes for shorter column widths; otherwise you can end up with lines of uneven length.

Changes space between words

Changes space between letters

Applies horizontal scaling to characters

Controls a single word occupying a line

Enter values to control how words are hyphenated

Amount of white space at the end of a non-justified line

How many consecutive lines can be hyphenated

**H and Js** Hyphenation and justification can be fine-tuned manually, giving an excellent level of control; here the dialogue boxes from InDesign are shown.

## JUSTIFICATION OPTIONS

**1. No H and J** This justified setting has no word breaks. You can easily see the problem of excessive word spacing, which causes rivers of space to form.

**2. Hyphenation** Using hyphens can help to reduce the problem of excessive word spacing, but don't hyphenate too often in a block of text.

**3. Unjustified** Excessive word spacing can be made to disappear with the ranged-left style of setting. With no word breaks you can shorten lines, giving a ragged look.

1. With justified setting – that is, alignment on both the right and left of the measure – the word spacing will vary because words are pushed out to fulfill the requirements of the measure. Herein lies the problem. The space can become excessive, particularly if the chosen measure is too small or the typeface too large. The result is often bad word spacing, which can cause 'rivers' of space to run down the page.

2. Hyphenation can be adjusted to even out the word spacing as far as possible and avoid ugly spacing. Hyphenation specifications are sets of automatic hyphenation rules that you can create and apply to paragraphs. You can specify the smallest number of characters that must precede an automatic hyphen (the default is 3), and the minimum number of characters that must follow an automatic hyphen (the default is 2). These controls do not affect manual hyphenation.

3. With ranged-left setting you have the decided advantage of being able to space words consistently – the inherent difficulties of justified text can be avoided. For this reason, many designers prefer this style, though problems of legibility can still arise. As mentioned earlier, style of type also plays an important part in the amount of word spacing to have. Percentage adjustments can be made within hyphenation and justification (H and J).

## Leading

This term derives from 'hot-metal' typesetting, where strips of lead were placed between lines of type, and it refers to the amount of horizontal spacing between lines of type. In display type, the designer will invariably have to adjust individual lines and not just rely on a constant setting. Each line of type is spaced differently, according to need. The role of leading becomes particularly important when setting large areas of text, notably in books. There are no clear rules regarding the adjustments of line spacing for display matter; it is a matter of skill in developing an even look and in letting your eye be your guide. Every time you use display type, analyse each case individually. For example, designers sometimes use negative leading (in which the leading has a lower numerical value than the type size). This can be effective in giving a dynamic visual appearance, but should be used with care. You can also set preferences for a baseline grid (a horizontal grid structure that helps guide text layout) and align your text to sit upon it.

All type settings are enhanced by the careful consideration of leading. Factors such as x-height, measure and weight of typeface will all influence the amount of leading you should employ.

### ⓘ Left versus right

Ranged-right text is considered harder to read than ranged-left text, because the eye travels to the end of the line and seeks a consistent location for the beginning of the next line. If the lines (on the left) are uneven, it's more difficult to do this.

### RAGGING TEXT

Creating ragging text, which is ranged left, takes time, practice and patience. The key is to create a 'soft' right-hand edge to the type, by bringing words down onto the following lines, and avoiding making harsh, obvious shapes – such as sharp diagonals – at the right edge of the text that distract the eye. A tried-and-tested rule of thumb is to alternate longer and shorter lines. Avoid putting in hyphenation to solve ragging issues; it is much better to work with the natural flow of the words in the copy and only break where it's absolutely necessary.

**⬇ Ragging** This typographic event poster embraces ragged text. Ranged-left, the ragged speaker biographies continue the ragged title treatment.

## X-HEIGHTS AND READABILITY

Helvetica Medium, designed in 1957 by Max Miedinger, a Swiss type designer, is a sans-serif typeface that has a relatively large x-height in relation to its ascenders and descenders. This means that when setting text in this font you may need to add extra leading (space between the lines) to ensure maximum readability.

Set in 8pt, with 4 points of leading, or 8/12pt.

The same size of type in Futura Medium, designed in the mid-1920s by Paul Renner and based on simple geometric forms, has a relatively small x-height for a sans-serif typeface. However, its long ascenders and descenders (see the 'l' and the 'y') mean that when setting text in this font you may need to add extra leading to ensure maximum readability.

Set in 8pt, with 4 points of leading, or 8/12pt.

This text is set in the same size of type, in the transitional serif typeface Times New Roman, designed specifically for *The Times* newspaper in 1931, by Stanley Morison. It has a smaller x-height in relation to its ascenders and descenders, and therefore an overall smaller appearance on the page, needing less leading.

Set in 8pt, with 3 points of leading, or 8/11pt.

The same size of type in the old-style typeface Bembo, originally cut by Francesco Griffo in 1496, has an even smaller x-height, although it is in the same size as before. This means that when setting text in this font you may want to reduce the space between the lines to ensure maximum readability. This typeface also looks less visually dense when set as text on the page, because the weight of its strokes is less heavy.

Set in 8pt, with 2 points of leading, or 8/10pt.

| PART 1 | PRINCIPLES |
|---|---|
| CHAPTER 3 | FUNDAMENTALS OF TYPOGRAPHY |
| MODULE 5 | **Readability and legibility** |

**Debate continues between traditionalists and modernists as to whether sans-serif typefaces are more or less legible than serif faces. Traditionalists argue that serifs aid legibility by helping to differentiate letterforms, factors that keep the eye moving along the horizontal line. However, modernists argue that sans serifs do not really decrease legibility; it is just a question of readers becoming culturally acclimatised to the sans-serif face aided by electronic devices.**

Certain rules have evolved about setting type and using letterforms that still apply. One rule is that long passages composed entirely of either capital letters or very bold text are difficult to read. Multiple capitals can be difficult to read because the words have similar visual shapes or outlines and all are the same height. Ascenders and descenders in capital and lowercase settings aid in the differentiation between words.

**Justified versus ranged left**
Another perennially hot topic is the relative virtues of justified and ranged-left settings. Justified text may be no easier to follow than lines ranged left. Ranged-right settings force the reader to search for the beginning of each line, which can get very annoying over long passages

and should generally be avoided. If you are reversing type out of black or a colour, then a sans-serif typeface might be a safer option than the alternative, with its finer lines and serifs. Of course, much will depend on the size of type, choice of colour and quality of paper or media.

Between 60 and 72 characters per line (on any given measure) is the best number for optimum readability. However, these parameters will change according to type size. When lines are too long, the eye loses its place; too short and the reader will become distracted by the constant returning to the start of a new line. The text throughout these paragraphs is set in Berthold Akzidenz Grotesk at 9 points, with a leading measure of 11 points.

**→ Contrast** Serif and sans-serif fonts can be used successfully in the same system. Sans serif is used here to emphasise the difference between the call-out and the body text, and is used again to highlight and separate the captions. Note that all of the selected typefaces are well proportioned, with the weights relatively balanced to keep the system elegantly consistent.

**Justified:** Lines or paragraphs of type aligned to both margins simultaneously, creating different spacing in between words.

**Measure:** The length of a line of text on a page, based in inches, centimetres, points or picas.

**Ranged left:** Paragraphs or lines of text aligned to the left-hand side margin.

**Ranged right:** Paragraphs or lines of text aligned to the right-hand side margin.

**← Systems** A change in the typographic styling can be used as a navigation device that separates elements in the extended system: pagination, captions, body text and, in this case, evocative display type used as part of the photographic image, all have distinct styles that work together.

**⊕ SEE ALSO:**
UNDERSTANDING AND SELECTING TYPEFACES, P66

SPACING, P72

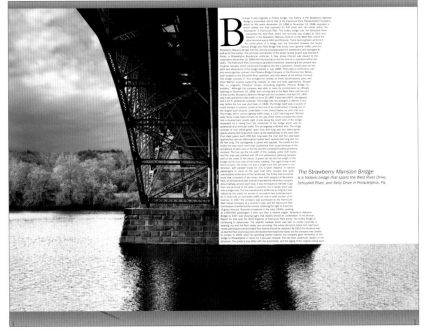

The Strawberry Mansion Bridge
*is a historic bridge that spans the West River Drive, Schuylkill River, and Kelly Drive in Philadelphia, Pa.*

⬆ **Structure and shape** Justified type can be used decoratively, but the lines and the H & Js need to be managed line by line, as does the tracking and kerning on each word. When it's done correctly, the results can be a stunning integration of type and image. Choose a typeface that is easy to read, in this case a clean sans serif, and manage your paragraph breaks carefully to avoid widows.

## KEY FEATURES: READABILITY

Measure (line length), type size and leading (spacing between lines) work in concert and affect readability.

- We have established that the optimum number of characters per line is between 60 and 72. Any more and the eye has problems picking up the next line; fewer characters per line can interrupt reading flow. Of course, the needs of different design types will influence these decisions; in fact, context is everything. In magazines, measures tend to be shorter because readers dip into articles rather than reading from cover to cover. Novels, which have to satisfy a criterion of continuous reading, look very different to advertisements, where immediate impact is a primary concern. Indeed, it is a useful exercise to ask why certain publications – newspapers, timetables, cookbooks, etc. – differ in their standards of readability depending on their function.
- Choice of type size and measure also depends on the amount of copy. Readers can cope with small amounts if the setting is smaller or on a narrower measure than the recommended optimum.
- Leading is a major element in readability. If there is insufficient space between lines, the eye will be hampered from moving smoothly to the next line. Increased leading is also required if the typeface is condensed, or if a serif typeface with a heavy or bold characteristic is being used.
- Typefaces with large x-heights have reduced ascenders and descenders, resulting in less differentiation in word shapes. Therefore, these typefaces need to have more leading.

| PART 1 | PRINCIPLES |
|---|---|
| CHAPTER 3 | FUNDAMENTALS OF TYPOGRAPHY |
| MODULE 6 | **Typographic emphasis and hierarchy** |

**Knowing how to solve problems of emphasis using type is a critical skill. This involves considering the relationship between multiple elements – the size and weight of type, the position on the page, and the dynamic between elements – as well as developing an understanding of how these decisions call forth some contents while suppressing others. These kinds of typographic decisions relate to what are called hierarchies of information, since in any design, some things will need to be read first, with secondary information to follow.**

Before starting any design, it is crucial to understand where the main points of emphasis fall in terms of headings, subheadings, intro copy, captions, quotes and so on. These levels of importance are called hierarchies. Once established, hierarchies can be indicated in various ways: by space, weight, colour and form.

• Adding vertical 'white' space in the form of a one-line or half-line space above or below a heading, separating it from the surrounding elements, creates emphasis.
• The density of black ink creates its own visual emphasis. Sans-serif typefaces, such as Univers, are good for this because they typically have various weight combinations you can use: light with bold, medium with extra bold, and so on. Bear in mind that a smaller size of bold type is visually 'heavier' than a larger size of regular-weight type.
• Changing the typestyle is a third method – switching from roman to italics, for example. Italics add informality and movement to a design and are also effective for highlighting key phrases within text. Because of their more delicate form, you will probably need to increase the size proportionally for readability where needed.
• Changing some lowercase to capitals can add formality to a design. Capitals need more letter-spacing, and so consume more space, though you

don't have the problem of ascenders clashing with descenders. Small capitals provide an even more subtle shift of emphasis.

**The power of contrast**
Other techniques involving the use of contrast can be applied to add emphasis effectively.

• Contrasting condensed with extended type can be effective, but use it sparingly with short, concise headlines. Remember that condensed type requires more leading, and that expanded type pushes out the length of the copy. Simple, effective paragraph styling adds emphasis, too, such as indents at the start of paragraphs or sections.
• Colour is a valuable tool and type does not have to be black and white to create contrast. Make sure that you have tested ink colour on the stock colour if you are printing. Transparent inks can compromise readability, and colours too close together in value or hue will not work. Colours with complementary values, such as red and green, can cause type to vibrate. When adding delicate colour to type, try using a typeface with more weight, and provide a larger area of colour. Experiment with reversing out type or adding rules to highlight parts of the text.
• Changing type size or weight is a popular option. Again, when using shifts of size for emphasis,

**⬆ Whispers and shouts**
The delicate serifs chosen for the brand's name complement the graceful illustration of a blackbird. The stacked and centred typography, the careful mixture of caps and lower case in serif and sans-serif fonts, and screened back colour stand apart like a wine label on a bottle.

**Contrast:** The difference between elements, which allows for comparison and emphasis. Contrast is closely related to hierarchy, since it allows different levels of information to be identified.

**Hierarchy:** In this context, the name for differing levels of text in a document. A page title, for example, is at the top of the hierarchy, whereas paragraphs of text are below.

⊕ **SEE ALSO:** SPACING, P72

ensure that there is a substantial difference between the main text and the heading. If the sizes are too close, then the point is not well made. The difference in size has to be great enough to make the point.

## Less is more

Try not to have too many means of emphasis going on at once. Too many techniques in one place will confuse the eye and detract, rather than add, to the concept. 'Less is more' is often a good principle when trying to work through problems of emphasis and hierarchy. Don't overstate your points by setting type in a large point size, bold, italics, underlined and at an angle. With computers, it is easy to change things, and you need to be disciplined to avoid creating a mishmash of weights, sizes, forms and indents. Resist the temptation to use all your techniques at once – and remember, you do not always have to shout to be heard.

**⬆ Customise and complement**
A slight parting in the negative space at the base of the logo's double letter 'l' is just enough to express the root-to-tip promise of swell haircare products, designed by Aloof. Keeping the rest of the type clean and simple allows the subtlety of the logo to shine and stays true to the brand.

## ANATOMY OF A PAGE

Work with your copywriter and your client to assign the page hierarchy before you begin your design work. If you have a system that repeats formats, as in book design, make sure you stay consistent in assigning fonts and weights to your style sheets.

## Type size

Your choice of font, weight of heading, or amount of leading all depend on other decisions you have made. The same is true of type size: point size is an absolute measure of how big type is, but remember the same-sized type can look very different depending on other factors – the amount of space around it, the relative size of the text copy, the weight of font used and so on. The central point about increasing type size is that it works as a strong form of emphasis, providing a focal point that attracts the reader's attention.

## Headings

Once agreement has been reached about the different levels of importance in the main text, they need to be translated into appropriate sizes and a format for the document should be designed. If headings are of varying levels of importance, try to make sure they are visually segregated.

There are numerous ways in which you can play with headings to improve the visual feel of a design.

• Breaking a line or word into different parts, or using alternating sizes with a heading, can look dynamic. For example, articles and conjunctions ('a', 'the', 'and', 'or') could be made smaller to give important words more stress.
• The logotypes of magazines (known as mastheads), billboards, newspaper headlines and posters are all working to catch people's attention in a short time span, so they often need to have large, well-differentiated typography to communicate effectively and quickly. Books, on the other hand, work on a slower timetable and their typographic presentation can be subtle.

**➜ Size variations**
A sidebar accommodates a pull-out quote set in oversize text. The hierarchy is tightly controlled by the use of black text on a nearly black background, effectively making the quote function as background information, but preserving the readability because of the size and weight.

**⬇ Titling components** Assigning importance to the components of the titling in this article adds interest. It also allowed the designer to keep the height of the word cluster equal to the height of the short columns, creating a 'sight line' to the image of the eye.

**ⓘ Sizing**
If you think it should be 10pt, make it 9. It's often the case that when we try to differentiate and create hierarchies through type, we overemphasise the importance of size. Try to use space and position before enlarging the size of your type. Depending on your client, market and product, keep the type slightly smaller than you think it should be until you have become really familiar with the details of your favourite fonts.

# Title 46pt
## Subtitle 28pt
### Subhead 18pt

Text 10pt

caption 8pt

**Number series** Some typographers determine a hierarchy of sizes by using a Fibonacci series, in which each number is the sum of the preceding two. This may result in a sequence such as 8, 10, 18, 28, 46 or 8, 12, 20, 32, 52. Do the mathematics if you like, but trust your sense of proportion and be true to the content.

**Establish a hierarchy** Choose a font family that gives you plenty of options such as light, book, medium, bold and Xtrabold weights, and good italics and numerals. Keep your choices limited to one to three fonts per layout.

**Call-outs and pull-out quotes** Both are used effectively to add emphasis to highlighted sections of the content in this architecturally styled page design. On the right-hand page, the emphasised phrase forms a bridge across the gutter, linking the two columns inventively, but maintaining the separation from the body text.

Title, sans serif, all caps, condensed

Navigation bar, lower case, serif

Subject headlines, caps, sans-serif condensed

Body text, serif

Subject headlines, caps, sans serif, colour change

Body text in two columns

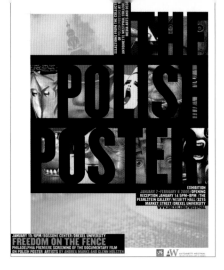

Typographic rules (lines) and ornaments have been inherited from the letterpress tradition of setting and arranging type matter. They are still invaluable to the designer today because they serve both functional and aesthetic roles.

Rules draw attention to specific parts of copy and break it into sections. Vertical rules can be used to separate blocks of text when other means of division are neither possible nor sufficient.

Generally, the weight (thickness) of the rules should match the tonal value of the text to which they relate. Horizontal rules work well for organising information and aiding readability. Examples can be found in tabular matter, such as timetables and contents pages, and sometimes between columns of text in newspapers and/ or in books, where they can be used between each entry and to help direct the eye from item to page number.

### Highlighting text – rules and panels

Rules have gained in popularity since computer commands can underline a word or words. Some designers argue that there are more subtle means available if you want to emphasise typographic elements. Nevertheless, rules can be effectively used to highlight a piece of copy by placing them in the margin alongside the text, or as a dynamic component in the composition of a design. Widths available range from a 0.5pt (hairline) rule upwards, and are often measured in points, so that we might use a 1pt or 2pt rule.

Tinted, outlined or solid-coloured panels are popular in magazines for their ability to provide in-depth focus on a particular editorial theme, while relieving the eye from the potential strain caused by reading column after

Poetica

**Confine** Heavy dividing bars bleeding into the headline letters create a strong sense of confinement. The message is reinforced by hints of the posters in the actual exhibition, effectively behind the bars of type, in this evocative poster.

**Exclaim** Paula Scher used matched weights of rules above and below each copy point to house each one in radiating shapes of near equal size. Note the control of the hierarchy through the point sizes and weights.

### GLOSSARY

**Ornaments:** Typed characters that embellish the page. Also known as flowers.

**Panel:** Device used to highlight information. Also known as a sidebar.

**Typographic rules:** Printed lines that direct the reader's eye.

**SEE ALSO:** TYPOGRAPHIC EMPHASIS AND HIERARCHY, P78

Zapf Dingbats

**Construct** Powerful words in tightly fitted boxes add sharp diagonals to this composition, and build an interlocked urban landscape of image and text.

Poetica

53

column of main text type in a single size. These 'sidebars' are most effective when they contain supplementary information and are used to distinguish separate content. However, rules and boxes can easily overtake a design, particularly when they are used 'decoratively' rather than functionally.

### Rules in display type

In display setting, rules can create emphasis by drawing attention. The Constructivist art movement in early 20th-century Russia pioneered the use of rules in this way. Very heavy rules were used, running alongside, or at angles to, the copy. The popularity of the rule is still evident in today's designs.

### Ornaments

Ornaments have been in use since the origin of printing. They give a decorative feel to a layout and invoke a sense of tradition. They can also separate information, as in the title pages of traditional books. Zapf Dingbats is a well-known digital font made up of ornaments, as is Whirligig, by Zuzana Licko. However, as with rules and boxes or sidebars, the overuse of ornaments should generally be avoided. If your content is unique, try to invent your own ornaments, icons or embellishments to enhance your type design and stay constant with your concept.

**Decorate** Printer's flowers and dingbats can be incorporated into a design system with great effect. The exuberance of these pages owes much to the enlarged ornaments that separate sections of information.

**Punctuate** The classic forms that serve as punctuation and ornament are celebrated as design elements in their own right. Given dimension and scale, they become the beautiful subjects of this article.

Wingdings

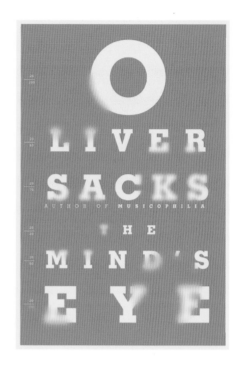

| PART 1 | PRINCIPLES |
| --- | --- |
| CHAPTER 3 | FUNDAMENTALS OF TYPOGRAPHY |
| MODULE 8 | **Text as image** |

**Contemporary designers know that type not only communicates specific meaning, but also possesses aesthetically powerful characteristics in its own right. If you think about how many expressive fonts are now available, and the way in which one can apply colour, weight, form and spacing to customise and achieve specific effects, it is possible to see type functioning as an image in its own right.**

Illustrative, photographic, calligraphic and shaped text are further variations that add excitement to a design and effectively convey the mood and concept. Working with text as image requires an understanding of both the communicative and aesthetic properties of typography, and beautiful, illustrative typographic artworks are considered a collectable art form as well as a form of visual communication.

**Display type**
Display type is chosen, in part, for mood, and each face has its own characteristics. Just as an artist can create mood through illustration, so can a typographer subtly illustrate meaning by choice of font, type size and weight. This effect of typography is normally seen at its fullest potential when type is used for display (above a certain size, for example 14pt), since smaller type is meant for reading. Display type exploits the specific characteristics of a given typeface.

**Symbolisation**
Designers can exploit the familiarity of type by carefully manipulating suggestive letterforms so that they become images in their own right. This means that type can actually stand in for objects. Conversely, objects that resemble images can replace letters.

**Form matching content**
Techniques for using type as illustration are numerous and transcend type as simple objects and vice versa. Certain words, such as verbs indicating action, particularly lend themselves to typography reflecting meaning. There can be word repetition; overlapping of characters; distorting characters to break them up, blur or roughen them; outlining or shadowing type; setting type along a curved path or in a circle; adjusting colour, weight or form; and so on. To be effective, however, positions and forms in type arrangement must reflect meaning and, as always, try to avoid clichés.

To be used effectively, our Latin alphabet, composed basically of straight lines, circles and part circles, has to be resourcefully manipulated. The decorative nature of shaped text transforms reading into a visual experience, and advertising and logotype design frequently use these techniques to give text enhanced visual impact to convey a specific message.

⬆ **Intelligent design**
This design concept by book designer Chip Kidd uses a recognisable typographic arrangement with a twist to illustrate points made by the author, Dr. Oliver Sacks. The book examines how the visual cortex processes visual information. The title was designed to evoke an eye-chart, then key areas were blurred in Photoshop.

**GLOSSARY**

**Onomatopoeia:** In typography, the use of type to suggest the sounds of a spoken language, such as adding a large 'o' to the word 'open'. Marinetti and the Futurists were effective in employing onomatopoeia, in the design of books such as *Zang Tumb Tumb*.

⬆ **Interpretive typography** In repackaging a classic tale of horror, the designer used raw chicken meat stitched together with thick twine and photographed the title for *Frankenstein*, bringing content into the concept and, in this case, to the process. Support text was added to the final image. A black-and-white half-tone minimises the gore and sets the image in an earlier time period.

⬆ **Media as message** Paper letters are edge lit and photographed to express the title word of the film: *Shadows*. Letters can be constructed out of different media, reconstructed from found objects, or hand painted to become illustrations.

⬆ **Information is beautiful** Peter Grundy's witty commentary on the statistics of death for *Men's Health* magazine arranges lines of type into a grinning and winking skull. Masterful scale management and excellent spatial relationships keep the illustration balanced and evenly coloured, and establish the headline hierarchy by the highest numbers.

⬅ **Found object design**
With a bit of imagination, letterform shapes can be found in everyday objects and pressed into service. In 'Beauty', the objects that help us define the standard spell out the word. They can be photographed, solar-printed or hand drawn.

DESIGN HISTORY

Having a good knowledge of design history enables you to pursue type-as-image concepts in a more informed way. Look at the work of Josef Müller-Brockmann, H. N. Werkman and Philippe Apeloig. Also, see examples of calligraphy and shaped text throughout history, and you will see how typographers, artists and designers have exploited type as image to enhance meaning.

# **CHAPTER 3** ASSIGNMENTS

## ◯ THE ANATOMY OF TYPE

**1** Select four typefaces, two serifs and two sans serifs.

**2** On a single 28- x 35.5-cm (11- x 14-in) page, in landscape format, select a suitable adjective for each typeface and typeset them along the same baseline grid. Using the same point size and leaving space between each grouping, identify and annotate as many parts of the letterforms as you can, taking your time to adjust the design and type setting as you see fit. Pay particular attention to uppercase cap, ascender line, lowercase, eye, cross stroke, bowl, ear, leg, crossbar, counter, serif, link, loop, bracket, descender line, terminal and beak.

**3** On a separate 28- x 35.5-cm (11- x 14-in) page, in landscape format, create a poster using a word of your choice. Copy this word four times, adjusting each to have a distinctively different colour and a distinctively different typeface, but keep them all positioned in the same place overlapping each other.

**4** Distinguish the differences made by the overlaps, and add any three of the following terms into your composition in a way you find meaningful: x-height; baseline; ascender; descender; and cap height.

## ◯ TYPOGRAPHY AND MEANING

You will want to do this exercise on a computer, and Adobe Illustrator software is strongly recommended. Working on a computer will allow you to create many variations, or electronic thumbnails, more rapidly than drawing the typeface accurately each time. This will keep your creative process moving and reveal a great number of options before you commit to a final selection.

Select two words from the list below:

> Transition
> Disruption
> Relaxation
> Migration
> Expansion
> Evolution
> Compression
> Exhilaration
> Repression
> Elimination

Take the time to consider their meanings carefully and think about how the meanings can be expressed typographically.

Create two distinct designs, one for each word, that best express the meaning of each word. Each type poster should be 28 x 43cm (11 x 17in) in a tabloid format, and only black and white or greyscale may be used. As you generate your thumbnails, consider all of your design decisions, including the placement on the page and the proportion and orientation of the word. Be aware of the interaction of white space and your design elements as you compose the page. You may elect any means of visual communication at your disposal – contrast and scale, cropping and proportion, letterspacing and repetition with (or without) variation – but you must work from a single principal typeface. You can mix the variations in a single font – bold, light, condensed, italic and so on – and you may also overlap, omit, slice, crop or tint the letters. You may not distort the type in any way, or use drop shadows behind the letterforms. The end result should be an engaging and well-designed page. It should also be legible, and the principal typeface easily identified.

## ◯ ADJUSTING LETTERSPACING

**1** Begin by visiting http://type.method.ac/ to see who can get the highest score!

**2** In 60-point sans serif typeset the headline:

## RAILROADS IN CRISIS.

Print out your page, and look closely at the spaces between each of the letters. Using some of the tips from type.method.ac, mark any spaces that seem uneven within the words, and return to your computer to kern the type. Print your second version, and compare the differences made by your adjustments.

**3** Reset the headline in 60-point serif type. Repeat the exercise, making special note of any differences encountered in kerning serif and sans-serif type.

## ◯ HISTORY OF TYPE DESIGN/ PARAGRAPH DESIGN AND HIERARCHY

**1** Research the work of one of the following type designers: John Baskerville; Giambattista Bodoni; William Caslon; Claude Garamond; Eric Gill; Frederic W. Goudy; Adrian Frutiger; or Paul Renner.

**2** From your research material, create a PechaKucha, a presentation style in which 20 slides are shown for 20 seconds each, totalling 6 minutes and 40 seconds. The format keeps presentations concise and fast, but also requires important design decisions for legibility at this speed. On each slide include information you have discovered about the designer or about a typeface they designed. Using the typeface you have researched, consider the following elements and how to include them appropriately in your presentation:

• Headline: the name of your subject.
• Body text: the paragraph you have selected.
• A complete alphabet of the typeface, with all numerals and select punctuation.

**3** In portrait format, create a dynamic page design that uses all three of the above elements. Your headline may be placed anywhere on the page, but you must use some element of contrast or scale to call it out as the headline. You may elect justified or ragged type for the body copy, and you may incorporate the alphabet in any way that is aesthetically pleasing, as long as the hierarchy is clear and the reader is able to clearly find each element in the proper order. As always, be aware of the placement on the page, the integration and sequencing of the visual hierarchy, and the legibility of the point size and leading. Remember to produce several versions before you finalise your finished artwork, and be true to the nature of the type designer's work: is the face old style or modern, formal or informal?

*Note: Always print your work. Type sizes can be very misleading on the screen. Always view your work in whatever format it is intended, so that you can see it as the audience will.*

**4** Show your exercises to a designer or to another design student and have a candid discussion about your intention with this work. As the projects and practices become more complex, it's easy to get caught up in designing to please yourself, and to forget about the necessary function of visual communication. Always make sure your intentions are clear, and keep an open mind as you exchange ideas.

## ● TYPE AS IMAGE

Select one of the following titles, or substitute one of your own favourite film or book titles. Make sure you select one that inspires visuals: Pride and Prejudice; The Bell Jar; The Alchemist; On the Road; Black Hawk Down; The Hobbit; Moby Dick; The Scarlet Letter; or Dr Jekyll and Mr Hyde. Using only the letterforms provided, create a typographic illustration that communicates the meaning of the title. You may use any media you find appropriate, such as traditional media, three-dimensional construction, photography or photomontage. Your finished work should be 23 x 30cm (9 x 12in).

Develop your concepts first, then collect the materials you need to create your imagery, but work with recognisable typefaces before you substitute your artwork for the conventional letterforms. This will help you to control the composition and to create your final artwork in the correct proportion.

Remember to look for inspiration in nature and the environment, as well as design history and museums. Letterforms can be 'seen' wherever geometry and spatial relationships exist – you just have to remember to look for them.

**Further Reading:**

Robert Bringhurst, *The Elements of Typographic Style*, Hartley and Marks Publishers, 2014
Robert Bringhurst and Warren Chappell, *A Short History of the Printed Word*, Marboro Books, 2000
Rob Carter, Philip Meggs and Ben Day, *Typographic Design: Form and Communication*, Wiley, 2015
Ellen Lupton, *Thinking with Type*, Princeton Architectural Press, 2010
Emil Ruder, *Typography: A Manual of Design*, Verlag Niggli AG, 2001
Erik Spiekermann and E. M. Ginger, *Stop Stealing Sheep and Find Out How Type Works*, Adobe Press, 2012
Herbert Spencer and Rick Poynor, *Pioneers of Modern Typography*, The MIT Press, 2004
Paula Scher, *Make It Bigger*, Chronicle, 2005
Andreu Balius, *Type at Work: The Use of Type in Editorial Design*, BIS, 2003
Vince Frost, *Design Your Life: Applying Design Principles to Your Life*, Penguin Books Australia, 2015
Stephen Coles, *The Geometry of Type: The Anatomy of 100 Essential Typefaces*, Thames & Hudson, 2016

# 4

# Fundamentals of Colour

A thorough understanding of colour is essential to expert design, and is one of the most important tools in graphic design. There are infinite variations of colours at the designer's disposal, and endless ways of combining them across many media, from printed inks to screen-based colours, each with their own characteristics.

Colour has a unique, complex language, and the ability to change its meaning when partnered with other colours. When choosing colours to incorporate into your design, you will need to consider issues of contrast and harmony, and how these might affect legibility in typography. You can also set the mood of a design by using the psychology of colour, but you must be sure your selected colours convey the correct message at an unconscious level, and that they are suitable for the audience your project is intended to reach.

To understand how to choose or assign colour for a specific purpose, designers must first develop knowledge of how colour works, how colours are classified, and the terms used to describe them.

Colour is differentiated in three main ways: hue, tone and saturation. 'Hue' refers to the colour's generic name – for example, red, yellow or blue. A single hue will have many variations ranging from light (tint) to dark (shade). This is called tone or value. A single hue will also vary according to its saturation or chroma (also known as intensity). Saturation ranges from full intensity to low intensity, or from brightness to greyness. Colour can also be described by its temperature and movement. Hues in the red spectrum appear warmer and closer to the viewer than hues in the blue spectrum, which appear colder and further away.

Complementary colours, such as red and green, lie opposite each other on the colour wheel, whereas analogous colours, such as green and blue, lie adjacent to each other. The former are associated with contrast; the latter are linked to harmony. Certain colours have a profound effect on each other when combined. They can vibrate or blend, appear vibrant when partnered with one colour and muted when placed with another. The more you experiment with colour, the more you will understand how to select and group various hues for meaning.

**Hue** distinguishes one colour from another. It is the generic name of the colour – red, say, as opposed to blue.

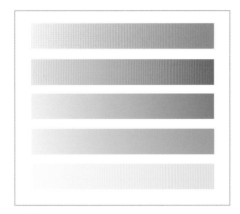

**Tone** (or value) is the relative lightness or darkness of a colour. A colour with added white is called a tint; a colour with added black is called a shade.

**Saturation** (or chroma) is roughly equivalent to brightness. A line of high intensity is a bright colour, whereas one of low intensity is a dull colour. Two colours can be of the same line but have different intensities.

**Colour wheel** Primary, secondary and tertiary colours of pigment are shown on the wheel. The primary colours are red, yellow and blue. Secondary colours are made by mixing any two primary colours together, producing orange, green and violet. A tertiary colour is produced by mixing a primary colour with the secondary colour nearest to it on the wheel. The tertiary colours here are red-orange, yellow-orange, yellow-green, blue-green, blue-violet, and red-violet.

**Subtractive colour** An acetate envelope printed with transparent primary colours transforms the cover of a publication and creates multiple triangles in varying hues and tones as it is removed. This same effect can be viewed digitally by working with transparencies and adding layers to your file. Experimenting with colour will help you learn to control the hierarchy in page design, create readability in typography, and set the mood and pace.

## GLOSSARY

**Additive colour:** System used on monitors and televisions, based on RGB (red, green, blue). When combined, these form white light.

**Analogous colour:** Colours that lie adjacent to each other on the colour wheel – for example, blue and green.

**CMYK:** Cyan, magenta, yellow, key (black): the four colours that make up the full-colour printing process.

**Complementary colour:** Colours that lie opposite each other on the colour wheel – for example, red and green.

**Gamut:** The complete range of colours available within one system of reproduction – for example, CMYK or RGB gamut.

**Primary colour:** Red, yellow or blue.

**Secondary colour:** A mix of any two primaries: orange, green or violet.

**Spot colour:** Any flat colour, like Pantone or Toyo colours, printed as a solid, and not made up of CMYK.

**Subtractive colour:** System used in printing, based on CMYK colours.

**Tertiary colour:** A mix of a primary colour with the secondary colour nearest to it on the colour wheel.

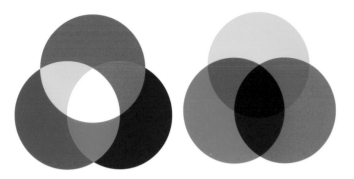

◀ **On-screen colour** Additive primaries and RGB light are used to create colours on computers, televisions and monitors. Combined, the additive primaries result in white light.

◀ **Printing primaries** Subtractive primaries and CMYK – cyan, magenta, yellow and key (black) – are the primaries used in printing. When combined, subtractive colours make black.

### Additive and subtractive primaries

To understand how colour works, the most important point to know is that coloured light (additive colours or the RGB system) and coloured pigment (subtractive colours or the CMYK system) do not work in the same way. To put this differently, if you are working with your computer, the colour on your monitor (RGB system) will not be the same as the colour that is printed (CMYK system). This phenomenon creates problems for printed projects, since colours on screen appear brighter than they do in print.

With printed matter you will be working with subtractive colour. Here, each colour printed onto paper stock subtracts from white, and if the three primaries overlap, black results. The colour wheel shows primary colours; the subtractive primaries are red, yellow and blue. Secondaries are a mix of any two primaries, resulting in orange, green and violet, while tertiaries are a mix of a primary colour with the nearest secondary colour on the colour wheel. The term 'full colour' refers to four-colour printing and to achieve a full range of colours, printers use cyan, yellow, magenta and black (known as CMYK; K = black = key colour).

### Pantone

An additional colour used in a design project is called a flat colour or sometimes a spot colour. When selecting colours for this, you should use a universal matching system known as Pantone Matching System (PMS). Pantone colour is mixed from 15 pigments (including black and white) and is primarily used for print colour matching. This system is different from the CMYK system and few colours can be matched between them. For more information, see pages 132–133.

### Process charts and modes

When printing in full colour (CMYK), you will find it useful to identify and specify the exact colour that you want to see printed by using a printer's process colour guide. This will show you all of the colours that you can make by specifying and combining different tints of cyan, magenta, yellow and black. When designing for print on a screen, make sure you are working in CMYK mode, not RGB. Once you have chosen your colour, you can make a new swatch on your document, specifying the different tints. This is the only accurate way to specify the printed colour that you will achieve when ink goes onto paper.

➕ **SEE ALSO:** PRINTED COLOUR, PAGE 132

### Printer relationship

A good relationship with a printer is a fundamental for getting the most out of your outcomes. Software is in a continuous state of updating, so it is easy to be left behind and have to address software conversion issues between computers. As a result, simple design elements such as colours, fonts, bleeds and pagination can all go wrong after the file is sent. Becoming familiar with a limited number of printers not only means they are aware of your preferences, but you'll have someone that is willing to catch mistakes before production.

### Communication

Communication is key; if your printer is using terms you are unfamiliar with, ask them to elaborate. When your printer says 300gsm cover stock or 4/4 perfect bound, do you know what they are talking about? Basic print terminology is important to come to terms with, not only for avoiding mistakes but also for understanding the print options available to you.

### Preparation

Prepress and file preparation can vary from printer to printer, so it is important that you have a conversation about file formats, colour palettes and bleed in advance of printing your work. If in doubt about your choices, ask the printer for a mock-up, although this usually comes with an extra fee.

### Calibration

If you are working on a project that requires very specific colour specifications you should talk to the printer about the possibility of calibrating your computer screen to the print machines, or being aware of the variety of colours when using different printers.

### Loyalty

And finally, loyalty is important. Printers do not usually turn a profit when dealing with student projects; you are an investment, so make sure you bring custom to them when you are working in the professional world.

⬇ **Greyscale** Squares in tones of black and white create halftones and can define light and shadow in both an abstract and a representational way. Subtle variations in the value of each square will create gradients that blend seamlessly.

⬇ **Movement and contrast** Reds, yellows and orange values come to the foreground of the composition, and blues and greens seem to be further away. This example adds scale change to colour theory to complete the effect of motion.

⬇ **Vibrating edge** When complements in red and green are adjacent, the eye perceives a faint white line along the edge. Vibrating edge is used to stunning effect in this design, but the same technique can render typography unreadable.

⊖ **Pastel tones** This set of provocative postcards from *A Traveller's Record* film screening uses a pastel palette to evoke subtle emotions. The gentle colour treatments result in the text becoming part of the image and more aesthetically pleasing.

PART 1 | PRINCIPLES

CHAPTER 4 | FUNDAMENTALS OF COLOUR

MODULE 2 | **Colour legibility, contrast and harmony**

Knowledge of the context in which finished work will be viewed is fundamental to the use of colour in graphic design. How that colour is perceived, and how legible it is, will vary greatly depending on whether it is viewed on a screen or in a print-based medium. Colour has a dramatic effect on legibility and needs to be considered very carefully. Contrast and harmony are ways in which a design can be further enhanced.

⬆ **Contrast** Large areas of flat, contrasting colour provide a perfect attention-grabbing visual, as demonstrated in the Romanian Olympic Sports Committee identity. The use of a very simple, limited palette can create a variety of different visual solutions for varying formats, while still being bold and cohesive.

⊕ **SEE ALSO:** READABILITY AND LEGIBILITY, P76
COLOUR TERMINOLOGY, P88

If you are designing a website or an onscreen project such as film credits, you'll be working with additive colours in the RGB mode. These are somewhat reliable monitor to monitor and have the lumens associated with onscreen colours. Very subtle variations may go unnoticed on screen, and care should be taken to avoid additional vibration when combining colours. If you are designing for print, make sure you are working in CMYK mode. This will enable you to come reasonably close to your intended selections, but test printing is the only reliable way to be sure your colours are correct. As explained in Module 1, problems can occur on translation to print in subtractive colours. Both clients and designers can be misled into expecting printed colours to have the same saturation and tonal range as those approved on screen. Don't rely on your monitor unless the finished design work is intended for the screen. Request scatter proofs and view your work in the same context as your intended audience to determine if your colours are successful before the final print run.

**Colour legibility**

Legibility refers to how clearly something can be read. Many factors can influence colour perception and legibility; for example:

- lighting and viewing conditions in the reading environment will have a clear effect on the legibility of both print- and screen-based work – compare viewing a monitor in a darkened room and under direct sunlight;
- selection of colours;
- background colours and textures on which colours are printed; and
- size and shape of type or image used.

Good colour legibility is achieved when ground and colour have contrast – for example, deep violet (the colour nearest to black) on a white ground. The legibility decreases by moving the image colour towards yellow, however, because violet and yellow are complementary and may cause a vibrating edge. Changing the contrast is key to legibility, and this means using your knowledge of the colour wheel.

### Contrast and harmony

Colour should both contribute to and support the content of a design, and it should reinforce the ideas you are giving visual form to. Therefore, it is important to understand how colour can work in contrast and in harmony. Both are related to legibility and colour associations, and affect design function and perception.

Allocating colour proportion is a critical decision. For example, a small amount of bright red in a complementary scheme can have a stronger impact than equal proportions of red and green. Equal amounts of a saturated red and green can actually result in unpleasant visual discord, and may bisect your composition in undesirable ways. You can avoid this by varying the saturation levels of the hues. By using a greater proportion of green with less saturation and a red with good saturation, the red is given extra emphasis. You can reduce the vibrancy of a hue by adding a bit of its complement to it, greying the colour effectively enough to change the relationship between your selections. With analogous schemes, the hues tend to have less vibrancy and therefore similar proportions can be used to pleasing effect.

Designers who develop an understanding of the complex and subtle ways in which colours interact will be able to explore new ways to express graphic ideas. Practical needs, such as legibility and the requirements of the work, should always be considered as a fundamental part of the design process. Experimentation will further your colour expertise; try a design project without using black or white, and use the values, tints, and hues of colour to solve your design challenges.

### GLOSSARY

**Analogous:** Similar, comparable, alike; for example, two colours that are near to each other, such as grass green and leaf green, are analogous.

**Contrast:** Differentiation between two or more elements, in this context, of image colour. For example, high contrast is between black and white, or blue and orange; low contrast is between two similar shades of blue, such as cyan and cornflower blue.

**Harmony:** Image with a balance of two or more colours that work together – for example, taupe and grey.

**⬅ Limited colours** By limiting your colour palette to a minimum you can create a striking, complementary visual. Badster use white, yellow and black to tie in with the brand identity and create various areas of focus – for example, the heavy black will draw your eye to the base of the product.

**⬆ Layers and texture** Layered design styles are exaggerated with the use of vibrant colours and screen-printed inks to create interesting textures. The varied intensity of the solid blocks of shapes and overlapping text in the Eady Forum event posters creates dynamic, bold and eye-catching visuals.

| PART 1 | PRINCIPLES |
|---|---|
| CHAPTER 4 | FUNDAMENTALS OF COLOUR |
| MODULE 3 | **Colour associations** |

**Why are certain colours preferred, or seen to be more effective? It is because colours have, throughout history, come to hold particular associations that most likely derive from nature, and have, over time, become rooted in human psychology. They have come to possess cultural, symbolic and often personal associations. To use it well, you need to understand how colour works both as a language and as a system of signs, and how it creates an emotional response.**

⬆ **Seeing red** The colour red is associated with caution in most Western cultures, but with good fortune and luck in China. This bilingual logo type uses the brilliance of a nearly primary red to evoke the imprint made by a traditional Chinese ink seal and to announce an American exhibition of contemporary Chinese artists. The strength of the colour also allows the viewer to see the letter 'I' in ink, even though it is bleeding off the edge.

Intelligence, memory, experience, history and culture all play a part in colour perception. Although individual people may perceive colours with slight variation, colour perceptions have different meanings depending on psychology and cultural background. Colours have symbolic associations in all societies, depending on context, and different cultures assign different meanings.

• Black is the colour of mourning and death in the industrialised West, whereas in China and India the colour of mourning is white.
• Red does not have the instant conventional association with 'stop' in those countries where automobiles are less pervasive, and is associated with good luck in China.
• Green was associated with poison in the 19th century through its links with arsenic, whereas today it is seen as the colour of spring and environmental awareness.
• Blue is associated with postage in the US, where the mailboxes are blue, whereas in Sweden or Britain you would look for the colour red.
• Yellow is the colour of courage in Japan.

The meaning of colour can change over time and across different cultures. If you are designing for international markets, you need to be particularly aware of such differences.

⬆ **Muted elegance** Sophisticated, muted values are often associated with a higher price point in retail packaging. Soft colour values and repeated forms combine with a sudden pop of vibrant green in these retail packages to add an edgy element to an elegant treatment.

**Colour in emotion and language**
While colour associations are highly subjective, despite local differences, colours and hues may have some universal characteristics. Reds, oranges and yellows stimulate the senses and tend to be perceived as warm, capable of exciting feelings of cheeriness, good health or aggression. Opposite on the colour wheel, blues and greens are seen as cool, with connotations of calmness, peace, safety and/or depression.

Other dimensions also influence perception. Compositions close in value may seem hazy, vague or introspective, whereas dark combinations might evoke night, fear or mystery. High colour intensities are dynamic and create a feeling of movement. Clearly, colour perceptions are rooted in psychology. They are even used figuratively to describe feelings. 'Seeing red' or 'singing the blues' are common descriptions of states of mind.

## COLOUR THEORISTS

**Josef Albers** (1888–1976) proposed that colours are never stationary; that is, they are constantly changing in relation to the colours surrounding them.

**Johannes Itten** (1888–1967) created colour experiments based on contrasts such as temperature or hue, and associations based on seasons.

**Wassily Kandinsky** (1866–1944) developed his colour usage in terms of spiritual moods and relations to musical instruments and sounds. His paintings are a synthetic colour expression of sound.

**Wilhelm Ostwald** (1853–1932) set up an order of colours based around the concepts of harmony and disharmony.

 **Hot palette** The right palette can associate the viewer with the message or the product immediately. This colourful display of gestural forms has a palette inspired by the actual ingredients of the hot sauce in the package. The concept image is resonating the heat of the peppers and is even suggestive of smoke. Text set in an acid-green colour has placement as lively as the illustration, with both offset by a deep background.

← **Chilling palette** The juxtaposition of the coldest and warmest of colours evokes a chilling message in this poster for the Coen brothers' story of murder in the great white north. The uninterrupted use of white space nearly obscures the typography, much as snow hides things in the landscape, adding a sense of the unknown to the mood of the image, and a touch of red predicts a hint of violence.

↑ **Sweet palette** Natural hues and soft contrasts produce a quiet, relaxed sensibility. The quiet of a garden is reflected in tones of moss greens and earthy browns, mixed with a dappled texture of cream and taupe in the background. Typography and illustrations are sized and placed to simulate the perspective one might see in a landscape, and no high-contrast images or type spoil the pastoral mood.

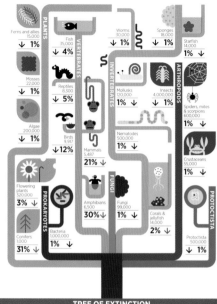

TREE OF EXTINCTION

PART 1 | PRINCIPLES

CHAPTER 4 | FUNDAMENTALS OF COLOUR

MODULE 4 | **Colour as information**

Colour is a powerful tool, especially in information design, where it is used to help the designer organise data into various structures, and to aid the experience of 'reading' a design. Psychologists have proved that the colour of an object is seen before its shape and details. Because colour works at this basic level, it is very good at keeping things defined, reinforcing informational hierarchies, guiding the eye through complex systems and data, and aiding navigation through physical spaces.

Systems are anything that contain a flow of complex information – maps, signage, sections, structures, web pages. Colour helps to categorise that information. Environmental graphic designers specialise in designing wayfinding systems, architectural signage, exhibition design and data mapping, and rely on colour as an important organisational tool.

• Complex buildings, such as hospitals and airports, need excellent signage systems to help people navigate through large, complicated architectural spaces. Colour is an obvious means to correct paths. Many shopping centres are so large that parking zones are now colour coded – a memorable way to help you remember where you left your vehicle.
• The London Underground map, developed by engineer Harry Beck, is one of the most famous maps in city transport. Beck used colour to differentiate lines, so that people could readily identify the right route. The map is schematic: it is a simplified diagram that uses abstract graphic elements (lines) to represent a complex real-world situation. This most original of designs is a model copied in various forms throughout the world, including on maps for the Paris and New York City metro systems.

• In finance, colour has traditionally been used in many ways. Debits in balance sheets would be in red to denote arrears, hence the phrase 'in the red'. This custom is still in use to separate trading figures from year to year.
• Charts apply colour to quantitative and statistical information, where differing quantities of data need to be reinforced.
• Catalogues and books often have different colour-coded sections to aid navigation through pages. Penguin Books introduced the first paperbacks in Britain in the 1930s using a bright orange background. This colour quickly became fused with the books' identity. Later, the same publisher introduced another imprint, called Pelican, whose books were given a blue background. Customers quickly came to recognise the differences through the use of colour. Such visual associations can also help to delineate sections within a body of text and highlight a number of different levels of importance. The designer can set crucial parts in a bold typeface and use a different colour from the rest of the text. The eye picks up this difference very quickly.
• Web designers use colour to help people navigate through the structure of a site.

⬆ **Charting info** Beautifully organised, well-designed information gets attention, and it is likely to be examined thoroughly. Here, a whimsical style is used in the infographic Tree of Extinction. The chart follows a six-column modular grid system and is colour coded for easy navigation.

**Data:** Facts or pieces of information of any kind.

**Diagram:** Drawing or plan that explains the parts of something, or how something works.

**Quantitative:** Related to quantities of things, or measurements (numerical).

**Schematic:** Simplified diagram or plan related to a larger scheme or structure.

**Statistical:** Related to the collection, classification and organisation of (often numerical) information.

**⬆➡ Finding the way** Navigating a city requires an organised map. The London Underground map, originally developed by engineer Harry Beck in 1931, was the first to use this schematic system and has served as the model for cities all over the world. The colour-coded navigation system in Shibuya Station in Tokyo, Japan (above), has a circuit board-like diagram and is seen by 2.4 million passengers on an average day. The colour coding extends to the directional signage in the Tokyo subway system (right).

**⬆ Menus** A well-designed extended system can create opportunities for the designer to encode navigation and still stay true to the coloration of the brand identity. Simple divisions on a restaurant menu will make it easier for consumers to select their meal.

**➡ Universal language** Colour is a universal way to communicate. In a setting where many languages are spoken, such as an airport or a hospital, colour-coding pictograms (see page 21) and information systems can be easily understood.

# **CHAPTER 4** ASSIGNMENTS

## ⦿ DEFINING COLOURS

This exercise can be done in Photoshop, Illustrator or InDesign. If you work in Photoshop, please make sure you are working in CMYK mode; that way, the colours should be the same if you export your files to Illustrator or InDesign later. In landscape format, set up a document to 28 x 43cm (11 x 17in). Create five squares in one aligned row, sized to occupy at least two-thirds of the width of your page. Make multiple pages, with your squares in the same position, to do the following experiments with colour.

**1 Advancing colour:** Select two different hues, one for the squares and one for the background, that will make the squares advance. Alter the tone on four of the five squares to see how it affects the advancement of the image.

**2 Receding colour:** Repeat the previous exercise with receding colour in the foreground squares.

**3 Tints:** Choosing tints of the same hue, fill the background with one and the foreground squares with the other. Create two variations, one that shows contrast and one that makes the squares barely visible. Add a small amount of the complementary colour to either the foreground squares or the background to see how it is affected.

**4 Simultaneous contrast:** Use the same hue for all five squares and the background. Then, alter the background hue in two different ways and note how the squares appear. Select one variation and alter four of the five squares to give them more and less contrast.

**5 Complementary colours:** Select two hues to demonstrate the term 'complementary colours'. Use them at full intensity on the foreground and background until you can see a vibrating edge. Change the complements to a different pair and see which combination is more vibrant.

## ⦿ CONTROLLING TINTS AND VALUES

**1** Using Illustrator, set up a document that is 35.5cm (14in) square. Along the top of the page, create a row of ten 2.5-cm (1-in) squares, evenly spaced. Do not add any colour to the background.

**2** Beginning on the top left and working right, fill each square with tints of cyan, dropping by 10% each time and working from 100% on the top left to 0% on the top right. Select and copy the entire row and paste it nine times below the original. You should have ten rows of ten squares ranging from 0% to 100% cyan. Do not use layers in your file, since they will make the file much too big.

**3** Beginning on the top right and working down, fill the first row with increasing percentages of yellow, beginning with 0% on the top right and ending with 100% at the bottom right.

**4** Now, working from left to right, begin adding the corresponding amount of yellow to each cyan square on the row, until all the squares on the second row across have 20% yellow added to them, the third row has 30% added, and so on.

**5** When you have completed the chart, change the background to black to see how the tints are affected.

**6** You can repeat the exercise with cyan and magenta, and magenta and yellow. If you do, save and even print the charts, since they will make a handy reference tool for you moving forwards.

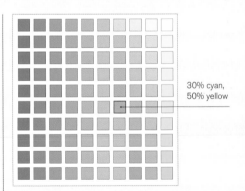

30% cyan, 50% yellow

## ● COLOUR AND LEGIBILITY

**1** Type the word 'legibility' in a landscape format on a white background in a colour that has great contrast, such as violet. Change the colour of the word gradually, working backwards through the colour wheel from violet to blue, green, red, orange to yellow, and note the legibility of the word.

**2** Show the word 'legibility' against a background of contrasting colours from opposite ends of the colour wheel. Reverse them until all legibility disappears, as with red on an orange background. Note which cause vibration, which become readable but subtle, and which ones just cannot be read at all.

**3** Repeat the exercise with a paragraph of 10-point type.

## ● COLOUR AND MEANING

**1** Explore your associations with each of the colours on the colour wheel. Make notes on which emotions you associate with each of them, and how you think most people perceive them. Research and record how these same colours are perceived in different cultures.

**2** Find examples of everyday things that are defined by their colour and photograph them in their surroundings as they are seen normally. They might be road signs, transit vehicles, street numbers, food or holiday items.

**3** If you are familiar enough with Photoshop to work in colour, upload images to your computer and alter the feeling of each by changing the colour of one object, leaving the surrounding area alone. Note how your perception of the object has changed. Does a glass of milk still look appetising when it has a pale green-grey cast? Is the emergency vehicle still obvious in traffic when the colour changes? Can you change a clear sky to threatening or peaceful? If your proficiency in Photoshop is still developing, you can work in Illustrator using tints and transparencies on your placed image, or you can simply print your photos and paint on them.

## ● WAYFINDING

**1** Using only black and white and tints of black, design a simple map, diagramming your journey from home to the nearest grocery shop and back again. Develop simple icons and/or labels to represent as many different landmarks as you need – street names, parking garages, retail shops, banks, ATM machines, car parks, bus stops, fields, bridges, and so on – and place them on your map. Include lines of typography along your route that describe your state of mind as you travel to and from your destination, and as you pass various notable points.

**2** Repeat the exercise using colour to differentiate the labels and icons, with the most important ones in the most contrasting colours. Add a background colour to the design. Assign a legible colour to your dialogue that does not disturb the readability of the landmarks. Use a key to help the audience find information. You may use any tints or colours you find appropriate. Note how important it is for information design to be clear, and immediately readable as you work.

Further Reading:

Josef Albers and Nicholas Fox Weber, *Interaction of Colour,* Yale, 2013
Chris Calori and David Vanden-Eynden, *Signage and Wayfinding Design: A Complete Guide to Creating Environmental Graphic Design Systems, 2nd Edition,* Wiley, 2015
Leatrice Eisman and Keith Recker, *Pantone: The Twentieth Century in Colour,* Chronicle Books, 2011
Adams Morioka, *Colour Design Workbook: A Real World Guide to Using Colour in Graphic Design,* Rockport, 2008
Pantone Formula Guide Books
Richard Mehl, *Playing with Colour: 50 Graphic Experiments for Exploring Colour Design Principles,* Rockport, 2013
Jim Krause, *Colour for Designers: Ninety-five Things You Need to Know When Choosing and Using Colours for Layouts and Illustrations (Creative Core),* New Riders, 2014

# Practice

In this part, you will be introduced to the tools and techniques of design, which form a key group of skills for professional practice in any field. No designer can ignore the requirements of technology, and while you may use powerful digital tools regularly in the production of work, it is essential that you familiarise yourself with the industry-standard technologies that designers utilise. However, these tools cannot generate the idea, nor can they execute the design for you, and the kinds of conceptual, intellectual and formal skills you bring are what will differentiate you from other designers. In short, you need both an excellent understanding of principles alongside outstanding technical skills. Being able to design formally and/or conceptually eloquent and innovative work is only half the story, since you then need to get the work into print, on screen, in three dimensions, or across multiple platforms, and so on. "Design is the battle, but printing is the war," used to be the designer's battle cry, describing the problems designers face when getting a design from the sketch stage to a final, printed piece of work. Those problems still exist but designers now need to be able to deliver graphics that will be viewed in multimedia applications, the screen being pre-eminent. Chapter 5 introduces basic image making and sourcing, followed by an overview of the key technical and software skills used in design today, including Photoshop and InDesign. In Chapter 6, various production issues, including colour for print, PDFs, paper stocks and press checks, are introduced. Chapter 7 is dedicated to design for web and mobile applications, and summarises the specific technical skills, tools and languages these platforms require. Here, you'll find design considerations for different styles of website, key software tools and how to bring creativity to an 'off-the-peg' CMS (and the acronyms are explained, too!). There is even a tick list of questions to ask a client during the website planning stages. Chapter 8 overviews seven of the key areas of design, including editorial design, web design and motion graphics. These 'tasters' aim to give a sense of the key skills and aptitudes needed to work in each field, and of the highs and lows of each profession, and to provide pointers to additional resources, including 'Best in the business', which highlights some of the most influential practitioners in that area of design.

PART

# 5

# Tools and Technologies

Graphic design production and practice is almost completely digital, and dependent on changing technologies. Previously, typographers would set type, pre-press production would be crafted by specialists at a printing company, and designers would commission a photographer. Now, one person can do all of these jobs on a computer, under the gamut of desktop publishing (DTP).

This chapter introduces you to the software applications and tools that are most commonly used in the graphic design industry. Each module focuses on a specific medium, such as photography, or a specific software application, such as Photoshop, grounding you in its unique tools, history and terminology, and giving you the opportunity to explore further. New applications, and updated versions of the ones in use now, will continue to be adopted into the practice of graphic design. The best way to prepare for a constant learning curve is to recognise the commonalities in the way they function, and gain proficiency through practice.

➡ **Frame your photos** The unusual perspective from floor level used in this image from the series Fitting Rooms, evokes an intimate perspective that may not have been considered if the image was framed in a more traditional way.

**Photography and image-making/sourcing are key skills for graphic designers. Not all designers are good photographers, but an understanding of the skills needed to compose and shoot images is essential. Your photograph may only serve as a placeholder, but having the image to hand will help you work out rough proportions, assign and design a composition, and can serve as research for drawing and/or digital illustration.**

Fortunately, the rules of good design – composition, contrast, hierarchy, rule of thirds and colour theory – don't change much for different design disciplines. Frame your photos the way you would approach any assignment, and compose each shot with purpose.

**Types of photography**
There are many broad categories of photography and image production that are relevant to designers. For our purposes, we'll focus on the most common, which are:

• objects and products
• portraits and images of people
• landscapes and buildings
• ephemera and texture
• reference and research

**Depth** The variance in depth and use of perspective of the viewer within this photograph evokes powerful sensations of being inside the football crowd.

**Contrast** Intense light and vibrant colours in combination create a compelling and striking composition.

Consider the purpose of your design challenge and what your needs might be before you shoot. Make sure the resulting images fit the purpose, and that you have considered all aspects of your image as it relates to your design work. For example, product images are generally brightly lit, sharp and clear, whereas land-scapes and portraits may have a variety of styles and convey a specific mood.

Your designs will be more powerful if you learn how to spot an effective, well-composed picture and can recognise a good tonal range. Think about how the image can combine effectively with typography, colour treatments and other illustrations.

There are many reasons why one image will make you stop and stare and another will make you turn the page without stopping to look at all. It certainly helps if a picture is in focus, correctly exposed, placed where it is shown off at its best, and has some interesting content, but images can be a powerful form of expression within a design. Try to capture images that reflect the design sensibility you need to communicate your message, and note that there are limits to how much you can alter them electronically in post-production.

**Symmetry** Centred and still, a symmetrical composition can evoke calm and emptiness. Drama is intensified in this case by the use of an ominous monochromatic palette.

**Asymmetry** Positioning the focal point off-centre can add dynamism.

**Layers** The framing of an image and the clever use of reflection, darks and lights add depth and drama to images.

| PART 2 | PRACTICE |
|---|---|
| CHAPTER 5 | TOOLS AND TECHNOLOGIES |
| MODULE 2 | **Page-assembly programs** |

Desktop publishing applications bring all your lessons in composition, page layout, contrast and typography into play. In these applications the elements you create in vector software, or the imagery you edit in raster-based applications, merge with your content. Using this layout-generating word processor, you can combine text and image to create brochures, magazines, posters or multi-volume novels, or publications for print and interactive.

Adobe InDesign is the industry-standard desktop publishing software and updates on a regular basis. Generally, Adobe files will open in any edition of the software; however, if using a higher upgrade of InDesign that will then be opened in a lower upgrade you will first have to save it as a mark-up or IDML file. There are many features that overlap in Adobe Illustrator, Photoshop and InDesign, but it is vital you are using the correct software. For example, typography should be handled in Illustrator, as this is a vector-based design program, and photographs in Photoshop as this is a pixel-based design program. Everyone has their own unique way of using these software applications; the key is finding what works best for you.

**Crop mark:** Vertical and horizontal lines at the corners of an image or page to indicate to a vendor where to trim off the bleed area.

**Gutter:** The inside margins or blank space between two facing pages in a publication. Used to accommodate binding, the amount of gutter needed changes depending on how the project will be bound.

**Handle:** An anchor point in a design program connected to the main vector path by tangential lines that can be manipulated to change the shape of the curve.

**Margin:** The usually blank space to the top, bottom and sides of a page between the trim and the live printing area. Headers, footers and page numbers are traditionally placed within this area.

## Work area

The main toolbar sits to the left of the screen, the canvas in the centre and the secondary toolbars to the right.

### Main toolbar

InDesign localises its main tools into one long toolbox. Mirroring many of the functions found in Illustrator and Photoshop, the tools in this panel can be accessed by clicking the icons or utilising the keystrokes assigned to each item, such as 'V' for the Selection Tool, 'P' for the Pen Tool and 'G' for the Gradient Tool. Note that some of the items with a small arrow also reveal other fly-out tools such as Rounded Frames, the Fill Tool and the Measure Tool.

## USEFUL TOOLS AND FEATURES

InDesign has many tools full of features and functions to help create compositions. Here are some of the more basic yet powerful tools that are the mainstays of any InDesign user. The keyboard commands for each tool are shown in brackets.

**1 Selection Tool (V)**
Selects the entire shape or line, which can then be stretched, rotated or moved anywhere on the page.

**2 Direct Selection Tool (A)**
Selects and manipulates specific lines, path points or handle ends distinctly to change the position of individual lines, points or curves of a shape.

**3 Pen Tool (P)** Enables you to create straight or curved lines by selecting two points on the page and 'bending' to your desired shape. By clicking the Pen Tool, you can reveal the Add Anchor Point, Delete Anchor Point and Convert Direction Point Tools to manipulate the points that make up curves and lines.

The Control panel can be docked at the top or bottom of the screen, as well as float freely, like all of the panels

Master pages are the page templates upon which you can program elements such as grids, header and footer elements, and automatic page numbering

**Swatches panel** This is where all the colours used in a document are located.

Click on Popup windows to activate

A simple coloured icon to the right of your swatch indicates if the swatch is CMYK or RGB colour

To modify a colour's mix – either by typing in its numerical values or PMS number – double click a swatch to reveal the Colour Mixer. You can also alternate between CMYK and RGB in these settings.

⬆ **Popup windows** Window organisation is important, because the amount of panels and tools necessary to do a job can easily fill up your computer screen. The Adobe CC applications help reclaim screen real estate by allowing users to 'dock' and minimise panels as they see fit. With a variety of options available under Window > Workspace, you can select one of the pre-organised panel arrangements or create your own. There is also a handy option to reset these workspaces if you lose something.

Standard colour swatches that accompany every document are 'None' or empty, 100% white, 100% black and Registration. They cannot be modified in InDesign. Registration black is formed by all four CMYK colours for printing on plates, as opposed to 100% black. It's called this because it is used to print the registration marks, which are those marks that the printer uses to align the four plates once your job is on press.

⬅ **Info panel** Displays layout information for the document or selected objects, including values for position, colour, size, text and rotation. For viewing only – you cannot enter or edit the information in the panel, but you can ascertain many qualities of an on-page object by hovering over it with your cursor.

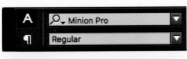

**4 Type Tool (T)** Used in the creation of text boxes and edits the type within them. By working in conjunction with the Control panel and Type panels, this tool will allow you to select and modify text to create headlines, paragraph blocks and captions.

**5 Control panel** Provides a customisable array of functions for the tool you have selected from the main toolbar. The Type Tool, for example, allows you to adjust the font, leading, tracking, text weight and style, paragraph alignment, column count and margin spacing.

**6 Rectangle Frame Tool (F) and Rectangle Tool (M)** Both create rectangular, polygon and rounded forms: the Rectangle Frame Tool creates frames to insert graphics and imagery; the Rectangle Tool is for drawing shapes to fill or outline with colour. Precise adjustments can be made to size and position using the Transform panel.

## Page layout

Creative layout design utilises different on-page items such as text boxes and image boxes to help place imagery and content, and assign colour in compositions on a generated pasteboard. These compositions can be sorted into a virtual pagination structure, comfortably up to hundreds of pages. The program also manages issues such as page size, orientation and output. The following tools are standard.

**➔ Guides** Imaginary rules are pulled over the page and viewed upon request. They do not print, but help in creating layouts and grids and lining up items. Usually gutters, margins and baseline grids are set with guidelines in the Master Pages.

**❶ Bleed**
When preparing imagery, remember to compensate for the bleed. If any of your pictures go to the edge of the page, remember to add about 3–5mm (dependent on print requirements) to that side of the image to be clipped off at press-time. This goes for background colours and lines as well.

Reoccurring graphics can be set up in the Master Pages

Page numbers and running heads are set in the Master Pages

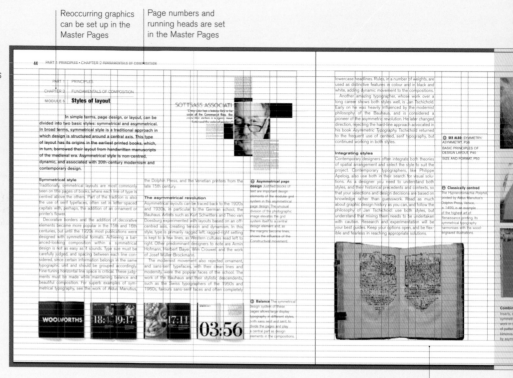

Grid lines can be switched on or off

Image bleed

## Page layout concepts

Beyond placing and sizing imagery, the designer can use desktop publishing programs to express content meaning with extensive control of typography. Through automatic flowing of text from multiple columns to multiple pages, hierarchy and information organisation is easily controlled and experimentation and changes are easily handled. Creative composition and invention in text layout require manipulation of the page items, and will cause countless ragging and adjusting. Make it part of your process to address this and leave time to fine-tune your typography when the document is completed. Magazines and newspapers around the world use desktop publishing programs to get as many words as is comfortably legible and aesthetically pleasing onto a page, with grids, layouts, templates and columns to make this happen.

Master Pages and Style Sheets will help you to create almost any composition and project. In Master Pages, you can create formats to be repeated throughout a multi-page document – for example, headers, page numbers and call-outs. In the Style Sheet palette window, you can select your typographic hierarchy and set it to be constant throughout the document.

**⬇ Master Pages** These template pages, upon which predefined pages mimic grid elements and on-page template elements such as text block items, header and footer elements, and automatic page numbering, are usually found at the top of the Pages or Page Layout panel. These pre-styled layouts help in creating uniform changes throughout a large document, but can be specifically changed on a per-page basis when necessary. To unlock a Master Page item select Command/Ctrl + Shift + click.

Click on drop-down menu > Override All Master Page Items to alter elements on the pages that are highlighted on the pages menu

Click on icons to get to Master Pages

Thumbnails show the content of each page

**ℹ Page numbering**
On a Master Page, create a text box and go to Type > Insert Special Character > Markers – Current Page Number. Now, that same text block on each page will reflect the appropriate page number.

**Style Sheets** Design and typographic styles such as colour, size, leading, position and decoration may be applied to text automatically with Style Sheets. Selections of text may be tagged with certain predefined meta-information at the click of a button. By naming a series of elements Headline, you can globally affect the styles and attributes of each selection, which is helpful and time-saving for last-minute design changes.

Object styles can be assigned to objects, groups and frames to modify the stroke, colour, fill, drop shadows, transparency, text wrap, and more

In paragraph styles, character and paragraph formatting attributes can be applied to a paragraph or series of paragraphs to adjust overall spacing, leading and style

Character styles are formatting attributes that can be applied to selected items of text, such as size, weight, tracking and italics

## Holding page

InDesign is a holding page. Unlike Photoshop and Illustrator, InDesign links images from the folders on your computer. If you move or rename these folders the links will break and will not export correctly. It is therefore vital that you are organised and have a good file management system (i.e. a folder for images, a folder for typefaces, etc.). To relink a broken link, select Window and Links. You will see a small icon alerting you to the broken link.

## Packaging

Exporting documents for proofing – most commonly with PDFs – and file preparation for publishing with an outside printing vendor are important details usually handled well by page-assembly programs, but you should know what vendors are looking for. Packaging allows you to group your updated InDesign file, PDF for proofing, and all the assets and links to the file, including a folder of imagery and a folder of all fonts in use. Make sure you check your font and image licencing before sending these files to your printer.

**⊕ SEE ALSO:** PHOTOSHOP, P110
ILLUSTRATOR, P114
PREPARING FILES FOR PRINT, P124

| PART 2 | PRACTICE |
| CHAPTER 5 | TOOLS AND TECHNOLOGIES |
| MODULE 3 | **Photoshop** |

**Photoshop is the industry-standard software package for raster-graphics editing and manipulation, and is frequently used for collecting images and to select elements for montage or photo retouching, both for print and digital. It also has the ability to perform basic 3D modelling, basic animation and a variety of output-for-web options.**

Photoshop replaces and enhances darkroom techniques such as retouching and editing brightness and contrast, and allows for ease of cropping while providing a cleaner, 'dry', chemical-free environment for editing. The most common tools used in Photoshop for photo editing are the Spot Healing Brush, the Clone/Stamp Tool and the Patch Tool. These allow the editor to remove imperfections and unwanted objects.

Photoshop's major advantage is that imported images can be moved, edited and layered over a potentially infinite canvas without loss of information, quality or resolution. Photoshop documents with multiple layers can get quite large and may compromise the memory allocated on your computer. Make sure you save and archive the original PSD version, and flatten and save the

**! Tablet**

A tablet with stylus pen is the preferred tool of many Photoshop artists. The pen gives the designer free range of hand movement and pinpoint precision by emulating the feel of using a brush or a pencil. The most common brand of tablet is made by Wacom.

**Work area**

This section shows the general layout of Photoshop. Additional pull-outs can be accessed through the 'Window' menu on the header bar.

**⊖ Main toolbar**

This bar has easy icon access to all of the main tools, some of which also have keyboard shortcuts.

Foreground/background colour selection. Clicking on the squares selects the colour, whereas the 'X' key swaps them over

USEFUL TOOLS
AND FEATURES

There are five main tools that enable you to edit an isolated area of pixels without altering the rest of the image. Each of these can be accessed through the main toolbar, and many have additional options to customise the tool, located at the top of your screen in the header bar. The keyboard commands for each tool are shown in brackets.

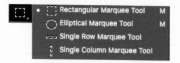

**1 Marquee Tool (M)** Selects an area or sets up a boundary within the layer that is being worked on. Different Marquee Tools can select rectangles and ovals, and, when holding down the Shift key, geometric circles and squares can be selected. This tool also allows you to select a one-pixel-width line down or across the entire layer. This is useful when making a striped page pattern or creating a boundary line.

**2 Magic Wand Tool (M)** Selects pixels of the same colour with the Tolerance option set to 1, but within a range of colour with Tolerance set to more than 1. If the Contiguous box is unchecked, the tool will select all the pixels in the entire document that are of the same colour value, regardless of whether they are joined together or not. Use the Shift key to add pixels to the selection and the Alt key to subtract.

Main toolbar

The canvas

Secondary toolbars

The colour pull-out lets you adjust the colour by altering the RGB or CMYK measures

The Layers pull-out details each canvas layer and which filters or additions are on each layer

SHORTCUTS

These keyboard shortcuts are helpful and save time:
• ctrl or ⌘/C Copy
• ctrl or ⌘/V Paste
• ctrl or ⌘/Z Undo
• ctrl or ⌘/M Marquee
• ctrl or ⌘/+ Zoom In
• ctrl or ⌘/- Zoom Out
• ctrl or ⌘/W Magic Wand
• ctrl or ⌘/T Free Transform
• Space key + mouse movement: move canvas around in window.

**◀ Colour editor** The Photoshop Colour editor, currently set to the CMYK (cyan, magenta, yellow, key/black) range that is used for print colour. The RGB (red, green, blue) colour editor is used when designing for the web/ television. Each range has different effects on the colour usage.

**◀ Preset colour swatches** The swatches are used as a standard range of colours, for example black, white, 10%, 20% and 50% greys. If you have mixed your own standard swatch, or have been set a range in a brief, you can save and keep it to select when you are working on a design.

**3 Pen Tool (P)** Creates vector-based lines and curves with control points (see Illustrator, page 114). These points can be dragged over the layer for a better fit, converting them from fixed points. An area enclosed by the Pen Tool boundary can be affected by various fill functions or made transparent to add texture and depth.

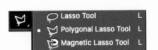

**4 Lasso Tool (L)** Draws and selects freehand shapes. Use the Shift key to add a new selection or the Alt key to subtract. The Polygonal Lasso draws straight-line sections. Use the Alt key to toggle between the Lasso and the Polygonal Lasso Tool, and the Shift key to draw perpendicular or 45° angles. The Magnetic Lasso is the fastest way to outline and isolate a shape. The Magnetic Lasso will attach to the pixels that describe the outer edges of any photographic subject, making it a simple matter to eliminate a background or copy and paste the object into a different layer or file.

**5 Brush Tool (B)** The size, shape and colour of the Brush Tool can be changed, as can its hardness and scatter range. Alter the brush's flow rate or opacity to achieve different effects for use in retouching, adding texture or digital painting. The Brush Tool options can be found under the header bar.

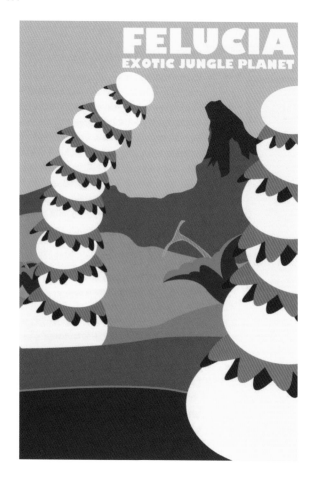

**Adobe Illustrator is a vector-based package used for illustrative, logo and page-layout design, because of its shape-rendering and text-editing capabilities. Its linear handling complements Photoshop's pixel-based format, and most designers have knowledge of both programs.**

Illustrator's main advantage is the resizing of vector-based illustration without loss of detail, from its 'point and line' function. For example, at billboard size a raster image becomes pixellated and blurry, whereas a vector image retains design by angle geometry and proportion, and remains sharp.

For the graphic designer, Illustrator offers a clean, crisp edge to the produced objects and brushes, and mapped along 'paths' can be moved, edited and recoloured easily. As in Photoshop, you can build layers of illustration using textures and transparencies, and typography, and create finished artworks to import into a desktop publishing program.

Illustrator has many great functions worth investigating further; these include changing type into an image, live tracing accuracy and setting up files for CAD (laser cutting/engraving, vinyl, etc.).

⊙ **Vector illustration**
Illustrator's vector-based format allows for a variety of image-making techniques, object edits and custom typography. This makes it an excellent format for many illustrations, such as those on this bold Felucia Exotic Jungle Planet poster.

## USEFUL TOOLS AND FEATURES

Many of the tools found in Photoshop are duplicated across the Adobe range, such as the Selection Tools, Lassos and Pen Tools. Here are five of the most commonly used tools in Illustrator. The keyboard commands for each tool are shown in brackets.

**1 Pen Tool (P)** Creates vector-based lines and editable points.

**2 Type Tool (T)** The most useful tool in the best program for creating crisp logos and typographic solutions.

**3 Rectangle Tool (M)** Creates customised shapes.

**4 Warp Tools (Shift + R)** These tools change the geometry of vector objects. The Warp Tool drags a specific area of an object. The Twirl Tool changes the local geometry/colour into a spiral. The Crystallise Tool changes the local geometry/colour to splines.

**5 Mesh Tool (U)** Creates colour graduations within a 2D vector object. For example, making a star with the Star Tool and clicking within the shape with the Mesh Tool sets up a gradient, which can then be edited.

Main toolbar menu. Tools that are used daily are situated in this toolbar menu

Composition Workspace is one of the most important panels in After Effects: this is where you can see the progress of your work

The Character panel is used to manipulate text. There are many panels in After Effects, which can be found from the Window menu

Layers are used to organise the workspace. Labelling layers with colours is an easy way to stay organised in After Effects

The audio icon indicates that the audio is present in the timeline

Audio waveforms. The height of the line indicates the strength of volume in the audio: long vertical lines indicate loud audio, small vertical lines describe quiet audio

---

### ⬆ Deconstructed Circle

The storyboard shows the key sequences for compositing the final animation. Deconstructed Circle was produced by Zak Peric in After Effects, and the animation can be seen using the weblink https://vimeo.com/85708559.

organised on tracks similar to video-editing programs like Adobe Premiere Pro and Final Cut X.

Transitions, effects and presets can be drag-and-dropped between compositions that will then render using computer RAM Memory (more RAM memory means quicker rendering times). After Effects has many filters, effects and presets, such as film scratches or blurring, to create a mood or tone in your project. What makes After Effects popular and powerful is the range

of third-party plugins that can be used to extend the functionality of the application (e.g. Red Giant Trapcode Suite and Boris FX Boris Continuum Complete), although it can argued that AE Scripts website (http://aescripts.com) is the most complete repository of current plugins available for After Effects and other animation, 3D and compositing applications.

---

**4 After Effects: Puppet Tool** Excellent for creating bone structure in bitmap images. Select the Puppet Tool and place pins in order to create hierarchy. Each pin can be animated separately to create complex movement.

**5 After Effects: Mocha** This stand-alone application that comes with After Effects enables you to motiontrack (planer track) objects within a film so that words, images or symbols can be spliced into the film, even if the film tracks fast or is blurred. For example, you could track a different billboard image onto a billboard as a car passes and the camera pans to follow the car (this method of tracking is called four corner pin).

**6 After Effects: Animation Presets Menu** Ideal for those who are new to animation and compositing, After Effects features pre-animated presets that can be utilised in any project. The benefit of using these presets lies in their flexibility: each preset keyframe can be changed to create a new effect.

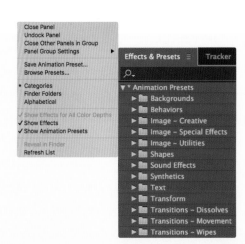

# CHAPTER 5: ASSIGNMENTS

## ● OUTSOURCING PHOTOGRAPHS

You should only outsource an image if you cannot make it yourself. No matter how complicated, consider it a creative problem to solve. You could stage a scene and capture your own image, or capture a series of elements to compile an image in Photoshop.

In your sketchbook draw five squares.

**1** Find a stock image online or cut one out from a magazine; it can be anything from a mountain scene to a small kitchen. Print and cut it (a demo version is fine for this exercise) to size and stick it in the square. This is the image that all your other squares will take reference from.

**2** Stage the stock image scene using materials around you; maybe it requires creating backdrops or an unusual crop of the image – for example, instead of an image of war you could capture a soldier's boot in the mud. Once happy with your set, light it appropriately and capture a photograph. Print and paste it into your second square.

**3** In the third square collage a series of imagery by breaking or cutting up previously created visual materials, be they your own photographs, photographs from magazines, previous artwork, textiles, advertisements, packaging or other materials, and rearrange them to create a new artwork based on your stock image theme.

**4** If proficient in Illustrator, create a series of vector layers to build up your scene. If you are not proficient, this can also be done with plain or textured coloured paper. Print and paste into square four.

**5** Finally, simply draw straight into the fifth square. What tools you use is completely up to you, but by practising and mastering your drawing skills you'll always have a plan B when it comes to sourcing imagery.

It is good practice to organise and store imagery for future use. Whether you print things out or keep them filed away on your computer, creating a visual reference library will result in much more scope and ideas for image making. Make sure you always have a camera, whether it be digital, film or on a smartphone, with you to take images that you find engaging and might be able to use for future projects.

## ● SETTING UP IN PHOTOSHOP

**1** When opening Photoshop you will be met with prompts to create a new document page or you can select File > New and enter the page size you are planning.

**2** To edit an existing image select File > Open [your image].

**3** It is important you know the output for your work before you get started; if in doubt, always set up as if you were printing to high quality as it's much easier to reduce than increase image size and quality. Select Image > Image Size > Resize to 300p/inch (not cm).

*Note: p stands for pixel (originated from the term picture element); it is the basic unit of programmable colour on a digital image.*

**4** Similarly, knowing if your work is going to be screen- or print-based will alter the way you set up the colour mode. To set Colour Mode, select Image > Mode > RGB (Screen), CMYK (Print), Greyscale, Mono/Duotone (you need to set your colour mode to greyscale first before having the option to Mono/Duotone it).

*Note: The specific colour that a pixel describes is made from Red, Green and Blue, which makes the screen format RGB. Printer colours are made from combining Cyan, Magenta, Yellow and Black – CMYK – and won't look the same on your screen as when you print them.*

## ● SELECTION TOOLS IN PHOTOSHOP

Photoshop layers are like sheets of stacked acetate. You can see through transparent areas of a layer to the layers below. When you move a layer into position the content on the layer slides like a sheet of acetate in a stack. You can also change the opacity of a layer to make content partially transparent.

The selection tools (Quick Selection, Magic Wand, Marquee/Lasso, Magnetic Lasso, etc.) isolate one or more parts of your image. By selecting specific areas you can edit and apply effects and filters to portions of your image, while leaving the unselected areas untouched.

It's also possible to make selections based on a range of colours in an image. Select > Colour Range > using the Eyedropper Tool select the colour you want selected, then alter the settings in colour range to increase/decrease your selection. In addition to pixels, vector data can be used to make selections. Use the Pen or Shape Tools to produce precise outlines called paths. Paths can be converted to selections. After your layer or selection has been created you have isolated that area to be duplicated, moved or edited in some way. Explore the adjustment options for hue/saturation, opacity/brightness and contrast, etc.

Select a photograph to experiment with these tools. For each tool save a new image of your photograph. Once you've experimented with at least six selection tools print your edited photographs and annotate what you have done and where this tool would most appropriately be used. Do you find one easier than the other? What happens if you start to alter the default settings of these tools?

## PHOTOMONTAGE IN PHOTOSHOP

Now that you understand how to remove or edit a selection you can create new images by combining elements from a variety of different photographs, textures or imagery.

**1** Select three to five images of objects and select three to five backgrounds and textures.

**2** Open a new Photoshop document. Under the File tab, select New and create an 21.5 x 28-cm (8½ x 11-in) document. Make the resolution 300dpi, so you can print it, and name the file 'Photomontage 1'.

**3** Under the Layers tab, select Background and change it to Layer 0. Import one of your backgrounds or textures.

**4** Create paths on your objects or subjects and copy and paste them onto a new background. Each one will come in on its own layer. Using the Move Tool, you can reposition or scale any of your imported objects. Hold down the Shift button to scale your images without distorting them.

**5** Create three photomontages, placing objects or subjects into new situations. Experiment with filters to affect your colour, and make your subjects look as realistic as you can in their new setting. Pay attention to the lighting in the foreground and background, and see if you can adjust them to work well together.

**6** When you have a file you like, save it with all of the layers intact. Then, flatten the image, crop it to suit your liking and, using the Save As selection, rename your file and save the compressed version with a different name. It will be smaller and easier to import, but always save the original, layered version, in case you want to make a change.

## PAGE ASSEMBLY IN INDESIGN

In this assignment you'll be creating an InDesign review in the form of a booklet, while learning the fundamentals of the program.

**1 File Management**
The most important thing to remember about InDesign is that it does not hold information you place in the file, but links it from an external source. If you rename or delete the original file the InDesign link will be broken and it will not appear in your InDesign document. Therefore, it is always advisable to set up a file management system. Create a folder called 'InDesign Assignment' and within this folder save the InDesign file and create sub-folders for text and images.

**2 Brief Overview**
Research the program InDesign online. What is it? What is it used for? Condense your research into a brief overview of 250 words. This text may change as you gain more insights into using the program. Save this text as a Word document (WORD.docx) inside the text folder. Similarly, choose an online image, photograph, or draw and scan an image that complements your opinion on the program. Save it in the images folder.

**3 Set Up**
Open InDesign and select File > New > Document (command+n). In the popup window set your document to 140 x 200mm (5½ x 8in) by entering the values and select the portrait option using the icon. Tick facing pages, this allows you to design spreads for a publication rather than a single page, and enter 4 into number of pages. You can also adjust Columns

By double clicking A-Master in the Pages tab you can set up a template that will flow throughout the whole body of your document. To unlock these elements to delete/edit, click command+shift

You should set up a margin and columns to ensure all your content is contained within printing parameters, and guarantee consistency throughout your designs. Bottom margins tend to be bigger in documents with a large amount of text, to increase legibility

Guides can be adjusted to create structure and visual balance on a page. Think carefully about what information your pages need to contain, and develop a system that complements the content

and Margins here if you wish, although there is another option once you're inside the program.

If you select More Options you will see there is space to enter value for Bleed. This is for the printers to control elements that run flush to the page; the standard tends to be 3–5mm, but always check with your printer first. Enter a value. Click OK.

**4 Master Pages**
Once you are inside the program and looking at the blank document, it is time to start thinking about setting up a framework. If you select Pages from the right-hand workspace (if you cannot see it go to Window > Workspace > Essentials. You may need to 'reset' Essentials if you're using a public computer), you will see the Master at the top. Anything edited or added to a Master page or spread will be implemented throughout your whole InDesign document.

Double click both pages on the spread to begin. It is important for any amends you make that you have both spreads selected to apply them to both pages.

Layout > Margins & Columns > Set your margins to 10mm except for the bottom margin to be set at 15mm. You may need to double click the lock icon to enter different values.

Layout > Create Guides > here you can set your columns. Set 3 Rows to 4 Columns to the Margins. Click OK.

# CHAPTER 5: ASSIGNMENTS CONTINUED

**5** Add Text

Now you have a framework set up, start to lay out your 250-word paragraph across a spread. In the Tool Bar, select the T (Type Tool) and draw a text box to fit one of your columns. Import your text using File > Place and locate the Word document. Your text will appear in the box, but it may not all fit. If there is more text, you'll see a small red plus symbol (+) in the lower right corner of the box. With the Selection Tool, click on the symbol and draw another text box on your page. The text will flow from one box to another and will indicate the connection with a thin blue line that connects each box.

You can now edit your type for size, font, and location – for more options select Window > Workspace > Typography. Change it at least once; just to see the differences in the type flow and word count per line. Add a headline and subheads if you need them. Give the text a title and typeset them in a way that complements the body copy you originally wrote. Think about how these four elements work together, have you left negative space, and have you used both pages in an inventive way that complements each other?

**6** Add Images

To insert an image select File > Place and draw to grids. Alternatively, create a shape and, while it is highlighted, select File > Place and the image will fill the shape. Use Control + Click > Fitting or use the Direct Selection Tool to experiment with how the image occupies this shape. If you need to alter the colour in your photo, go back into Photoshop and change it; as long as you save the file in the same place with the same name it will update automatically. If in doubt, replace the image.

**7** Personalisation

Now that you are getting to grips with the fundamentals, experiment with the colour of the document using various tools. Add a title page and a back cover. Could you add more pictures? Or do something inventive with the typography? It is always difficult to design on the computer so take a step back into your sketchbook. Think

about what you are trying to say and to whom. What is your opinion of InDesign? Can you turn this booklet into a useful reference material? Sketch out some layout examples and apply them to your design.

## ● VECTOR TYPOGRAPHY

In this assignment you are going to use Illustrator to manipulate a vector-based letterform and draw one from scratch.

**1** Select the Type Tool and type a single letter of your choice, in a typeface of your choice.

**2** Select the text box with the Direct Selection Tool and click Type > Create Outlines. Illustrator has just turned your letterform into a vector shape. This technique is often used when printing vinyl or creating screen prints; make sure you keep an un-outlined version to one side in case you need to go back and edit.

**3** Using the Direct Selection Tool you will notice the letter now has handles. Grab the handles and start moving them around to experiment with how the letterform changes.

**4** Using the various Pen Tool options, add and subtract handles and add and remove curves.

**5** Using these tools, and retaining the fact this is a legible letter, make an abstract shape.

**6** Next to your final abstract letter use the Pen Tool in isolation to draw the new shape you have created. Is it difficult? How can you make it easier? Could you use existing shapes? Grids? Experiment.

## ● CREATING A LEAF IN ILLUSTRATOR

**1** Select the Arc Tool and make four lines as shown. Make sure that the two outside lines, the inside lines that create the 'stem', and the other end of the leaf all end at the same point. You will need to use the White Selection arrow to move the anchor points into place, as well as move the handles on each of the lines.

**2** Select the two inner lines by holding down the Shift key and clicking on each of them with the Black Selection Tool. Then give the lines a mid-green colour or C80 M15 Y100 K5. Next, select the topmost line and give it a yellow colour or C5 M0 Y100 K0. Finally, select the bottommost line and give it a rust colour or C40 M70 Y85 K35.

**3** Select the bottom two lines with the Black Selection arrow. Go to Object > Blend > Blend Options, choose the Smooth Colour option, and press OK. Next, press Alt + B and either ⌘ (Mac) or Ctrl (PC). The bottom half of the leaf should now be filled.

**4** Select the top two lines and repeat stage 3. The whole leaf should now be filled. Finally, select both sides of the leaf and go to Object > Group. The leaf is now one object.

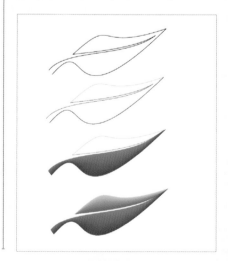

## ⊙ ANIMATE SHAPES WITH AFTER EFFECTS ANIMATION PRESETS

Set by Zak Peric

In this assignment you will create a three-second animation from scratch using presets in After Effects.

**1** From the Composition menu select New Composition. From the Preset drop-down menu select HDV/HDTV 720, 29.97. Next change the time of the animation by editing the duration to 0;00;03;00 (3 seconds). (see image 1)

**2** Find the Effects and Presets menu (right side of the screen), then collapse Animation Presets > Locate Shapes folder > Sprites–Still > Fan Blades preset. Use your mouse to drag and drop Fan Blades to your composition. (see image 2)

**3** Go back to Effects and Presets; this time locate the folder called Behaviours and click on the disclosure triangle to collapse that menu. Now find the preset called Rotate Over Time. Drag and drop this preset to Shape Layer 1 in your timeline. To test the animation press the enter key on your keyboard. (Pressing the enter key on the keyboard plays the animation on/off.)

**4** Now, let's change the speed of the animation. In the Effects Controls panel (top left of the screen), locate the Rotate Over Time effect, then change the rotation from 0x+10.0 to 0x+80.0. To test the change of speed to animation, press the enter key on the keyboard again: the flower rotates faster. (see image 3)

**5** Next, go back to Effects and Presets and this time find Behaviours > Fade In+Out–Frames. Drag and drop this preset to Shape Layer 1. Move the Current Time Indicator in the main timeline window to 0 frames. You will notice that the flower has disappeared. You have successfully added fade in/fade out. Test your animation by pressing the enter key. (see image 4)

**6** The next step is to make a QuickTime movie. Go to File > Export > Export to Render Queue. You will be presented with a new Render Queue window with three options highlighted. (Render Settings: Best Settings, Output Module: Lossless, and Output To: Not Yet Specified.) Click on Not Yet Specified; this will open a new finder window, the file will be called Comp1.mov. Use a desktop or documents folder to save the animation, then press Save. When the Save button is pressed the window will disappear.

**7** The final step in this exercise is to press the Render button in your Render Queue window. After the render is complete the movie will appear in the desktop or documents folder, as specified in Step 6. Play your final render to test your animation.

1

2

3

4

**Further Reading:**

Peter Lourekas, Elain Weinmann, *Illustrator 6: Visual Quickstart Guide*, Peachpit Press, 2012
Corey Barker, *Photoshop Down & Dirty Tricks for Designers*, Peachpit Press, 2011
Barbara Brundage, *Photoshop Elements10: the Missing Manual*, Pogue Press, 2011
Adobe Creative Team, *Adobe InDesign: Classroom in a Book*, Adobe Press, 2011
Nigel French, *InDesign Type*, Adobe Press, 2014
Brian Wood, *Adobe Illustrator CC Classroom in a Book 2015 (Classroom in a Book)*, Adobe Press, 2015

# Print Production and Presentations

When working in the realm of printed media, print production is the last stage in the design process, but it can be the first to be overlooked by the junior designer focusing intently on 'design'. It is really the final oversight of the creative decision-making process, and there are still options to be considered, even with the most detailed planning. If you have considered the project carefully and chosen colours, paper stocks and processes to suit, this final phase becomes a shared creative experience between designer and vendor.

Familiarity with print-production techniques and issues is vital to ensure the final printed job looks and feels the way it was intended. Planning for the use of a special-effect ink, stock or particular finish will only be achievable if you have a thorough (and up-to-date) understanding of the print-production process and a good relationship with your printer. Make it a habit to make a plan or enlist your production representative early in the process. Whoever takes on the task can provide dummy booklets on various stock samples, help to adjust packaging templates, solve bindery and fastening challenges, and provide ink-on-paper samples (ink draw-downs) so you can see how a Pantone ink colour might behave on coloured stock.

**Proofing** Be the first one to spot mistakes. Print your PDF files and check them for typos and colour fidelity, and assemble them to a finished artefact to avoid mistakes.

Keeping your digital work habits pristine will restrict to an absolute minimum the need to tidy up files just before sending them. By this stage your bleeds should be set, your colours checked against samples and swatches, all photography should have been purchased/prepared, page items should be aligned, ragging adjusted, and the spell check complete. Creating a positive workflow, from design stage to finished product, will help ensure a successful outcome every time. A true measure of a designer is not only apparent in your conceptual design and typographic skills, but also in your handling of the process from start to finish, including preparing and sending out files to service bureaus and print vendors.

After a final proof is signed off by the client, many issues often remain before work can be printed. Remind yourself that because every piece of design work is unique, it creates a unique set of problems: this stage is your last chance to check your work before handing it over to a printer.

## PDF ADVANTAGES

- Highly compressed files can be generated – with optimised imagery and fonts embedded – to create a very close copy to the original working document. This condensed and mobile format can be easily emailed *en masse* to clients and co-workers for feedback, with edits and mistakes more easily caught during the production process.
- To print, the recipient needs only the free Adobe Acrobat Reader download. Many systems have this pre-installed, but it is always best to get the latest version.
- Newspaper and magazine publishers often receive ads as high-resolution PDFs only, with properly embedded fonts and images at the correct resolution and profile. Advanced tools in Adobe Acrobat Professional, such as Preflight, optimiser and fix-ups, can be key to achieving a successful run.
- Email and Internet creators can link files to web pages for online viewing or attach files to emails.

**Note:** Keep in mind that you cannot easily edit a PDF document. Any changes that might be needed after a PDF leaves your computer will require the original document for editing. That means edits can only be done by the designer, in the original format, unless you decide to provide the native file to your vendor, but be aware of image and font licensing when you do this.

## PDF OPTIONS

When Preflighting, you can bring your PDF to PDF/X and PDF/A standards. These file types, defined by the International Organisation for Standardisation (ISO), adhere to standards that facilitate reliable PDF transmission. They apply the wills and will-nots of a file. Using a PDF-X1, a file generated from Acrobat Preflight (a recognisable preset option in the Pre-Flight menu), is considered the best way to ensure that your file is correct and secure, and is an option in InDesign.

- Be meticulous. It is your responsibility to check everything from tint specifications and image colour spaces to tidying up unused colours in your palette menu, style sheets, unintentional indents on justified edges, extra spaces and missing fonts. Programs such as InDesign have spell check, an option to show hidden characters (such as spaces and paragraph breaks) and Preflight capabilities.
- Have a conversation with your printer about printer's marks, crop marks, bleeds, single pages, and other export options.
- Printers are often sent postscript or PDF files – locked documents including all fonts and images – thereby reducing the potential for error. PDFs play an important role these days in near-instant proofing, and are the primary format used for sending files.

### The role of PDFs

The Portable Document Format (PDF) has come a long way from the aim of the 'paperless office', and is now a means to instantaneously review in-progress drafts and final sign-offs (or soft proofs) with clients, vendors and colleagues. PDF has become the standard for version editing, as well as submitting ads and media to newspaper and periodical publishers; the final output for the printer is itself a high-resolution PDF.

Many programs create reliable PDFs automatically, ensuring correct colour profiles and linking to final images and fonts. In creating PDFs using Acrobat, InDesign or Illustrator, you should start the press optimisation process using predefined settings. In InDesign you can go to Adobe PDF Presets > Press Quality. To customise the PDF settings, first go to File > Export and choose your format for print from the drop-down

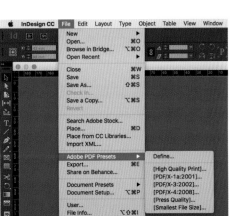

**PDF presets** Select the correct PDF Preset setting for your file. Choose low-resolution, 72-dpi formats for sending files for email review, and high-resolution files for production.

window. When you select Save, another option window will allow you to select Compression > Do Not Downsample; then select Marks and Bleeds to set your crops, bleeds and printers' registration marks. Always double check the PDF in Acrobat to make sure everything is correct.

**Font embedding** When a font is not embedded, it is usually because it is missing from the document folder or has vendor restrictions; when opened or printed, a generic typeface might be substituted. Nothing is worse than opening a publication with your client's advertisement – a masterpiece in Gill Sans, say – and being greeted with a horror dripping in Courier. Proper embedding during your process prevents font substitution at the viewing stage, and ensures that vendors reprint the text in its intended font. Preflight tools in InDesign and Illustrator usually help you steer clear of errors before reaching PDFs, and you can always check Properties when viewing PDFs to check that fonts are embedded.

### What to send

When collecting a project for output, essentially you are mirroring requisite elements that make up the design: fonts, images and page layouts. However, you are also augmenting these with as many items as possible to help translate to your vendor what you are trying to achieve in production. You can do this by including a satisfactory comp (comprehensive) printout to be used as a guide.

Traditionally, elements such as images and fonts were strung together in desktop publishing programs such as InDesign; naturally, these included a suite of Preflight and Packaging capabilities to check and collect everything for output.

### File types and compression

Different applications store and compress data in various ways. Misunderstand or misuse these formats and you are heading for trouble. For example, you might spend hours scanning-in files and creating artwork for a magazine, only to save your hard work in the wrong format. At best, this will cost you hours; at worst, the job. A working knowledge of file formats and the process of compression could go a long way in preventing this scenario.

---

## PRINT CHECKLIST

**To send a file electronically, be sure to include all of the following.**

- **Your final approved document** (InDesign: .indd; high-res pdf and an .idml mark-up if your printer is not using the most up-to-date software.)
- **A folder of all linked images** (.eps, .tif, .pdf), entitled either 'links' or 'images'. You should also include original files in .psd or .ai, in case your printer needs to make an adjustment.
- **A folder of all fonts** (PostScript, TrueType, OpenType). Be wary of typography sharing licences.
- **Printer instructions and profiles** (included in the Preflight and Packaging options).

- **Output or a low-resolution PDF** for the printer to use as a guide, clearly labelled as such in order to avoid confusion.
- **A detailed comp dummy** that tangibly demonstrates folds and sequences.
- **Ink swatches**, additional material samples and a paper sample, if needed.
- **A note to the vendor** that may include specific instructions, a copy of any relevant correspondence and job numbers.
- **Email information** reiterating agreed-upon specifications with the files attached or a notice of online upload.

---

Electronic files appear to travel many distances around the city or around the globe, when in fact one computer is just copying from another. During this process, corruption can occur, especially to page layout and font files. Compressing files before sending via email or FTP (File Transfer Protocol) is an effective way of preventing this.

Most files that are not native application formats can include some sort of compression to facilitate use in other programs or transmission via the Internet. The amount and type of compression, especially with imagery, video and audio projects, can affect the quality and performance of your final file.

.ZIP compression file types reduce the number of bytes by removing the redundant areas of underlying code that make up every file. These repeated and replaceable areas are put back into the file using a program such as WinZip or Stuffit to 'unzip' or 'unstuff' the file back to its original format. The final, expanded

### FILE NAMING

- Do not put any spaces in the name or extension; if you need to separate words, use an underscore: 'my_ file.jpg'.
- Use lowercase, not uppercase, characters.
- Use only alpha (abc) or numeric (123) characters. Avoid characters such as @%^&*(), and use a full-stop (.) to separate name and extension.

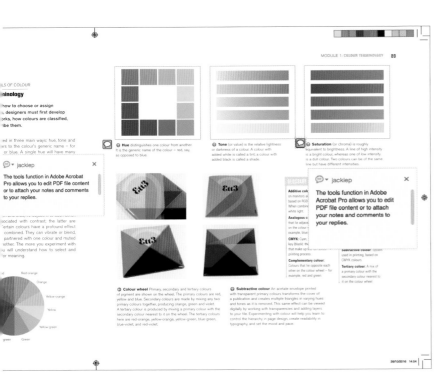

file is identical to the original before it was compressed. Macs and PCs natively create and open ZIP files, whereas Stuffit file creation and expansion needs a separate program.

Sometimes called archives, these compression formats are in all walks of design and production because they speed up and simplify data transmission across the Internet. Used primarily to send large files within emails, many studios and companies utilise an FTP set-up on their web server to easily transfer files online.

There are many online transfer sites that enable you to send large files and avoid compression. Dropbox and Google Drive are file-sharing programs, so will update in your recipient's folder when you update them in yours. WeTransfer is a great resource for sending one-off files.

**PDF Tools** PDFs are commonly sent as email attachments for approval and opinion during the design process. The Tools function in Adobe Acrobat Pro allows you to edit PDF file content or to attach your notes and comments to your replies.

## Key graphic file formats

 **PSD** and **AI** are the file formats for Adobe Photoshop and Adobe Illustrator used for image creation.

**Compatible with:** Photoshop, Illustrator and InDesign with minor restrictions.

**Tip:** Make sure you always save an unflattened master version of your Photoshop files to fall back on, and save Illustrator files with unoutlined text.

 **EPS** used to be the most widely used file format in artwork preparation for print. It can contain either vector or bitmap information and is best used when dealing with logos and illustrations as well as vinyl printing and one- and two-colour jobs.

**Compatible with:** Illustrator for edits and InDesign for layout.

**Tip:** EPSes themselves can contain font data that may need to be backed up with a font file at the collection stage, or font outlines can be created.

 **TIFF** creates one of the largest files because it saves an alpha channel in the file, which allows for transparency at the art's edge, not at the pasteboard's edge. Best when dealing with monotone, greyscale or watermarks for colour toning, TIFF is the highest-quality image format for full-colour photography as well.

**Compatible with:** Photoshop for editing and InDesign for layout.

**Tip:** Make sure you check with your printer as to whether they accept files with LZW compression, which is an option while saving.

 **JPEG** is a format that uses lossy compression – meaning that a certain amount of the image quality is lost during the saving process. With a complex photographic image this would usually remain unnoticed (unless the image is over-compressed).

**Compatible with:** Photoshop for editing and InDesign for layout.

**Tip:** Nowadays, most digital cameras save as large JPEGs, which can be resaved as high-quality images for print due to advances in image resampling and printing. For large, high-quality reproduction, you should be using .tif files.

| PART 2 | PRACTICE |
|---|---|
| CHAPTER 6 | PRINT PRODUCTION AND PRESENTATIONS |
| MODULE 2 | **Creating a convincing presentation** |

⬆ **Presentation** Packaging prototypes for retail, food and beverages should represent how they will look and function at the point of purchase. There are software packages that will render images onto a digital object, but your client may want to simulate the consumer experience to help them decide.

It is critical that your client approve the final version of the electronic file, usually a **PDF** document, but presenting the idea clearly at the concept approval stage can influence the client's choice on which concept to produce. A comp, or comprehensive, is the designer's finished concept shown in the closest possible approximation to the produced product as is possible. Good craft skills are essential and, although a bad concept can't be saved by good craft, a great concept can sometimes suffer if it is poorly crafted.

**Colour**

Electronic output from a high-quality desktop printer can come close to matching the four-colour process intended in production. Matching Pantone colours can be trickier. Colours on screen can be misleading, and will only come close if your monitor is perfectly calibrated. A Pantone number encoded in your document will ensure the colour ink that prints, but to show that exact colour to your client in comp form you may need to depend on a custom blend that adjusts the colour for comping only. Make a separate file named 'Comp' and adjust your colours there. That way you won't send the wrong document to the supplier. Alternatively, although expensive, it is worth investing in a Pantone swatch book so you can show the client the exact colours without having to fork out for Pantone scatter proofs.

**Format**

With your colour perfected, you need to assemble the document into whatever form the product will take, such as a booklet, poster or package design. Output papers come in various weights, and some colour printers will accept the stock you intend to use in production. If you can, print on stock samples, which will give you and your client the best representation of the final product and will show you how duotones and tritones will be affected by the stock colour.

Unfortunately, it's nearly impossible to register output on both sides of the paper, so you'll need to use a dry mastic sheet, like 3M mounting material, to glue – or dry mount – the sides together. Always leave some bleed and printers' registration marks, and trim your pages after you have assembled them. Cut and score the paper for folding after the assembly is completed in a clean, dry studio space.

**Craft**

Some techniques can't be imitated digitally and need to be done by hand. Die cutting will require careful handwork with a thin utility knife, and practising your cutting and comping skills will lead to cleaner presentations. Metallic stamps will need to be hand cut and applied, also. In some cases, a poster, or board, of your intended materials and colours can help in the presentation, but there's no substitute for a clean comp.

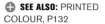

### ⬅ Present appropriately

Determine where you will be presenting, and how many clients will be attending. At a small meeting you can use a tabletop presentation, but with a larger group, you may need to post images or project them. Be prepared, and bring your tablet or laptop to the meeting.

### ⬇ Match colour and paper stock

Simulate the look of your recommended print process, as well as your format. You can come very close to simulating the four-colour process with a good laser or ink-jet printer. Assemble the product, even if you are showing it on screen.

### ⬅ Form and function

Work out the logistics of assembly, in simple and in complex constructions, as best you can. If it helps, consult a print vendor during the design process and determine the best way to commercially assemble your concept, then create your prototype.

### ⬇ Craft is art

Die cutting, scoring and folding by hand take practice and patience. Laser cutters have simplified the process, but if you don't have access to one you'll need great craft skills. Be true to the product line and make sure you carefully create each element in the design system.

⊕ **SEE ALSO:** PRINTED COLOUR, P132

| PART 2 | PRACTICE |
|---|---|
| CHAPTER 6 | PRINT PRODUCTION AND PRESENTATIONS |
| MODULE 3 | **Paper stocks and finishing** |

**Paper is absolutely part of the picture, and it can enhance or diminish the vibrancy of your imagery. Paper stock is manufactured in a large assortment of weights, colours, textures and finishes, and selecting the correct one can really add to the success of the finished product. Sampling is the ideal way to determine whether or not a particular stock will work for you. You should also be aware of the common terms used to describe paper, including the various attributes and how they apply to a particular job.**

Paper is produced from pressed pulped wood, cotton or recycled paper. Seven standard attributes describe different characteristics.

• Weight describes the density of the fibres that make up the sheet, and is measured in grams per square metre (gsm or g/m2) or pounds (lb). Letter weights vary from 24 gsm or lb to 140 lb cover weight. Speciality stocks can be even heavier.
• Thickness is measured in caliper (inches) or millimetres; however, greater thickness does not mean better quality.
• Texture depends on the size or quality of wood fibres and the method of construction. Tightly pressed, fine fibres result in a smoother paper normally used for writing or printing; less pressed, bigger fibres form board and fibrous card.
• Strength (tension and resilience) is affected by texture, density, weight and thickness; for example, tissue paper and cardboard are both used for packaging, but in different contexts.
• Opacity depends on density and thickness, and refers to how much text or image on the overleaf page can be masked. Vellum paper is highly translucent and is made by immersing good-quality paper in acid, which alters the fibres.

• Brightness depends on how much the paper has been bleached before it is pressed. Brighter stock reflects more light and results in a fresher look to a page. Environmental concerns have resulted in a return to unbleached paper in recent years.
• Colour is produced by dyeing the fibre pulp before it is pressed. Coloured stocks can be more expensive than white stock.

**Matt, satin and gloss surfaces**
Different paper qualities affect the intensity of printed ink – there is a stark difference between printed matt and gloss surfaces. When ink adheres to matt paper, it is absorbed and has no shine. Matt finish is used for printed-word texts such as newspapers and books. It is usually easy to read, but does have a tendency to make images and colours duller. However, ink printed onto gloss paper stays on the surface, so more light hits the paper below and bounces off, giving a deeper, more intense colour. This quality is used for book covers, magazines, brochures and packaging. Satin paper (or dull coat) comes somewhere between the two, giving a slightly less intense colour than gloss but without the shiny surface.

⬆ **Add flavour** Deeply textured cover stock in cocoa brown is a tantalising entrée to the individually packaged chocolates on the inside of this package design. Beautiful typography and delicate matt colours partner to establish the brand as a luxury item.

✳ **Paper samples**
Printers and paper suppliers have a range of paper samples to distribute to existing and potential clients. Each booklet has samples of the available colours, weights and surface finishes on each sheet. The big suppliers, such as GF Smith and Fedrigoni, make beautifully designed publications that are worth getting your hands on. Alternatively, some design magazines, such as *Eye Magazine*, advertise paper stocks inside their issues.

ⓘ **Going green**
Concerns about sustainability mean that many designers now use recycled papers, or sheets made from cotton, not wood pulp. This is not the only concern for sustainable design; there are also environmental issues based around paper bleaching and certain inks, all of which are important considerations when designing.

## Finishes and coatings

Finishes and coatings are added either to protect printed ink, or in patches to emphasise an area of ink.

- Varnishes are coatings applied 'on press', either with other inks or as a separate run, and can be matt, satin or gloss, and tinted with added pigment.
- UV coatings are spread on as a liquid, then hardened with ultraviolet light. They can be matt or gloss, and applied accurately in spot form or as complete coverage.
- Aqueous coatings – matt, satin and gloss – are relatively expensive and are laid at the end of a run. As such they cannot be controlled to be put in specific areas, only as a complete coat.
- Laminates are layers of sheet plastic or clear liquids that bind into the paper to protect it.
- Paper can also be embossed and debossed to emphasise lettering or an image, and it can be stamped with metallic foil or glossy, flat or shiny colour, a beautiful effect on matt paper. It can also have a painted edge, which is a particularly beautiful addition to publication design. It can also be laser cut or die cut to expose pages underneath. These are beautiful but expensive techniques, so make sure your budget allows for the technique you choose.

**⬇ Texture and light**
Die cuts add surprising pops of colour and use light and shadow to add detail to an extended system. Consult your print vendor or paper merchant to choose the right stock for your project.

**↗ Surface texture**
Business cards are personal items. Adding a tactile element, such as a raised embossing, adds memorability and delicate light and shadow to the surface of the design.

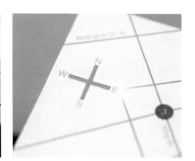

**⬆ Impression** Add texture and tactility to your composition by embossing or debossing the surface of your stock. Uncoated, textured stocks work well, with or without ink coverage.

Various factors determine how many colours you use to produce a job. Aspects such as aesthetics, budget and branding come into play when you make your selections, and you want to be sure the colours you choose are the ones that appear accurately on the finished product.

**Pantone Colour Bridge** This not only shows you what a particular solid PMS colour will look like, but also its full-colour printed counterpart, while giving the CMYK, RGB and hexidecimal formulas for typing it in.

**PMS book** Keep one of these books to hand when designing, attending client meetings and going on press check, as a guide to help choose and validate colour.

Any printed image we see is an illusion of light, paper and patterns of ink that rely on the visual cortex 'blending' the information our retinas perceive into a logical image. Many different kinds of printing types have been created in order to mass-produce this 'illusion' over the decades.

Single-colour (monotone or monochome) printing can be used when there are budget constraints or when there is a particular colour that must be used. For instance, many companies specify a particular Pantone ink for consistency across all their printed work to ensure brand recognition.

Two- and three-colour printing allows for interesting mixtures of Pantones: overprinting two translucent inks can generate a third colour, and printing black-and-white images in two colours (duotone) and three colours (tritone) can enhance their effect.

Four-colour process printing uses cyan (C), magenta (M), yellow (Y) and black (K) inks specified in percentage tints to create a huge variety of other colours. This more popular method is used for reproducing full-colour imagery, photographs or flat colours.

### PMS

The Pantone Matching System consists of colour reference manuals, or books, used for selection and input, either by PMS number or by precise CMYK formulas. Printers have these books and the corresponding matching inks.

Pantone colours, or spot colours, have different ink options, since colour reacts differently with different printing processes and surfaces. To help approximate this, PMS swatch books come in many versions, made for different papers such as coated and matt, and in solid or process colours.

### Workspace, monitor and calibration

The key to consistent colour is to work in a well-lit room with a properly calibrated monitor. Using colour conventions such as PMS and composing colours using CMYK breaks help you achieve correct colour from screen to press. When in doubt, do it by the numbers.

With colour you can mix cyan, magenta, yellow and black in any image-making program or by selecting colours from an image. This mimics the pioneer press person's experimentation with inks that forged the path for printing today. However, PMS is a more reliable way to ensure you are going to get the colour you choose.

**Calibrating your monitor** The best place to begin a successful colour workflow is with the monitor. Correct calibration and profile usage ensure that what you see on screen is what turns out in print. Reliable translation of material from scanner or camera to monitor and printer means proper communication from one device to the next. Many modern monitors come with presets and programs to help you get basic values, but in recent years colorimeters have become readily available to ensure every colour point and setting is consistently and dependably adjusted to standard. Colorimeters cycle through a series of modes to read the current state of display and adjust the video card correctly, creating a new profile, called an ICC profile, for the monitor to create colour from.

### ⓘ Global standard

GRACOL is currently the standard colour profile, but ask your service bureau which profile they prefer you to work with – they may even have created their own.

### ← Tints and opacities

Screen colour doesn't always translate exactly in print. Proofing your design on the actual stock will give the best indication of the final outcome.

Every device has its own set of ICC profiles. Set up by the International Colour Consortium, these standards facilitate the translation of colour information of an image from one device to the next. When a screen, scanner or camera is recalibrated, each is given a new profile and the image produced picks up that profile. Images opened in Photoshop can be reviewed; if a profile setting is different or missing, then the working profile of the monitor is used.

### ⓘ RGB to CMYK

Printers often insist that you give final image files converted to a CMYK format. Generally, it's best to keep images in RGB format until you are ready to send the file to the printer, since image-manipulation programs such as Adobe Photoshop work best with RGB files for correction and effects. Printers recommend the Image > Mode > CMYK function to change an image from RGB to CMYK. They may also prefer to do their own pre-press production check to ensure that all electronic files are prepared to their satisfaction.

### ← Surface and ink Coated paper

allows the ink to sit on the paper surface so the shine of the stock is evident. On uncoated stock, the ink sinks into the paper fibres and dries to a matt finish. PMS coated and uncoated swatch books show you the differences on each PMS numbered ink.

## PMS AND PANTONE BOOK PAPER CHOICES

### PMS

- **Solid** Over 1,000 PMS spot colours are contained in either the fan guide or the chip book, with speciality versions for metallic colours, pastels, neons and tints.
- **Process** Over 3,000 Pantone Process Colours with their CMYK percentages are contained in these books.
- **Colour Bridge** Formerly known as the Solid to Process Guide, this book provides a larger colour swatch and tint comparison showing how solid colours will look in CMYK, and also gives print and web formulas.

### Pantone

- **Coated** This book contains PMS numbers followed by a 'C', indicating that a colour can only be matched by printing on a coated (glossy) surface.
- **Uncoated** This book contains PMS numbers followed by a 'U', indicating an uncoated (matt) surface.

### ↑ Calibration Many factors

such as time, usage and heat cause a monitor to go out of calibration – many colorimeters, such as the Spyder, are available to recalibrate.

**DPI:** Dots per inch is a measurement of printer resolution revealing how many coloured dots are available to create a square inch of an image. The higher the DPI, the more refined the text or image will appear.

**LPI:** When printing halftones, such as in one-colour newspapers and reproductions, the lines per inch is the number of lines that compose the resolution of a halftone screen.

**PPI:** Pixels per inch or pixel density is interchangeable with DPI, but usually refers to the resolution of an unprinted image displayed on screen or captured by a scanner or digital camera.

⊕ **SEE ALSO:** FUNDAMENTALS OF COLOUR, P88

### ← ⟳ Limited colour The two-colour booklet has

a friendly, environmentally conscious and no-fuss appearance. Radiant colours in transparent inks create gorgeous value and hues when overlapped on the package design. Limited colour can be used for its appearance as well as for value.

100% yellow

100% cyan

100C 100Y

100Y 100M

100C 100Y 100M

100C 100M

100% magenta

100K

**◤ Full-colour printing** CMYK is the most popular form of print used daily in book and magazine production. Be aware that 100C 100Y 100M combined does not equate to 100K.

| PART 2 | PRACTICE |
|---|---|
| CHAPTER 6 | PRINT PRODUCTION AND PRESENTATIONS |
| MODULE 5 | **Print media** |

In all traditional printing methods (that is, everything except digital printing), your digital artwork needs to be separated into the constituent colours in which it will be printed.

**⬆ Printing on plastic** Different printing methods are provided for different materials, so consult your vendor and research your options. Consider how many colours you will be printing and how many impressions you need. Most surfaces can be offset printed or screen printed, but new digital technologies are rapidly adding options.

To accomplish this in traditional lithography the printer will make plates, a separate one for each of the four process ink colours or an individual plate for each Pantone, or spot, colour. Most large presses have room for at least six inks and can accommodate varnish as part of the process. Requesting too many spot colours may cause the job to run through the press more than once, and can really affect your printing costs.

**The offset printing principle**
This printing process is based on the principle that water and oil do not mix. The digitally produced printing plate is treated chemically so that the image will accept ink and reject water. The simplified diagram below shows an exposed plate wrapped around the rotating plate cylinder, where the image is dampened and inked. The inked image on the plate is then transferred onto the blanket cylinder. The rubber blanket transfers the image onto the stock, which has been carried around the impression cylinder (adjusted depending on the stock used). This planographic process is rapid, and the plate is inked on each rotation.

**➡ The principle in action**
This press diagram shows an exposed plate wrapped around the rotating plate cylinder, where the image is dampened and inked before being transferred onto the blanket cylinder.

**⬅ On a roll** Most presses feed one sheet of paper through at a time, but larger web presses, which are used for long runs, draw paper from a roll.

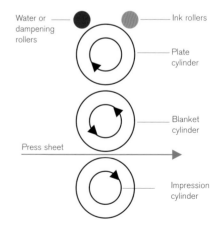

Water or dampening rollers

Ink rollers

Plate cylinder

Blanket cylinder

Press sheet

Impression cylinder

## OFFSET ADVANTAGES

- High-quality images can be achieved by providing a higher-resolution print.
- Works on a wide range of print media such as paper, fabric, plastic, wood, metal, leather and glass.
- Cost per printed piece decreases as the quantity increases.
- Quality, cost effectiveness and bindery finishing are fully controllable in large-run jobs.
- Modern offset presses use computer-to-plate technology, increasing economy and quality.

**● Black**
Many designers and printers prefer the 'mega-black' or 'super-black' formula for large areas of black. This formula, at 60C, 40M, 40Y, 100K, should be used in imagery, not text, and provides a much richer interpretation over 100K alone to create black.

**⬆ Full black** Choose this process when your halftone photographic subjects have significant expanses of black and a full greyscale range to add richness to the subject. Printed body text and fine lines should be printed in as few colour separations as possible to avoid registration issues. Use 100K or choose a Pantone black.

### GLOSSARY

**Flexography:** Method of printing that uses rubber relief plates.

**Gravure:** Method of printing that uses plates with recessed cells of varying depths.

**Offset lithography:** The digitally produced printing plate is treated chemically, so that the image will accept ink and reject water.

**Plates:** Separate plates enable the printing of separate colours.

**Relief:** A printing process that uses a raised surface, such as letterpress.

**Screen printing:** Method of printing that uses stencils.

**⊕ SEE ALSO:**

FUNDAMENTALS OF COLOUR P88

## Screen printing

Screen printing is a printing technique using a mesh to transfer ink onto a surface, except in areas made impermeable to the ink by a blocking stencil. After this photosensitive ink has dried and been exposed to halide light, the screens are washed out with a pressure washer, ensuring that unwanted blocking ink is removed. Each colour in the design needs its own screen, and therefore is only worthwhile when running large numbers of prints.

## Risograph printing

Risograph printing is environmentally friendly and cost effective, using stencils made from thermal-sensitive paper. The Risograph is extremely energy efficient and generates a minimal amount of waste. The underlying technology of a Risograph is very similar to that of screen printing. The original image file is sent to the machine and is burnt onto a master. The master is then wrapped around a print drum. This drum rotates at high speed, which pushes the ink through the screen and onto the paper as it is sent through the machine.

**⬇ Screen print** The use of a mesh as opposed to a printer makes screen printing an ideal option for printing onto fabric or unusual surfaces.

**⬇ Riso** Risograph printing was originally created for high-volume photocopying, but due to recent trends it is now back in fashion, and offers a cheap solution for printing large runs of minimal colours.

| PART 2 | PRACTICE |
|---|---|
| CHAPTER 6 | PRINT PRODUCTION AND PRESENTATIONS |
| MODULE 6 | **Digital printing** |

With conventional offset lithography almost a century old, digital presses – emerging in the early 1990s with the ability to create print directly from a digital file – have opened up new frontiers. Forward-thinking printers have embraced any technology that enables them to provide more options for their customers. Different than traditional offset, from speed to price to flexibility, digital printing has worked its way into the workflow of many designers and print houses as clients' needs, wants and timeframes accelerate with the changing times.

75dpi at actual printed size

300dpi at actual printed size

Digital presses reproduce documents through a process of toner-based electro-photography – a technology inherent in the common desktop laser printer. This not only speeds up the process but also removes a variety of margins for error.

Generally used for print runs of fewer than 1,000 pieces, for economy, digital printing also opens up per-piece customisation for direct mailing, variable data jobs and frequently updated publications such as newsletters and timetables. Personalised printing and printing on demand are therefore growth industries, allowing for print-on-demand books and other items of varying printed details, page quantities and binding techniques.

Vendors include online-and-on-demand service bureaus, traditional sheet-fed and web-offset printers, screen printers, sign manufacturers and point-of-purchase display producers. Allow yourself and these agencies a margin for error in production stages as you prepare and oversee your digitally printed project. Always check a digital proof and discuss the options with your printer.

◐ **CMYK and resolution** When a full-colour image is needed for print, it must be generated as a CMYK file. For full-colour, duotone and greyscale images, image size is reproduced and digital file resolution should be twice the lines per inch (lpi). The standard for high-resolution print is 300dpi.

**Ink versus toner**
With digital printing the toner does not permeate the paper like conventional ink, but instead forms a thin layer on the surface. Some designers and printers believe that digitally printed colour can appear more saturated. This happens due to lack of light absorption by the paper when ink 'sinks in', as in traditionally printed items. It is not necessarily a bad thing, because 'more saturated' to a printer can also mean 'more vibrant' to a client. Make sure you discuss project adjustments to match your intended output more closely, since some newer presses use a combination of toner and ink to achieve more exact colour values.

Some digital presses that use toner may produce large areas of solid colour with banding and blending problems. Ask your printer to run samples, so you can review for yourself what may or may not work.

**Timeframe**
Digital printing cannot be beaten for production timing, since there is no set-up and clean-up of the press for each job. Some offset print houses are now offering

➔ **Complete systems** Colour matching a complete identity system can be tricky. Digital colour works wonderfully well on photographic subjects and is less expensive for shorter press runs.

## DIGITAL OR OFFSET OPTIONS

- **Quantity** Short-run jobs can prove more cost effective with digital printing; larger quantities are likely to have a lower per-unit cost with offset printing. The rule of thumb is: over 1,000 pieces – go to offset.

- **Colour** Digital presses are like large four-colour process (CMYK) desktop printers. With monotone or duotone printing, offset printing may offer a more cost-effective solution. If Pantone colours are needed, traditional offset is the only way to go. However, digital printing may offer economical and scheduling advantages when it comes to full-colour pieces.

- **Paper and finishing** Special paper, finishes, surfaces and unique size options are increasing every year for digital, but offset printing still offers more flexibility because of the variety of print surfaces available. Also, most digital presses can only handle 35.5 x 50-cm (14 x 20-in) press sheets, whereas offset goes up to 100 x 70cm (40 x 28in), increasing the number of impressions you can group on a sheet.

- **Proofs** Digital offers more accurate proofs, since you receive a sample of the final printed piece using the exact process and paper that will be used for the intended final run. In offset printing, the proofs are generally being produced by digital printers.

shorter print-timing by utilising such techniques as gang-run printing or shift-scheduling. Newspaper Club, for example, have litho and digital print runs on certain days, with certain turnaround times and costs to reflect both jobs.

### Personalisation
Database-driven variable data printing allows digital printing to offer the most economical way to customise marketing materials, direct mail pieces, newsletters and other items with different information or designs on each individual printed piece. Finally, all that information that companies have been collecting for years can be easily used in print!

**Multiple formats**
Digital printing can be used for all types of projects as long as you are working with digital files in CMYK mode. Printing can be done in many formats, including large-format printers that accommodate much bigger surface areas for packaging, posters and banners.

**Complete systems**
Desktop digital printers are essential for printing comprehensives for client approval. A good-quality inkjet or laser printer will also help you to check your work in progress and simulate your intended printing effects.

| PART 2 | PRACTICE |
|---|---|
| CHAPTER 6 | PRINT PRODUCTION AND PRESENTATIONS |
| MODULE 7 | **Correcting colour proofs and press checks** |

The arrival of colour proofs from the printer is second only to the arrival of a finished printed piece of work you have created. However, at colour proof stage, it is still possible to correct some flaws in photographic reproduction, both digital and conventional.

Your proof should be carefully examined for density, colour, registration and dots or spots that may appear on the surface, in addition to any potential text errors you or your client may have missed. It's better to catch them at the proofing stage, when they can still be corrected fairly inexpensively, than during the press check. Keep your comp with you and check the proof to make sure the trim, fold and assembly have been detailed properly. Whenever possible, ask for a proof on the actual stock you will be imprinting, so you can check the colour accurately. Circle anything that worries you, and ask your printer about it.

**Press check**

Printers are usually very receptive to clients overseeing their jobs at the beginning of the press run, and this almost always turns into a learning experience. It is especially helpful when aesthetic judgment is needed. The press person will pull a sheet off the press for you to review, approve and sign off on. At this point you should take your time, pay attention, ask questions and have a checklist to keep you focused.

Remember that at a press check time is expensive – egregious errors such as misspelled words and unaligned edges should have been handled at the proof stages. This will help to avoid any extra correction costs, set-up charges and rescheduling for you and your client. When you are 'on the floor' in the press room, you should focus on overall aesthetic considerations, although a keen eye is always on the hunt for an errant inch-mark instead of an apostrophe, or a random double space.

Greyscale density patches are printed in steps from no tint through to black. They are used to check black-and-white photography and black text in a similar way to that of a colour control strip

The colour control strip tells the designer whether the proof is faithful to the film being proofed. For example, if the printer has used too much yellow ink, so that the proof looks too yellow when the film is correct, the colour bar will help to show this

Check trim marks for position and that the bleed allowance is correct

Check registration marks to see if the job has been proofed in register. If it is correct, all you will see is black. If it is out of register, one or more colours will show next to the black

**Linen tester (loupe)** A magnifier called a linen tester, or a loupe, is used to check colour separations, transparencies and proofs. It will clearly show the dot screen of your half-tone images and will allow you to check the sharpness and dot registration easily. The built-in folding stand keeps the lens at the exact right distance from the sheet surface and leaves your hands free, so no fingerprints are confused with potential flaws.

**❶ Printer's marks**

When setting up a file for printing, a number of marks are needed for the printer to determine where to trim the paper, check calibration and dot density, etc. To add crop, registration, colour bars, page information, bleed and slug, in the Export dialogue window select Marks and Bleed and select either All Printer's Marks or individual marks, depending on your requirements.

⬅ Tints, transparencies and overlays can be deceiving if you only check them on screen. Be sure you are satisfied with the effects you see on the proof. On press, you can ask the printer to hold back slightly on individual CMYK colour values but it will affect the whole sheet, not just the image in question. The best practice is to make the adjustment to the proof before the plates are made.

## PRESS CHECK CHECKLIST

Be prepared; bring these with you.
- An extra copy of electronic files or, even better, a laptop you can work directly from (with requisite fonts and imagery installed).
- The Pantone book (coated/uncoated, or spot or process). See page 133.
- The colour proof that you signed. Although many vendors may want this back, make sure you ask for it again at press time.
- A linen tester or loupe to check for such things as registration, dot bleed, dot gain and font clarity. It usually has a folding stand to hold the lens at the correct distance from the page.
- Patience. A press check on a multi-page document can be lengthy, especially on large print runs. Be prepared for down time, and settle in for the long run.

⬅ **InDesign** Check the swatch colours in your native files if they need adjusting. In the InDesign main menu under Window > Colour > Swatches, you can see the four-colour breakdown of your tint.

➕ **SEE ALSO:** PREPARING FILES FOR PRINT, P124
PRINTED COLOUR, P132

On first specifying a tint, always give percentages of the process colours, obtainable from a tint chart, rather than a Pantone colour swatch or reference number to match, because many special colours cannot be achieved from the four-colour process. The tint on the proof can then be checked against the tint chart. Watch out for mottled tints, which can be caused by the film or plate being exposed out of contact

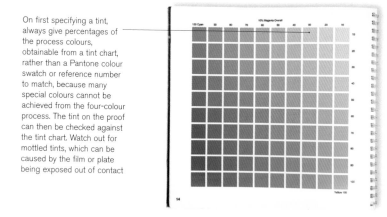

## BACKGROUNDS

If a common special colour or tint background is required for several pages in a publication, the designer should be aware of problems the printer might have in maintaining consistency between pages. For example, if a taupe background is used, consisting of a percentage tint of process yellow, and there are some pages that require a heavy weight of yellow to be run for the pictures, the tints on those pages may be heavier than on the other pages. The use of a special fifth Pantone colour for the backgrounds only should prevent this problem – but remember that it is more expensive to run five colours than four.

# CHAPTER 6: ASSIGNMENTS

## ○ PACKAGING A FILE FOR THE PRINTER

**1** In InDesign, create a poster summarising your favourite film that features: a solid-colour background; a series of sketches you've drawn, scanned and edited in Photoshop; and body text and a headline and captions for each sketch. Use your design skills to create an interesting page, but bear in mind that this exercise is centred on packaging the file for reproduction.

**2** **Check for the following:**

**• Resolution and colour mode**
The most common problem at the printing stage is bitmapped pictures due to low-resolution imagery. The standard dots-per-inch resolution for printed imagery is 300dpi, which is much higher than you see on your computer screens (a mere 72dpi, which translates to 72 rows of 72 dots). The 300dpi rule goes for photography as well as images and illustrations. Low resolution is also associated with the RGB colour mode, the web-based resolution. Check your colour subjects and convert all to CMYK mode before continuing.

**• Bleeds**
With imagery and colour reaching the end of the paper, an actual section of that colour 'bleeds' into the outer margin of the larger print sheet. Printers ask for at least 0.3175cm (⅛in) around the page. Make sure your photographic subjects are sized accordingly and that you have enough material for the bleed areas. When positioning photo imagery, remember to compensate for the bleed by placing the image to be trimmed in the full proper space. It may appear slightly off-centre in the electronic file, but when printed and trimmed, it will equalise.

**• Fonts**
In Illustrator-rendered pieces, you can change your type to artwork by selecting the Type > Create Outlines function to retain consistency. You will not need to send a font if the type has been converted. Do not assume that printers have the same fonts that you do. Fonts of the same name come in different versions and from different foundries, and so can have minor characteristic changes. You may also be in breach of your font licence if you send original font files, so outlining is a safe option; just make sure you save an un-outlined version for possible text amends.

**3** When you have completely checked your file, go to File > Package and follow the steps to create a new folder for the work. When you have electronically packaged the file, you'll see that InDesign has collected all of your assets and automatically placed them in titled folders. Open each folder and check the contents. If you make a change to the design work after this point, remember to package it again, or to save changes in images to the individual folders that house your assets.

## ○ CREATE PDF FILES

Preflight tools in InDesign, Photoshop and Illustrator will allow you to save in PDF format. Each one offers preset options that allow you to optimise the PDF and customise it according to use.

**1** Open a file in each program and explore the Adobe Preset options available, then create PDF files in low resolution for electronic approvals. Check them for errors, correct any you find and try again.

**2** Email them to yourself as attachments, and make sure they are travelling well electronically.

**3** Using the same native files in InDesign and Illustrator, create high-resolution files intended for reproduction. Remember to add your bleeds and printer's marks. Save the files and check them on screen before printing them to see how accurate they look.

## ○ CREATE AN EIGHT-PAGE ROLL-FOLD DOCUMENT

**1** Start to prepare an eight-page roll-fold document by measuring it carefully. Each page will measure 10 x 21cm (4in wide by 8½in tall). Each of the end panels will fold in, so they will need to be slightly shorter than 10cm (4in) to clear the centre fold.

**2** Set up the file electronically if you have paper large enough to print on – 33 x 48.4cm (13 x 19in) – or draw it out by hand using a T-square, metal ruler and triangle. You will need a sheet of paper approximately 23 x 45.5 cm (9 x 18in) to complete it by hand.

**3** Using an exacto knife with number 11 blade, carefully cut out the whole form, scoring the folds lightly with your knife. Your first try may be less than perfect. Make the adjustments and try again. Make sure the blade is sharp, and change it if it begins to drag on the surface.

## ○ COLOUR COMPS

**1** Create a small multi-page document in InDesign, either a simple four-page document with front and back cover and inside spread, or a trifold.

**2** Create a PDF when you have finished, and print the document. If the document is double-sided, you'll need to adhere the sides together. Do not trim it yet. Use a dry mounting sheet, such as 3M mounting material, burnish down the material and then attach the back. You can also use rubber cement, but make sure you let it dry completely before you attach the back.

**3** Using the encoded printer's marks on the PDF, trim the document, score it and fold it.

**4** When your comp is complete, think about which parts of the product you would discuss at a large presentation. Photograph your comp on a seamless white background and upload the image. Select two details of your project from the native file and create large detail images that explain your talking points. Then create presentation boards or an electronic presentation for a meeting.

## ⬤ PAPER SAMPLES

**1** Collect as many examples of print techniques on various stocks as you can. Try to collect examples of effects as well, such as stamping, embossing and die cutting. Cut them into 9-cm (3½-in) squares, or as close to that as you can without destroying the sample.

**2** Score them across the top, 12mm (½in) down, to make a flap, and paste the flap into your sketchbook, leaving the bottom free. You will be able to feel them for weight and surface texture and use the swatches as inspiration when you are brainstorming. Visit a local paper merchant and request sample books. Build a library of coated and uncoated samples that you can use as references.

## ⬤ TEST SHEET

Find two images: a photograph and an illustration (preferably one with only a few colours, such as a logo).

**1** Open the photograph in Photoshop and go to Save For Web and Devices in the File menu. You will see the image with a variety of controls to the right.

**2** Explore the drop-down selectors, choose between JPG and GIF, and modify the settings for each format to see how the image is re-rendered. Watch the file size change in the lower left as you make adjustments.

**3** Repeat the process with the illustration and make a note of which option best suits each image.

**Further Reading:**

Trish Witkowski, *Fold: The Professional's Guide to Folding*, Finishing Experts Group, 2002

Taka Nakanishi, *Special Effects: A Book About Special Print Effects*, All Rights Reserved Publishing, 2007

David Bann, *The All New Print Production Handbook*, Watson-Guptill, 2007

Gavin Ambrose, Paul Harris, *Basic Design 06: Print & Finish*, AVA, 2014

Paul Jackson, *Cut and Fold Techniques for Promotional Materials*, Laurence King Publishing, 2013

Maria Da Gandra and Maaike Van Neck, *InformForm: Information Design: In Practice, and Informed Theory*, Mwmcreative Ltd, 2014

Mike Perry, *Pulled: A Catalogue of Screen Printing*, Princeton Architectural Press, 2011

# WEB DESIGN

If you assemble a group of website designers and ask them to provide concrete perspectives that relate to designing for the web, you will often get the same response: "Well, it depends."

For newcomers to the field, this vacuous response elicits more frustration than comprehension. But, at the core, this is the essence of what makes designing for the web so exciting. Each client brings with them new material, with varying project goals and functionality requirements. While some projects require the active participation of a full development team, most are the collaborative product of a few key members, or perhaps a well-rounded individual. Therefore, it is increasingly common for a modern website designer to not only have a working familiarity with the varied steps of a website's development process, but also to be ready to take the lead and make sure that each step is accomplished successfully.

How many different development roles will a website designer be expected to command on a given project? Well, it depends.

Website development processes can vary greatly from individual to individual and from firm to firm. However, to ensure that a project runs smoothly for all parties involved, including the client, it is essential that you develop – and follow – a structured game plan, broken down into phases and related steps.

### The planning phase

The planning phase in a website development project is the most crucial, because these initial steps serve to define the process for the entire project.

**Review** Initially, the designer and client should get together to define the client's goals, establish who the target audience is, and discuss required specific features and/or functionality of the site. You should work together to establish the metrics for which the site's success will be determined – such as increase in site traffic, sales, contact or social media reach – with the goal of maximising the return on the client's design investment (RODI).

**Content gathering** The next step is to summarise the information that will be presented on the website. Include the site content (text) as well as defining the visual elements (logos and branding elements, imagery).

**Flowchart** A flowchart is a graphical representation used to display the overall scope of the website. It defines the elements that make up the site's navigational structure (shown as boxes, one per page), as well as the structured flow of traffic through the website (the lines connecting the boxes). It is the crucial foundation for a successful website.

**Software, technology and resources** You will need to determine and identify the programming format in

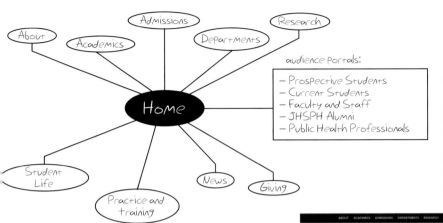

audience portals:
— Prospective Students
— Current Students
— Faculty and Staff
— JHSPH Alumni
— Public Health Professionals

⬅ ⬇ **Flowcharts** These are used to document the anticipated site structure. Flowcharts can be subject to numerous revisions before the project begins. Pages are added (or removed) and topics can be combined on the same page, as logic dictates.

which the site will be developed. Anticipate the range of devices on which the site will be viewed, then summarise additional resources that may be required (web font usage, stock photography, etc.), which may add expenses to the overall project rate.

**Training requirements** If instructional documentation, phone support or onsite training will be required in order for your client to maintain their own website, this should be defined in the initial planning phase, as it will add additional time to the project's development.

**Contract** The contract is the end product of the planning phase. Extra care should be taken to make sure that all items discovered and defined in this phase have been factored in to the project's development framework. Successful contracts clearly define the goals, deliverables, roles, timetable, flowchart, copyright and financial information for the project.

### The design phase
The design phase uses the information that was gathered in the planning phase and brings it forwards to define the appearance for the final project. Generally speaking, traditional websites are developed around two to four different layout variations, or templates: one for the initial (home) page, with one to three additional, standardised layouts for the project's interior pages, as dictated by the varying types of information that will need to be displayed throughout the website.

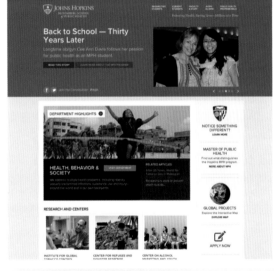

## THE CLIENT QUESTIONNAIRE

In most cases, project information is obtained by leading a client through a web-development project questionnaire, of which many can be found online. They are usually grouped by category, such as general questions, functionality questions and design questions. Avoid using technical lingo, which may confuse your client; for example, instead of asking "Do you require an e-commerce solution?" try "Do you plan on selling anything on your website?".

➕ **SEE ALSO:** SCHEDULING, ORGANISING AND FINALISING, P26

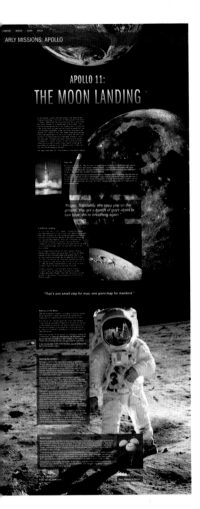

**↑ Embrace the scroll**
When designing for print, artists make use of the entire canvas. On the web, the layout expands and contracts, defined by the content being presented on each page. Sometimes the content fits neatly within the browser window. Other times, as in this example, the visitor would instinctively scroll in order to discover the full scope of the presentation. Be wary of the first impression your site gives and try not to hide the important information with a scroll.

**Image prep** Image prep involves cropping/resizing supplied or purchased images for insertion within the layout, then optimising the resulting files in order to generate smaller file sizes that help ensure faster page download times. There is a Save for Web option in Photoshop.

**Coding** Most websites are created using a foundation of HTML and CSS code. HTML (Hypertext Markup Language) is similar to the architectural structure of a building, defining the foundation, wall placement, and so on. The CSS (Cascading Style Sheets) is the code that controls the appearance of features within the building, equivalent to wall colour, furniture placement and the inclusion of decorative elements.

**Additional functionality** As defined in the planning phase, the project may require additional programming. For example, if the website content is controlled by a content management system (CMS), additional code – typically PHP (Hypertext Prepocessor) or ASP (Active Server Pages) code – will need to be inserted within the HTML template structure so that the web page can 'call' content from the website's database (text and images) for display on the page when it is viewed in a web browser. For those uncomfortable with coding in general, you have two options. The first is to collaborate with a developer. The second is to modify existing web templates. WordPress, Wix and SquareSpace are all good starting points, but they usually come with limited features and additional costs.

**Content integration** For smaller websites this step will not be time consuming, because the information will be copied and pasted from a supplied text file and inserted into a web page template. For larger or e-commerce-based websites this step can involve significantly more work; for example, sizing numerous product images or creating inventory listings for inclusion within the e-commerce platform.

**Test and verify** Using the flowchart as a roadmap, walk through each page of your website to make sure that it functions correctly. It helps to have a fresh pair of eyes to assist you in this step. Test using current browsers (Chrome, Firefox, Safari, IE), platforms (Mac/PC) and devices (desktop, laptop, tablet, smartphone).

**The launch phase**
The purpose of this phase is to prepare the site for public viewing.

**Upload to client's web server** Developers usually create a website in a testing, or production, environment, at a different web address from the client's actual web address. Once the website is ready to be launched, the files must be adjusted for the move to the final storage location, the client's web server (or 'host').

**Hosting and domain names** Depending on budget, it is always advisable to buy up as many domain names as you can, joebloggs.co.uk, joebloggs.com, joebloggs.org, etc. 123-Reg offers lengthy packages for reasonable prices and provides a step-by-step guide to linking the domain to your hosting. There are numerous hosting sites available, so shop around to find the best for your money. Be aware that, usually, the cheaper sites do not have the most attentive customer service.

**Code adjustments** If the project requires the inclusion of third-party code, such as Google Analytics (for tracking site statistics), it will be inserted after the site has been uploaded to the client's web server.

**Testing** A final round of usability testing should be conducted. Again, a fresh pair of eyes from individuals not familiar with the project will help point out issues that might have been missed in the project's development. [Client review. Revise as necessary. Client sign-off]

**The post-launch phase**
This is the final step in the web project's development, when the designer provides a 'clean' hand-off of the project to the client. It represents the closing of the project development contract, so be prepared to process all last-minute client requests and make sure that all contractual obligations have been met before you define the project as being complete.

Depending on the type of project, the post-launch phase could include the following:

• **Packaging source files** This task involves organising and assembling all files to be returned to the client, such as stock photography images, font purchases, and working Photoshop and Word documents.

**⬇ ➡ Concept to execution** This student's senior thesis project began following the developmental structure of a traditional web design project. Rough sketches were used to define the main navigational structure, as well as desired features and visual imagery. A series of compositional grid systems were explored and the most successful approach was brought forwards to create the final website.

Include a site map of the final site structure, a summary of the project's technical requirements – including languages used, web fonts and style documentation – and a separate listing of site access passwords, since one site may require different multiple passwords, including passwords to third-party services such as hosting and social media.

- **Documentation and training** If the site is going to be maintained by the client, the developer must compile and document the process for the client, including access to passwords and technical instructions for processing site updates. If personalised training or phone support has been specified as deliverable within the project's development contract, it takes place at this step.

- **Satisfaction check** Immediately following the initial website launch, most clients will begin receiving feedback from associates, clients and friends. Follow up a few weeks after the launch to make sure that your client continues to be satisfied with your work. A little extra effort here will serve to solidify a positive experience and increase the likelihood of client referrals. Additionally, because you have adopted this step into your project development process, you can incorporate a rough estimate of support into the original project pricing.

**⬅ Online and offline** At the planning stage of any project it is important to know what formats your visuals will be applied to. This identity for Chiswick needs to be applied online and in print. Note how the photographs are of similar tone and sophistication, and the typographic vector logo is handled with subtlety in both scenarios, to show the cohesion across the brand.

PART 2 | PRACTICE

CHAPTER 7 | WEB DESIGN

MODULE 2 | **Project structures**

It often falls on the designer to define the appropriate project structure in the beginning, since decisions will cascade into both the design and development processes. Your clients may often cite buzzwords relating to what they want, but it is your role as the designer to listen to and decipher what your client actually needs. This module looks at a range of project structures that may define, or be combined to define, your client's project.

### Brochure

This is the most straightforward type of web project. Brochure websites are usually the result of a rapid deployment, meeting the goal of quickly establishing an online presence. First impressions via branding and visual imagery are in the forefront, since the text-based content is typically less developed. Technically, we're referring to static content, HTML and CSS.

### Portfolio

An online portfolio shares many similarities with online brochures, with an enhanced focus on presenting the visual examples. Clicking on an image in an online brochure may take you to a page with product details, whereas clicking on a portfolio image may simply display a more detailed view in the same screen.

### Event/campaign site

You may be asked to develop an event, or campaign, website, which corresponds to a strategic marketing push or to promote an upcoming event such as a concert, lecture or exhibition. These websites typically have a short shelf life, because they are usually attached to a specific date or campaign life cycle. These sites focus on the visual branding, with the addition of actionable items such as submitting RSVPs or purchasing tickets.

### Blog

A weblog is an online journal of posts, or news items, presented in a linear, dated format. Blogs often utilise a content management system (CMS) in order to display the site content dynamically, and, by employing the option to allow your site visitors to comment on specific blog posts, you can engage your viewing audience in an evolving conversation.

### Community

Community sites are focused around a need to share information and/or support for a specified interest or topic with their member audience. These sites have the goal of engaging their members to interact with each other by submitting comments, user reviews and aggregated content through social networking and message boards.

### News/reference

A news site is highly driven and based upon information. It is usually controlled by a CMS and can feature an editorial structure for managing content inclusion (contributor, editor, moderator levels). News sites are typically monetised by advertising placement. Banner ads, badges and buttons are designed elements to be included within the layout structure.

### E-commerce

Websites created with the goal of selling products online offer the benefit of being open 24/7, reaching a wider audience than an actual shopfront location. These sites can be created from a range of solutions, from Google/PayPal shopping basket buttons to customised CMS, connected to a merchant gateway (merchant account) featuring a layer of SSL security. E-commerce sites can incorporate many UI display components such as cross-promotional banners, used for 'You May Also Like' and 'Recently Viewed' listings. Popular systems include PayPal, Google Checkout, Magento and Zen Cart.

**GLOSSARY**

**SSL (Secure Sockets Layer):** Provides communication security over the Internet.

**UI (User Interface):** Where interaction between humans and computers occurs.

⊕ **SEE ALSO:** PROJECT DEVELOPMENT PROCESS OVERVIEW, P142 WORKING WITH CONTENT MANAGEMENT SYSTEMS, P173

POPULAR CONTENT MANAGEMENT SYSTEMS (CMS):

**WordPress** An open-source CMS with a reputation for being easy to use. Websites can appear as linear, post-based blogs, or as the administrative back-end for more traditional websites.

**Joomla** Best for medium-sized sites that don't require a lot of complexity. Extensions – free and commercially available – add enhanced functionality to the default system.

**Drupal** Used in larger websites that require more complex features. Enhanced functionality is added by installing modules. Has a steeper learning curve, so most designers on Drupal-based projects team up with a developer.

**1**

**2**

**3**

**4**

**5**

**6**

**1 Dark, not black** Site visitors prefer reading dark paragraph text on a light background because it is easier on their eyes. However, this layout does not feature an abundance of text, so they made the decision to break from the norm. The sophisticated use of a dark grey field (instead of black) provides enough visual contrast for the white text to be easily read.

**2 Editorial structure** Blog content is intended to be read. This blog echoes layout styles common to printed publication design, with a strong visual hierarchy, the use of a playful grid structure, thoughtful typography and the flourish of using an initial capital letter to lead off the first paragraph.

**3 Communicating visually** When presenting an online portfolio, your selected work examples should do the talking.

**4 A full home page** The home page of a news website serves as the gateway for presenting site content. A variety of topics are being presented to a wide audience within a limited space. A structured grid system with clearly delineated content areas is used to organise the presentation of information. Content rotators and tab-based navigation structures are used to efficiently group similar content within the available space. Online newspapers are usually designed to match their printed counterparts; arguably there may be different ways to tackle this design problem.

**5 Featured images** The pairing of a featured image with a specific article topic serves to visually reinforce the subject matter of the article. It is presented at a large scale on the home page to visually convey that the website is fresh, with new content. On the interior pages, the featured image can be presented in thumbnail form for category listings or as the main visual accompanying the full article.

**6 Keeping it simple** For e-commerce projects, a successful user experience would provide clear access to review the available products and complete the purchase in the shopping basket. Access to review the shopping basket is usually located in the top-right corner of a web page layout and remains present on each page of the site.

| PART 2 | PRACTICE |
|---|---|
| CHAPTER 7 | WEB DESIGN |
| MODULE 3 | **Web tools** |

**As a web designer you will be relied upon for your production and technical skill sets, in addition to the strategic creativity that you bring to every project. Whether working on your own or in a collaborative environment, you will need to keep abreast of software and technological advances; maintain clean and well-organised source files; and possess a working knowledge of current code standards.**

As the Internet and the function and use of online media develops, the tools that are used to create them develop too. As the subject area advances it is becoming more complex, usually requiring the need for teams as opposed to a sole worker.

Teams often include a web designer, who will focus on visual elements such as colour theory, typography, composition, etc., and how the page will work. They often know little or no code. A developer will write the code; front-end developers will use CSS, HTML, JavaScript, etc., and back-end developers will use database management, etc. And finally, UX, which stands for user experience. This role is heavily research led, focusing on user behaviour and motivation, investigating business and users, and verifying the design decisions to make the site functional rather than attractive.

There is no 'correct' way of making a website; in fact, you will find web designers and developers that approach it in all manner of ways. However, it is important that you understand the tools that are used in all stages of the process, and how to provide files to each member of the team involved.

**Adobe Illustrator** is a vector-based drawing application for creating graphics that are used in print and/or on the Web. Web designers use this application for the rapid creation of wireframe layouts and flowcharts (exported and shared with the client as PDF files).

Illustrator can also be used for rendering graphics that are incorporated into websites, such as logos or icons, because it's more efficient and intuitive to create complex graphics in Illustrator than it is in Photoshop.

File set-up: RGB colour mode, with 'pixel' as the unit of measurement, and 72ppi (screen/web resolution).

Create your artworks in Illustrator at the size they will be used, paying special attention to generating shapes that remain within the pixel-based grid structure. Then copy your artworks from Illustrator and paste into Photoshop as 'Smart Objects', which preserves their ability to be edited or updated at a future time.

**Adobe Photoshop** is used by the web designer to visualise the site, but it is the developer who will be responsible for 'slicing up' and coding the web page layout, and for this reason they also need a working familiarity of Photoshop. Industry wide, this is why most request that the final files, from designer to developer, be supplied in a layered Photoshop (PSD) file.

File set-up: RGB colour mode, with 'pixel' as the unit of measurement, 72ppi (screen/web resolution) and the desired length-width dimensions.

Layered PSD files can often grow to more than 100 layers, with elements present across different views. Even when relabelling and organising your layers into a coherent structure, it can be quite complicated to work with the file. Photoshop's Layer Comp feature lets you take snapshot views depicting which elements are visible/hidden when viewing a specific web page.

**⬆ Adobe Photoshop**
As with the other Adobe applications, the appearance and positioning of the palettes, toolbars and document windows on a website mock-up can be adjusted to suit your individual preferences. The default layout is optimised for working on a laptop, but can be expanded to take advantage of larger monitor sizes.

**✷ Photoshop file etiquette**
This website offers a valuable lesson in organising and labelling your Photoshop files for working in a collaborative environment.
www.photoshopetiquette.com

**✷ Adobe TV**
Online video tutorials relating to all Adobe products are an excellent resource for discovering features that have been added to recent software releases.
www.tv.adobe.com

◀ **Illustrator** is an ideal application for drawing and modifying letterforms and vectors. Live, editable text can be converted into vector shapes from original sketches and further modified to create unique visuals. In this example, the Grand Café logo has been drawn systematically with shapes from the letterforms.

◀ **Using Illustrator**

This image of an elephant has been made in Illustrator as a vector-based illustration that can be used for a variety of applications – scaled larger or smaller with no loss of image quality.

## GENERATING PIXEL-PERFECT ARTWORK

Illustrator will let you render graphics that can break from a pixel-based grid. For example, if you created an icon that was 20 by 20 pixels and, later, manually resized it using the bounding box, the resulting dimensions may become fractions of a pixel (30.565 by 30.565 pixels). While it may look fine in Illustrator, when you placed the artwork into Photoshop (or export it for the web), the artwork will become aliased (or feathered), as opposed to maintaining a crisp edge. Web designers maintain a pixel-based grid in Illustrator by working with the grid turned on (View > 'Show Grid'), based on one-pixel integers (Illustrator > Preferences > Guides & Grid > 'Gridline every: 10px/ subdivisions: 10'); using the dialogue box to define the desired width/length dimensions of rendered shapes; and reviewing the dimensions in the Properties panel to make sure that any resized shapes remain comprised of solid integer values.

## EXPORTING GRAPHIC ELEMENTS

Until you get a feel for which specific file format you should use, you can take advantage of the 'Save for Web' export feature in the applications above to preview the visual results, while making sure that the file size stays as low as possible. The file sizes of images included in a web page layout will have a direct impact on a web page's loading time. **GIF and PNG** Traditionally used for buttons, logos and simple artwork, GIFs tend to yield smaller file sizes, while PNGs tend to provide better visual results. Both of these file formats support transparency (if needed). GIF also supports animated content (banner ads). **JPEG** Primarily used for optimising photographic images. Usually, the default 80% quality setting generates the best result without loss of image detail. Avoid using a 90% or higher quality setting, since this may actually increase file size.

◀ **Visual compression**

Photoshop's 'Save for Web' feature gives you the ability to review different image compression options to see how they will affect your original image. Using their '4 up' display tab (as shown), you can visually compare the compression results and the corresponding file sizes. Your goal is to reduce the file size as much as possible without reducing the visual integrity of your image. Additional features available in this interface include image resizing, as well as image compression to match a specified file size – typically used for creating banner ads.

## Coding

Web pages are usually made up of textual documents, which are annotated in a specific manner indicating to the web browser how they should be displayed – this is known as coding. The most common language used is HTML. Extra stylistic methods such as CSS and JavaScript can be applied along with the backbone of HTML to improve the look and feel of web pages.

**HTML and CSS** To use an architectural reference, the combination of HTML and CSS creates a complete house. The HTML represents the structure of the building, while the CSS is used to define the visual appearance.

A benefit of obtaining a basic comprehension of the programming language HTML is that it provides a means to create the skeleton and structure of text-based information, images and interactions contained in your site. As with any technology, HTML is always on the verge of an upgrade. The newer HTML5 builds on the HTML4.1 code structure, while organising the code differently, based on revised semantics, as opposed to the traditional structure of 'head', 'body', and so on. HTML5 also adds animation that is controlled program-matically – replacing the reliance on additional programs for animation and effects such as sliding elements, colour cycling and 3D extrude effects.

The positive of achieving a level of familiarity with CSS is that the style sheet language (written in HTML) pro-vides flexibility in the presentational look and formatting of the design. CSS code is more versatile (and more complex) than HTML, but CSS cannot live alone without the HTML. It would be like trying to paint a wall that does not exist.

CSS has evolved over the years to not only define the style elements of a specific web page, but to be used as an external library of stylistic definitions for an entire website. This strategy allows developers to make modifications quickly, and have them applied globally.

While 'living' in a separate file, the use of CSS also helps speed up the loading time of a web page, reducing the amount of code that the viewer's browser must download for each page.

Designers should endeavour to learn even the very basics of HTML and CSS, since these coding structures have been with us for quite some time and it is likely that you will come across them in your workload. However, as

Content management systems (CMS) and templates are becoming prominent due to their ease of use, there are ways around not even looking at code. Adobe Dreamweaver CC, for example, now has CMS built in, which makes site construction more straightforward.

**JavaScript framework** Scripts are another kind of web language, which sits externally to your site, and is refer-enced in the code, defining how the website behaves and functions in response to certain click requests sent by the user. MooTools, Scriptalicious and jQuery are lead examples of libraries within the JavaScript frame-work. Animated slideshows, Apple-style touch interac-tions and display/hide content options are examples of functionality that can be added to a website through scripts.

**Animate CC /ActionScript** Animate CC, previously known as Flash, is a timeline-based application that can be used for animating vector content. It is supported by a robust back-end programming language called ActionScript. For a long time, animation and design in Flash were considered essential skills for web designers and developers, and it is still widely popular. Today, emerging languages/formats such as HTML5, CSS and JavaScript are gaining traction in creating presenta-tions that used to be only feasible in Flash. However, learning to use the updated Animate CC is still an important skill to understand the concepts and practice of timeline-based animation.

**Website code** HTML code is an organised structure of opening and closing tags that tells your browser how to present your site content.

**Website structure** This diagram shows the typical organisational structure of an HTML document.

**Code academy** A highly regarded resource providing free, step-by-step, online courses in Web Fundamentals to introduce novices to coding using HTML and CSS. www.codecademy.com

**SEE ALSO:** FLOWCHARTS AND WIREFRAMES, P158

**Dreamweaver** Adobe Dreamweaver is the HTML/CSS editor of choice for creating web pages. It remains the industry standard because it generates the cleanest code.

**Adobe Muse** Adobe Muse is a part of Adobe Creative Cloud., and enables designers to build websites without writing a single line of code. The application functionality is extended due to its capacity to use HTML5 scripts via use of Widgets. The Widgets library can be extended with new scripts downloaded from the developer's website (http://resources.muse.adobe.com/collections/widgets). Adobe Muse works seamlessly on all platforms and across all new versions of web browsers. One of its main features is the implementation of Master Pages, responsive design and the use of Scroll Effects.

**InDesign** Adobe InDesign, a vector-based application for creating multi-page documents, can now be used to produce iPad apps. Apps can include audio, video, touch-based interaction, alternate layouts (based on device orientation) and other interactive features.

**Bootstrap and Foundation** Before major developments, browsing the web on mobile phones or any smart device other than a computer was a challenge. Besides all the different formats of different devices manipulating the look and use of a site, it also introduced content-parity problems as the change in device often meant that information was hidden or skewed. Speed was also an issue, as loading a lot of content drinks your mobile Internet data fast. Ethan Marcotte decided to challenge these issues by proposing to use the same content, but the coding would offer different layouts for the design on each device. He coined the term Responsive Web Design.

HTML and CSS are still used in responsive design, so it is more of a conceptual advancement than a technical one. For a web designer, responsive means mocking up multiple layouts for multiple devices. For the client, it means it works on the phone. For a developer, it is the way in which images are served, download speeds, semantics, mobile/desktop first, and more. The main benefit here is the content parity, meaning that the same website works everywhere.

Bootstrap (available in Dreamweaver CC) and Foundation are both front-end frameworks that handle responsive design tools that allow you to build a site in one format (it is advisable to always start with the computer screen) which automatically reformats your designs for multiple devices. The down side is that designs often look the same and designers still can't access them without knowing how the code works, so it is usually left to a developer.

**⬅ Adobe Dreamweaver**
The Dreamweaver interface can be adjusted to preview the appearance of the web page, a code-only view or a combination of both.

**⊕ SEE ALSO:** RESPONSIVE DESIGN AND DISPLAY SIZES, P167

FILE-NAMING CONVENTIONS

When creating graphics for the Web, all files should be named using criteria that both facilitate proper image indexing by the search engines and correspond with accessibility requirements for special needs visitors. Naming your source files properly will save you from having to rename them each time you export your images.
- Always use lowercase letters.
- Never use spaces.
- Use a hyphen (-) to separate word combinations.
- Use an underscore ( _ ) to separate concepts.
- Do not use full-stops, commas or any other characters.
- Use keywords and/or descriptive phrasing that corresponds with the project's established taxonomy.
- Source files can also be dated (012313) when maintaining version control is a concern.

| PART 2 | PRACTICE |
|---|---|
| CHAPTER 7 | WEB DESIGN |
| MODULE 4 | **Initial consultations** |

Web designers are usually invited to preliminary client consultations, where they can provide insight into the project's development based on their previous experiences. They assist in defining the technical requirements and content organisation, in addition to visual approaches.

## MEETING TIPS

- Limit the number of detailed questions you ask. Most clients won't be prepared to focus on specifics at this time.
- Avoid relying on technical jargon.
- Take thorough notes. Nothing communicates the fact that you value your client's time more than pausing to document the points they are discussing.
- Actively listen. Ask your prepared questions and listen to your client's replies. Brainstorm in your own time as part of the proposal process.

These meetings – usually limited to an hour-long discussion – can take place in the agency, at the client's location or via conference call. The purpose of this initial discussion is to meet the client and understand their goals for the project. Follow-up meetings may be required to address specific items, but the focus of this step is to clearly define the project requirements for the development proposal.

### Preparation

Before you attend the first meeting, make sure you have a basic understanding of the project. Different project structures (see pages 148–149) will require that you ask different questions.

Prior to the initial consultation, it is common to ask clients to submit six websites for review.

- **Three competitor websites**

  In reviewing these sites, as well as the comments on what the client liked/disliked, a designer can see how high (or low) the bar has been set for defining the anticipated complexity of the project. The designer can also reference technical features, such as banner advertising, e-commerce functionality, social media integration and mailing list opt-ins, which will be discussed in the initial consultation.

- **Three aesthetic reference websites**

  These websites are supplied to efficiently communicate the client's thoughts on the visual styling of their own project. As with the competitor websites, a short dialogue should be supplied that

defines what they liked/disliked about the designs. While the goal is not to replicate an existing website, a designer can use this information to derive useful design cues, such as colour palette, layout structure, typographic styling and use of imagery.

### Consultation topics

**Project goals** Ask questions that guide your client through explaining who they are and defining their current business challenges.

- What is the website supposed to do for your business?
- What sets your company apart from your competition?
- Is clearly defining the benefits and features of your organisation a challenging task?
- Who are the decision-makers on this project?

**Metrics/RODI** Understanding how a client will determine the success of their project and the return on their design investment (RODI) will help you determine the items that will require your focus.

- Increase in sales? Social media following? Site traffic?
- Increase in email newsletter registration?
- How will clients find your website?

**Technical requirements** Use 'plain-speak' to ask questions that define the technical features for the project. From reviewing the competitors' websites, you should have compiled a basic list of items that will be discussed. In addition, you can draw from your own

◀ **Research** Consultations with clients and other members of the design team work hand in hand with visual research. Whether it be hand rendering typography or pinning examples to the wall for an overview, these conversations are vital to get the most out of your design.

expertise to recommend new features and approaches that may benefit your client.

• How do you currently communicate with clients?
• How often will your website need to be updated? By whom?
• Will you be selling items directly from your website?

**Scope** The size of a website has a direct impact on the project pricing. Guide your client through defining the different sections and subsections of the site. For reference, it can help to review the navigational taxonomy of their competitors' websites. This will serve as the first step for creating the initial flowchart (see pages 142–143).

• Define the sections and subsections of your website.

Additionally, determining your client's level of preparedness will assist you in scheduling the project's development, by clearly defining the client-supplied deliverables.

• For a new site: how much time will you require to generate the dialogue (text) that will be presented throughout your site?
• For a site redesign: how much of your current site dialogue/imagery will remain the same (or be changed) in the revised site?
• Will your website require photography/illustrations? Will you be supplying these items or will you require my assistance?

**Turnaround** You should have an idea of a comfortable development timeframe for developing a project at your own pace. If you do not, make an estimate, then triple it, to include time for unforeseen delays, as well as client delays. A shorter turnaround time requires that you be more aggressive in managing the development of the project.

• Do you require the site to launch by a specific date?
• Is this date flexible or does this date correspond with an event?

**Budget** Don't be afraid to ask this question before you go through the process of crafting a thoughtful proposal. Some clients will be up front about their budget range. Some will have no idea. Others will prefer that you define your pricing range – so you should give this some thought prior to your initial conversation.

### Closing the meeting

The meeting closes with a recap of the current actionable points.

The designer follows up by emailing a list of questions that the client was not able to answer. The designer also explains the next step, which could be a more detailed conversation or submission of the project proposal, which incorporates the points raised in the client consultation.

**✹ Smashing idea**
SmashingMagazine.com offers many resources that relate to questionnaires and project checklists, specific to varying project structures.

**✹ The Plan B**
If the client's budget is unrealistically low, be prepared to offer an alternative solution, such as a DIY service from a web host (or WordPress.com). It's not only polite, but it's good business. Once they grow frustrated by the limitations, they will often return to you.

PART 2 | PRACTICE

CHAPTER 7 | WEB DESIGN

MODULE 5 | **Information architecture (IA)**

The information architecture (IA) of a website is a major component of designing the overall user experience (UX). It is a balance of the intrinsic nature of a website and established user expectations, combined with your client's overall goals. This is the practical and functional expertise that a web designer brings to a website development project and has a strong impact on the perceived success of the endeavour.

### Define the critical pathways

Defining the critical pathways of a website involves understanding the goals for the project and making them clear to your site's audience. This could be in the form of presenting clear calls to action within the page layout. Or it could be guiding your viewers through the navigational structure in order to quickly locate the content without forcing them to 'click' through an excessive number of pages.

### Navigation

Navigation is one of the most important attributes of online design, yet varies so dramatically between websites. The site requirements could result in a simple or complex navigation bar, a few main pages or hundreds, and even different navigations for different types of users. As a result there are no set rules for how to construct your navigation.

Avoid presenting too many different navigational options, which may leave your audience confused about which link they should click on next. Instead, use visual cues (such as prominence, positioning and/ or scale differences) to visually guide your audience through your site's navigational options. Group similarly themed, secondary pages together into subsections and present them using a drop-down (or fly-out) navigational structure.

It is worth considering, especially if your website is large, the use of primary and secondary navigation. Primary navigation will point the user in the direction of the content that they came to the site for. Secondary navigation is for any additional information needed through navigation that does not serve the primary goal of the site. This could include 'About us' or 'FAQs', and be in a footer or below the main emphasis of a site.

### Create polite user experiences

A 'polite website' reacts the way your audience expects it to behave.

When users click a hyperlink, they expect a new web page to load in the same browser window. If your navigation element launches a new browser window (popup) or abruptly launches an application like Adobe Acrobat (or your email client), it is considered polite to warn your audience what to expect when they interact with that specific link.

View Application Form (PDF)
View Full Article (via pop-up window)
Email Us: info@website.com

Vary the colour of visited hyperlinks to let visitors see where they have already been within your website. Avoid using the underline decoration style for non-hyperlinked items.

Let users control their own audio/video experience. Don't force audio/video elements to auto-play as the page initially loads. Give your viewers time to adjust their speaker volume before they choose to press the play button.

### Present digestible content

While writing site content rarely falls on the shoulders of the web designer, it is often your responsibility to guide clients in crafting dialogue for their websites, as

### First impressions

An average user will make the decision to stay on your web page within the first three seconds of visiting. Make sure your landing page has impact. The Bitdefender landing page is straight to the point, with clean graphics and several obvious calls to action.

### Reduce the number of clicks

Try to limit the number of links that your typical viewer would have to click through in order to get to the information you want them to have.

### Usability

Jakob Nielsen is widely recognised as an authority in web usability. His website presents findings from many usability studies. www.useit.com

there are differences when writing for the web versus traditional media.

Online audiences are on the hunt for information. They approach a web page by scanning through the content, starting with the taxonomy of your navigation structure, continuing through your series of headlines and subheadings, and eventually landing on the desired paragraph content.

- Use descriptive keywords in your navigational taxonomy. Avoid using generic names like 'products' or 'services'. Select words that more accurately describe the products and services that relate to your client's business. For supporting information (contact, about us), it is considered appropriate to employ the traditional naming conventions.
- Use visual devices like headlines, subheadings, lists and call-out text to guide your viewers through the information.
- Be up front in your dialogue. Have the first two paragraphs of a page contain the most important information that your viewers are hunting for. Stay on point by defining what the product/service is, what it is used for and how it will benefit your client's site visitors.
- Review your site dialogue and infuse it with relevant keywords. Within reason, limit the amount of pronouns – he, she, it, they – in favour of including the actual names. This will help your site generate higher organic rankings from the search engines.
- Keep your paragraph text short and concise. Avoid compound sentence structures. Divide long paragraphs of text into smaller groupings of sentences.
- Use bulleted (unordered lists) or alphanumeric lists (ordered lists) to allow your audience faster access to the information they are seeking. Additionally, these lists facilitate comprehension between groupings of similarly themed items (bulleted list) or an implied sequential order (lettered/numbered list).

### Establish structure and visual hierarchy

Divide your layout into clearly defined content areas. Create visual relationships by grouping themed items together (for example, a list of recent news items).

Vary the scale of your type. The traditional size for paragraph type should be 11–13 points. Headline and subheading type should be presented proportionately larger, in order to make it stand out. Limit the use of bold or italic formatting, only to provide occasional emphasis within paragraph text. White space is your ally. Controlled and generous vertical white space within a web page layout is your best friend. It segments content areas and helps to control visual noise within your compositional structure.

### Be inspired

Innovation in web design is driven by the desire to create a better user experience (UX), not just change with the goal of appearing to be different. Review the websites that you visit most often and question everything. Look for patterns and similarities. Adopt (or reject) trends as you deem appropriate.

🔼 **Hierarchy** When creating mock-ups for any website or mobile app it is important to think about the hierarchy of information. What is most important, what do you want the viewer to get from the site, what are your main goals/calls to action? Once you have questions like this confirmed through research and conversations with the client, your hierarchy should be a factor in all of your design decisions.

| PART 2 | PRACTICE |
|---|---|
| CHAPTER 7 | WEB DESIGN |
| MODULE 6 | **Flowcharts and wireframes** |

Flowcharts and wireframes enable both designer and client to visualise the structure of a website and throw light on possible problems. It is recommended that both are tackled before the project begins and are included in the project development contract.

### Flowcharts

In the initial planning phase, flowcharts are created to illustrate the navigational structure of the website, the critical pathways for the site audience, and to define the overall scope of the project. These foundation elements are used in establishing a meeting of minds between the designer and the client.

Experienced web designers will caution you not to skip this step. Having a visual representation of the website's structure will facilitate discussions relating to detailed considerations that clients may not be able to immediately grasp. Work with your client to establish what pages are needed, write them on cards, and physically decide upon a framework together before you take it onto the computer.

**Navigation structure** By presenting a flowchart with the defined navigational structure, the client can review the specific taxonomy, the presentation order of the links as well as the distribution of content among primary, secondary and tertiary page structures.

For example, does a primary page ('our services') present an overview of the content found on the secondary pages (each of the services)? Or will it serve as the first page for the section (service #1) and provide links to the other secondary pages?

**Critical pathways** Every website has a purpose and the client's goals for their site should have been defined

⬆ ⬇ **Critical pathways** Working with flowcharts and diagrams to help visualise the hierarchy and connections between different pages or areas might seem unnecessarily excessive. However, this is a simple and valuable way of making sure that all aspects of the common-sense organisation of your site have been fulfilled and nothing is accidentally overlooked. Working in this manner helps to explain planned connections to your client and also helps to confirm the minimum number of steps necessary to get from one page or area to another. This is an important factor, since you don't want your client to lose their audience within an overly complex navigation system.

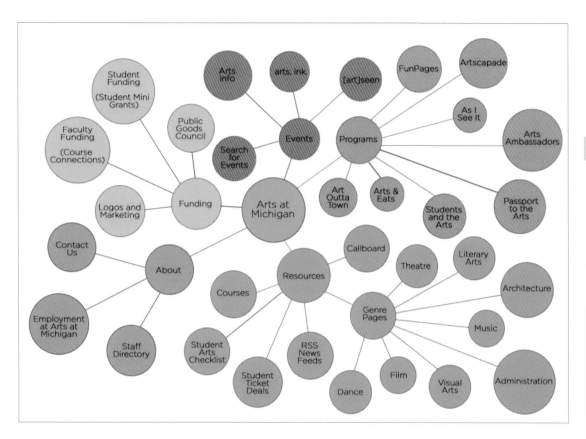

**GLOSSARY**

**Flowchart:** A visual organisational tool used to plan the structure of a website.

**Wireframe:** A basic grid framework for a web page on which design elements are positioned.

### Useful links

**960 Grid System**
Download free templates that feature a structural layout grid based on 960 pixels.
www.960.gs

**Wirify** This free, browser-based app lets you convert any web page into a wireframe view. This can be quite helpful for seeing how existing sites are structurally organised.
www.wirify.com

**I (Heart) Wireframes**
A Tumblog for wireframe strategy with many examples of how designers are using wireframes to define their projects.
wireframes.tumblr.com/

clearly in the Q+A phase, via the Client Questionnaire (see page 143). In creating a flowchart, the designer's goal is to limit the number of pages that a visitor needs to view before arriving at the desired content or call to action. A generally accepted rule of thumb in web design is three clicks or fewer. However, some calls to action can be incorporated, globally, into the site layout. For example, it would be much more efficient to list the desired contact information on every page, as opposed to isolating it on the 'contact us' page. Footers, which are located at the bottom of a website, are particularly good areas to repeat information. Once users have established what is in the footer, it will become a point of quick navigation.

**Project scope** In providing a visual representation that defines the size of the project, all parties involved will be able to review the anticipated scope. If the project is

↑ **Communicating visually** Flowcharts are an efficient way to communicate the scope and organisation of a web project. This example uses colour to define related sections, and change in scale to identify the critical pathways within the website structure.

amended – as they often are – both parties can refer to the previously approved flowchart to discuss how this may affect project pricing and turnaround.

⊕ **SEE ALSO:** PROJECT DEVELOPMENT PROCESS OVERVIEW, P142

⊙ **The grid** A 12-column grid is a common starting point in a website design due to the principles of web standards (see page 145). By aligning elements to a structured grid, the coders will have an easier time bringing your project to fruition.

⊙ **Establishing visual hierarchy** Define content regions for the elements of your layout. Balance spatial relationships with the goals of presenting content in a hierarchical form.

⊙ **Incorporate text and navigational elements** Consider the critical pathways through the website. Guide your audience through these pathways by making options clear, using changes of scale and visual prominence.

⊙ **Greyscale values** Assigning corresponding greyscale values will help you check to make sure that you are presenting your content with the appropriate level of contrast. As colour palettes can be modified as project development continues, you can refer back to your greyscale wireframe to determine the appropriate values that will work with your layout.

## Wireframes

The wireframe is a purposefully under-designed representation of the layout structure of a website's main pages. Similar to an architectural blueprint, it incorporates all structural elements, as well as defining the visual hierarchy and their proportional relationships within the layout. With a reduced focus on visual style choices, both the designer and the client can have productive discussions that relate to the layout structure without getting stuck on visual distractions such as typefaces or colour choices.

Traditionally, wireframes are created in Adobe Illustrator, because designers are already familiar with it, approaches can be revised quickly, and the artwork that it generates can be imported directly into Photoshop when they are ready to begin the visual design process.

**Start with a grid** Most web designers use the 960 Grid System, a streamlined approach to web development using common dimensions based on a width of 960 pixels, which can be divided into a series of equal columns (8 columns, 12 columns, 16 columns). See Web Standards on page 145 for more information.

**Add regions** Insert a series of boxes into your grid that will define the different content areas of your layout, from logo and navigation placement, through the body content, down to the footer area. These boxes should serve to define the proportional relationships between content within your layout.

**Add typography** Define the visual hierarchy between type elements within your layout. Create proportional relationships among your headline and subhead type to guide your viewer through the content. Mix it up and establish a flow. Traditionally, lines (instead of actual words) are used to represent lines of smaller body copy.

**Add links** Define the interactive elements. Will the main navigation menu feature drop-down menus? Will the layout feature buttons, text-based links or a combination of both? At this stage you are not defining the visual appearance of these links, just their form through annotation.

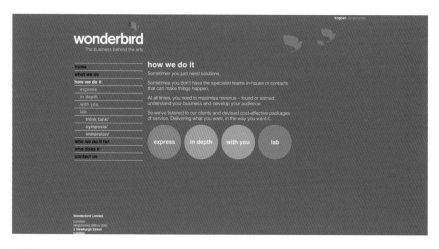

**Incorporate greyscale values** Your last step in the wireframe process is to assign greyscale values to your content. This step will help you determine the visual strength of your elements without having to focus on the colour palette. This will also help you assign colours, later, based on their relative values.

Don't be afraid to experiment. The purpose of the wireframing process is to quickly discover what isn't working and make adjustments.

**High-definition wireframe (optional)** A hi-def wireframe means adding additional details without getting too specific on the visual elements. It usually refers to inserting actual text to determine ideal type sizes, line lengths and leading.

**← 12-column grid**
The design of Wonderbird by Rebecca Foster illustrates well the scope and flexibility of her selected 12-column grid. She consistently uses two columns for left- and right-hand margin spacing throughout. From page to page, as she accommodates different kinds of information and imagery, Rebecca allows detail to extend across varied column widths as appropriate to the information in hand.

TESTING RESOURCES

There are several online resources that will help you troubleshoot your work by validating the HTML and CSS code structure, or by checking your website's navigational structure for broken links. The World Wide Web Consortium (W3C) is regarded as the leading mark-up validation service. validator.w3.org/

| PART 2 | PRACTICE |
|---|---|
| CHAPTER 7 | WEB DESIGN |
| MODULE 7 | **Common elements of a web layout** |

Above the fold

Below the fold

**All web pages have certain elements in common.
These features make up the basic building blocks of a web page.**

Before getting down to building and assembling the elements of a web page, let's take a moment to identify the structural zones common to most website layouts. The top area of a website is often referred to as the header. It usually contains a few key elements, such as branding visuals and the main navigation links. Immediately below the header, you have the body area. It is within this area that content will be changing as you navigate through the pages of the website. And at the bottom of the web page, you have the footer area. It typically contains items relating to site ownership and a recap of the main navigational structure, eliminating the need to return to the top of the page to access the links.

\* **Page title** The descriptive title for the website also identifies the specific page that is being viewed. It is presented at the top of the browser window, or in the browser tab; in the user's bookmark list (if they bookmark the page); and serves as the identifying page title within the search-engine results.

\* **Favicon** This is a small, branding graphic that appears to the left of the web address. Hosting sites usually require your favicon as an .ico file and 32 x 32 or 16 x 16 pixels. Using a non-standard size will not work in all browsers, and will appear distorted.

\* **Header** The top area of a web layout. It typically features the company logo in the top-left or centre position due to web standards (see page 145). The upper header area can feature call-out navigation elements such as login/logout for websites that require user registration, or provide access to shopping basket details for e-commerce sites.

\* **Main navigation/top nav/left nav** Navigation should be kept to a minimum, be easy to identify and easy to use. The main navigation is usually located horizontally across the top area of the screen, under the header. This design pattern (trend) is popular because the abundance of space across the width of the layout usually affords the ability to add additional links to the navigation, as needed, over time. An alternative is to present the main nav, stacked vertically,

along the left side of the web layout. However, this design pattern is becoming less popular as designers prefer to position the subnavigation links in this column space. Depending on the type of site, aim for around five to ten navigation buttons.

\* **Drop-down navigation/fly-out nav** As their names imply, these methods of subnavigation represent ways to visually organise related links, based on the site's organisational structure. Initially, the drop-down menu is revealed (on hover/rollover/tap) to show a series of secondary pages associated with the main navigation link. From those options, related tertiary links are displayed, flying out to the right of the drop-down list. An alternative to the drop-down, which features a full panel of stylised content ranging from subnavigation links to social media feeds, is called a mega menu.

\* **Breadcrumb navigation** This is a navigational wayfinding element, usually located below the header, presented globally, throughout a website. It helps communicate where the viewer is currently located within the site structure, while providing clickable access to return to a main page. It is most useful in sites that feature a navigational structure that goes at least three levels deep. On websites that feature only a primary or secondary navigation structure, this element would be superfluous.

⊕ **Extending 'below the fold'** As this website example demonstrates, site content often continues past the bottom of the immediate browser window, revealed as the visitor scrolls down. Web designers have a sensitivity to place important elements within the top of the website layout, so that they are visible when the page initially loads. Site visitors take visual cues from content being cut off at the browser window, as an indicator that they should scroll down.

✻ **Learn the lingo** Designers rely upon an ever-increasing list of terminology to communicate among collaborators and also with clients. While there are many glossaries available for review, we recommend this list as a great starting point, compiled by the design firm Motive. www.motive.co.nz

⬇ ⬇ **Multiple navigation sources** This website features a combination of both primary and secondary navigation links for navigating within the website as a whole, and the current section of the site. Although the navigation is not positioned in a traditional way, it is consistent throughout.

⬇ **Structure with animation** The Bike British website employs a fixed layout. The menu is in the top left, with animated shapes and graphics as you scroll. This structure is consistent throughout the website. Large vector shapes and a photographic cycle are employed as background images to add bold visual interest as viewers navigate through the site.

⋆ **Feature panel slider** This image slideshow is a visual marketing device that can serve a variety of purposes. Most often it is used to spotlight new products or updated site content, to keep the site looking fresh. Or, it can be used to visually communicate a marketing message, such as product benefits, ease of use statements, and so on.

⋆ **Body area** The body area presents a series of content and subcontent that is specific to the type of website being developed and/or the specific page being viewed. Most websites organise content presented within the body using a vertical column structure, ranging from two to four columns.

⋆ **Call-out/call-to-action elements** Pull-out quotes, special notices and/or buttons with calls to action are usually positioned within the body area, above the fold.

⋆ **Below the fold** Pulled from newspaper terminology, 'below the fold' refers to content that appears lower on the screen, which viewers do not immediately view when the page loads unless they choose to scroll down. While once it was a firm belief that viewers rarely thought to scroll down a web page, we now know that most do. Usually a visual cue, such as content being cut off, serves as a subtle indicator that the viewer should scroll down.

⋆ **Inline text links** Text-based links interspersed through the body copy to facilitate cross-linking among the website's pages, based on topic relevance.

⋆ **Anchor link/jump link/top of page link** A navigation element that, when clicked, directs the viewer to a specific area of a web page. Typically used on pages that present an abundance of dialogue, such as FAQs, or to give the viewer quick access to return to the top of the page without having to scroll.

⋆ **Footer** This area identifies the lower section of a web page. Content in this area is presented globally throughout the website and allows the user to navigate certain fundamentals without getting in the way of the design. It can repeat the main navigational elements that are presented at the top of the page, removing the need to scroll to the top in order to continue. Some websites utilise this area to present dynamic content, such as social media feeds, recent news, recent comments and/or special announcements. Corporate websites usually include a series of required, subordinate links to such topics as legal notices, disclosure details, site map, and so on. Additional elements often found in the footer area include address and contact information, dated copyright statement and developer credit-free advertising. Whether you opt for a little or a lot of information, the footer should be designed in keeping with the site, but may have a more minimalistic feel. Make it easy to use.

⋆ **Space** Space is essential. It dictates everything, from flow of navigation to readability and willingness to engage. Key spatial relationships, between information and lines of text and general use of open space, all need to be approached with consistency. Space is also important when deciding upon your focal points. An image or piece of text in the centre of white space will appear optically larger and more dominant than one that has been condensed into a smaller space. It is also worth noting that space doesn't always have to be white. Space is the lack of elements rather than the lack of colour or texture.

| PART 2 | PRACTICE |
|---|---|
| CHAPTER 7 | WEB DESIGN |
| MODULE 8 | **Designing for the web** |

Designing for the web is often a clever mixture of reflecting client goals, understanding user expectations, keeping up with current trends and infusing the project with your own insights and creativity.

**⬇ Web trends** The inclusion of a large slideshow element on the upper part of the home page is a popular trend for communicating the purpose of the site, reinforced with imagery. An alternate reason for using this element is to spotlight new content, so the site looks fresh to repeat visitors.

**➡ Style boards** Presenting varying stylistic design options – independent of a website's structural layout – is a popular strategy for keeping the focus of the discussion on the stylisation options such as colour palette, typefaces, navigation and image appearance.

## COMMON LAYOUT STRUCTURES

**⬅ Fixed-width layout** Most popular among contemporary websites, this layout structure features a defined pixel width, typically positioned within the centre of the browser window.

**⬅ Liquid layout** This layout is designed to be fluid and repositions the elements in response to the width of the browser window.

**⬅ Floating layout** This layout is based on a fixed width and height within the browser window. Typically, the background remains visible on at least three sides (left, right, lower) and the need to scroll to view content has been eliminated. Popular among high-end retailers, or as interstitial landing pages, this layout style can be problematic over time, since space can be limited.

### Client goals

In your initial consultations for the project (see pages 154–155), you will have defined the client's goals and reviewed the expected scope of the website. With the flow chart to hand (see pages 158–159), these points of information are brought forwards to define the critical pathways of how the visitor moves through the site.

### User expectations

The foundation of web design is rooted in adopting globally accepted sets of behaviours, also known as web standards. Novice designers may feel restrained by following these behaviours, but their acceptance and continuation serve to deliver a consistent user experience as visitors interact with different websites; for example, when the branding element in the header is clicked, the viewer is taken to the home page.

### Web trends

The web is fuelled by innovation. Trends are often rooted in logic: a clever solution that repeatedly springs up across the web because, frankly, it just makes sense. Of course, not all trends should be followed

GLOSSARY

blindly: this is where your own aesthetic judgment as a designer comes into play.

## Flat design

As a result of responsive design, flat design is currently a web trend. Responsive design requires layouts for a variety of formats to be designed, and therefore takes more time than if we were just designing for a computer screen. Due to time constraints with the extra workload, designers naturally began to streamline certain elements, including ditching drop shadows and other dated design trends to prioritise content. Simplifying visual elements, or so-called 'flat design', means that glossy buttons are replaced by vector images and icon fonts that not only load faster, but also look cleaner. The funny thing is, this is the way the web worked at the very beginning. We have come full circle!

## Layout structures

The most common layout structure is a fixed-horizontal layout, whereas vertical positioning is more fluid, dynamically expanding and contracting to accommodate varying amounts of page content. Alternative options include: proportionate width, such as 80% of the browser window; full-width, 100% of the browser window; flush left, a fixed-width layout aligned to the left side of the browser window; and fixed horizontal and vertical, a 'floating' layout that is popular among online retailers but extremely challenging to maintain in the long term, since content presentation needs may evolve over time, requiring more vertical space.

## Where to start?

The generally accepted starting place for designing a website is to focus on the traditional 'laptop view' at 1024 pixels wide (at screen resolution/72ppi).

Designers usually create a Photoshop document that is 1200 pixels wide by 2500 pixels tall, with an understanding that they're not designing to fill the entire canvas vertically. Some pages will require the insertion of a lot of content, and this height means you don't have to reposition items later on. The more space you dedicate to the elements at the top of a website layout, the more information you will be pushing below the bottom of the browser window, requiring your site visitors to scroll to reveal. A header (with navigation bar) over 200 pixels tall would be considered excessive. Most website designs are compact, using less than half that height.

### SUPPLYING CLEAN FILES

In an agency environment, most likely you will be supplying your layered Photoshop files to a team of coders. Keep your files organised. Name your layers using a consistent system. Delete unused layers. Organise related content into named folders.

If you find yourself lost and hunting through layers, most likely your developer may also. Use the Notes and Layer Comps features to define complicated items or settings.

---

**Critical pathways:** Defining the desired route of a website's audience, as it relates to taking an action (purchasing, contacting, registering, etc.).

**Drop-down (menu):** A navigational element that is revealed when a visitor clicks a main navigational link to reveal related links (subsections) that are displayed below.

**Fly-out (menu):** A navigational element that is revealed by extending out to the side of a main navigational element.

**Layer comps (Photoshop):** A feature that allows the user to record which items are viewable in a complex, multi-layer document.

**Style board:** A presentation of proposed website stylisations for review by a client, independent of the overall website structure.

**Tool tips:** A message that displays when a user hovers with a mouse over a linked element.

---

ⓘ **Start with paper**

Work out your concepts on paper before you move on to use a computer. Identify all regions where content will be displayed and the amount of visual real estate that specific elements will require.

---

⊕ **SEE ALSO:**

FLOWCHARTS AND WIREFRAMES, P158

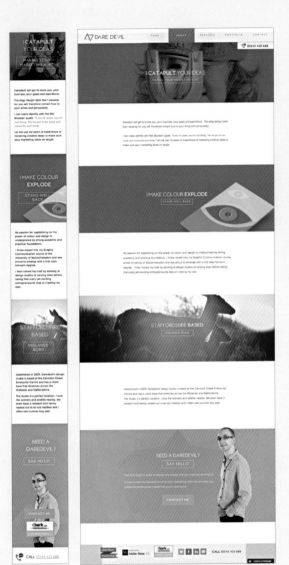

**Structuring your information** As digital devices expand and formats change, websites need to be able to expand and change with them. The Dare Devil site has a number of different platforms; each has a slightly varied grid structure and navigation elements, but the general design consideration stays the same throughout to provide familiarity for users accessing the site multiple times from different platforms.

**Hamburger** This collapsible navigation menu is called a hamburger. It has become the main indicator that there is a hidden or compressed menu so as not to distract from the site design. Most commonly used on mobile sites due to lack of space.

**Structuring your navigation** Over time, websites grow and present more content. The navigational structure of a website can be designed to grow with the size of the website by implementing a series of drop-down and fly-out navigational elements.

### Grid structures

The compositional grid (see page 160) is a design concept that is pulled forwards from traditional, print-based graphic design. In web design, a vertical grid structure is used to provide visual consistency and make the transition from design to programming phase less complicated.

The 960 Grid System is the leading system, because it can be divided evenly into 12 and 16 columns. The width of website layouts using this system is 960 pixels. The additional space would be used to display the background.

### Web typography

Type presentation online is more fluid than its print-based counterparts. Current technological advances in web design now afford designers the ability to present more thoughtful type solutions, but always check your font is web-friendly before you begin your mock-ups!

The width of paragraph text is controlled by defining a fixed width for the type container, typically reflected in your grid system. If your visitor decides to increase the viewing size in their browser settings – and they will – the content will reflow accordingly.

With the advent of web fonts, designers have access to an ever-increasing library of typeface options that have been optimised for onscreen viewing. Gone are the days of labouring to create pixel-based graphics with typeset words. This is the era of quickly swapping in new typefaces (globally, via the CSS) to text that can be understood and indexed by the search engines.

### Design to evolve

Unlike designing for print – where the project is considered complete when the files are sent to the printer – web design projects will continue to evolve over time. A designer must plan ahead for revisions, including the insertion of additional content, new pages and revised project goals. Failure to do so may require that the site be completely re-engineered at a later date in order to accommodate the requested adjustments.

It is because of this anticipated growth that a web designer should focus on a template-driven approach, distributing content consistently across a series of structured layouts.

It would be unheard of – and quite expensive – to

design a 24-page website where each page features a completely different layout structure. The traditional route would be to design a home-page layout and one (or two) interior pages. The presentation of content and imagery can be adjusted per page, but the overall structure remains consistent with the established template structure – not only for cost implications but also for coherence and design consistency.

## Responsive web design

Responsive web design is the innovation whereby the elements within a layout are modified in response to the device on which the site is being viewed. Primarily, this feature is controlled by the back-end coding of the website, which calls a media query to apply the appropriate CSS code to reposition the elements accordingly.

Developing a responsive website often stems directly from the client's request. It requires more labour than a traditional project and this can affect the overall project pricing. Responsive website designs will require the artist to create multiple versions of their designs (separate PSDs), which can be reviewed by the client, and eventually submitted to the coding team.

### ⬆ Reposition and edit

This is a great example of how a browser-based layout has been modified when viewed on a smartphone. Many of the core elements are still present within the composition, but they have been rearranged to accommodate the smaller viewing screen. Some elements, such as the menu icon, are condensed in order to reduce visual clutter.

### ➡ Responsive design

A responsive design can reposition elements to the orientation of the device, portrait or landscape view.

## TYPE TIPS

- Audiences prefer dark body text on a light-coloured background, as opposed to light text on a dark background, which tends to 'burn' into your retinas.
- Use solid numeric integers for the type that you specify in your Photoshop document. The typical size for paragraph text is 12 to 13 points, with an open leading of 16 to 18 points.
- The width of a paragraph should be limited to 'an alphabet and a half' (between 20 and 40 characters is ideal).
- While not an absolute, usability experts recommend using a sans-serif typeface, such as Helvetica, for paragraph text and a complementary typeface of your choosing for heads and subhead systems.
- Avoid applying the attributes bold and/or italics to entire paragraphs. Instead, limit these to occasional use in order to highlight specific elements within the paragraph text.
- Avoid using underscore formatting for non-linked text.

## RESPONSIVE DESIGN AND DISPLAY SIZES

At the publication of this book, the current display sizes are:
- Desktop (1600 pixels wide)
- Laptop (1024 pixels wide)
- Tablet (768 pixels wide)
- Smartphone (320 pixels wide)

A traditional (non-responsive) website, when viewed on a smartphone, might be revised to maximise the viewing experience on the smaller screen.
- Reposition/resize the brand mark (logo) and, perhaps, align it to the centre.
- Condense a main navigation bar into a scrollable drop-down menu.
- Remove rollover effects, because there is no cursor to roll over content.
- Space out links to avoid accidental activation.
- Adjust the alignment of subhead titles to be centred within the screen.
- Adjust images to fit in the screen by cropping or proportionately scaling them down (or a combination of both).
- Reposition multi-column content into a single-column view by stacking elements.
- Display content focused on the smartphone user's anticipated needs; for example, a restaurant spotlighting their hours of operation and reservations number on the home screen.

To review how a responsive website could behave, visit the larger websites you view most often from your computer. Resize your browser window, making it narrow. Responsive websites will reposition the elements in order to maximise the screen view. Traditional websites can still be viewed on these devices, but require the viewer to 'pinch-to-zoom' the site in order to get a better view.

### Documenting the details

In a web design project, the list of elements that need to be designed (and specified for the coding team) can grow to be quite large. Some elements may not be an anticipated factor in the site launch, but will need to be added at a later date. The following list can be used to make sure you have defined the traditional elements of a website.

### Main navigation

Traditionally, the main navigation of a website will appear horizontally across the top. Design for growth and leave space to add an additional navigation link or two.
- Positioning
- Alignment (aligned left, centred, indented)
- Text appearance (typeface, size, colour, spacing, etc.)
- Background appearance
- Active link appearance
- Graphic elements (vertical dividers or a triangle – typically used to identify the availability of submenu links)
- Drop-down submenu appearance (text appearance, horizontal rules, background colour, background opacity, graphic element, etc.)
- Fly-out sub-submenu appearance

### Background

A subtle tint is preferred over stark white.
- Solid. Pattern. Gradient
- Alignment
- Locked into position or scrollable?
- Blend image to solid background colour
- Does the background vary by page?

### Vertical positioning

- How will the layout reposition when the browser is resized?
- How much vertical space should be placed between elements?
- What is the shortest vertical layout size?
- How much space will be consistently above the footer content?

### Footer content

- Appearance of hyperlinks
- Appearance of text (copyright statement)
- Additional elements

### In-line hyperlink states

- Link appearance (typeface, size, colour, underline, etc.)
- Hover link appearance
- Active link/tab appearance
- Visited link appearance

### Navigation button states

A website could feature a wide range of visual buttons, from 'Read More' links to form submit, to adding items to a shopping basket.
- Default button appearance (height, width, colour, padding, corner radius, typeface, size, type colour, drop shadow)
- Hover button appearance
- On-click button appearance
- Disabled button appearance (typically displayed with incomplete forms)

### Submenus

Submenus are usually stacked on the left of interior pages, for navigating within a subsection.
- Interior page position (right column, left column, horizontally under top navigation)
- Styling (typeface, size, colour, background, graphic elements, etc.)
- Active link appearance
- Fly-out menu appearance (for sub-submenu)

## Text styling

- Body (typeface, colour, size, line spacing, bold/italic, etc.)
- Headings (H1, the largest, to H6, the smallest)
- Paragraph spacing
- Lists (ordered – with numbers/unordered – bulleted)
- Quote appearance
- 'Read More' link appearance
- Excerpt text appearance (and length)
- 'Top of Page' navigation link

## Horizontal rule

- Appearance (weight, colour, etc.)
- Spacing (above/below)

## Image styles

You will notice a trend for displaying images in a wide format. This is more common than displaying tall-formatted images, because it reduces the amount of vertical space within the layout.

- Display sizes
- Corner radius
- Drop shadow
- Margin
- Caption text appearance (typeface, size, colour, line spacing, etc.)

## Tables

Tables offer a way to pre-format structured content such as charts.

- Border
- First column, first row appearance
- Padding
- Typeface
- Type size

## Banner advertising

- Display sizes
- Number of ads presented within the layout
- Location of ads (header, side column, footer, with content, etc.)

## Forms

A form can be used by visitors for sending a message or submitting a request, such as joining an email list.

- Overall appearance (background, border, padding, spacing, alignment, etc.)
- Types of input fields (text field, multi-line text field, tick box, radio button, drop-down menu, etc.)
- Text label appearance
- Required fields
- Submit/reset button text
- Validation/error message (location, text appearance, message)
- Destination of form content (email, database, etc.)

## Animated content

- Buttons/button transition appearance
- Tool tips
- Image slideshow
- Lightboxes (title and caption display, previous/next icon, etc.)

## Social media

- Twitter feed appearance (text styling, link appearance, Twitter logo/emblem, etc.)
- Facebook badge appearance (include 'Like' button, display fans, number of fans, include 'Like' total, show recent post feed)
- Flickr badge appearance (number of images, thumbnail size, etc.)

| PART 2 | PRACTICE |
|---|---|
| CHAPTER 7 | WEB DESIGN |
| MODULE 9 | **Mobile application design** |

Due to the surge in responsive design, web designers are invited into mobile applications (apps) development to work on projects that are extensions of a client's existing brand. Be it smartphones or tablets, our clients are moving into an exciting new arena and taking us along for the ride.

↑ **Indygen** is a telecommunications company running across several print and digital platforms. The web app and website work simultaneously together, attracting the device-alternating target audience.

### App categories

Currently there are three categories of apps that a designer could be assigned to work on. It is crucial to understand the differences among the categories as the development process can be quite varied.

**Native apps** These apps are software developed to run on a specific operating system (Apple OS, Android, Windows Mobile). A designer working on a native app project would be collaborating with, at least, a programmer (of C++) for the project. In order to be approved for inclusion into the marketplace, native apps must first comply with a firm set of development guidelines, as defined by the individual device manufacturer. While that may seem limiting to a designer, the focus is on maintaining a consistent user experience from one app to the next.

**Web apps** A web app lives on the Web. Think of it as a mini web page that has been optimised for viewing on a mobile device. When the app is launched, it subtly loads in the mobile device's browser window – you will know by seeing your browser's bookmark/navigation bar at the bottom of your device screen. Using a JavaScript framework, such as jQuery Mobile, you can incorporate a similar touch-optimised framework that is present in native apps.

← **Cheerity** is a social media awareness and fundraising platform. The app has been designed to work effortlessly for desktop and mobile devices, linking to your social media channels and tracking your impact as your campaign grows. Cheerity has been designed in an online app design program called Sketch.

⊙ **App icons** Icons are the main branding element for an app project. The rounded corner is applied automatically by the device manufacturer. The glossy highlight is also a default appearance, but this setting can be deactivated programmactically.

**Adobe Illustrator Draw**

A handy Illustrator app for work on the go. Not ideal for final, professional outcomes, but a great resource to mock-up rough visuals.

**Instagram**

A user-generated photo library, great for inspiration and self-promotion if used appropriately. Use hashtags (#) to promote images.

**Pinterest**

An extensive catalogue of inspiration and of-the-moment design styles. Be wary you do not use Pinterest to steal ideas.

**Evernote**

A handy organisational app that helps you keep track of and prioritise to-do lists. A must-have to help any student keep on top of things!

⊙ **Device GUI** This is an example of Apple's GUI for their iPhone. These elements reflect the structural relationships and common interactions involved with app usage.

## Designing apps

The app development process usually begins before the designer gets involved. The project's producer compiles a project script, or content document, that defines the content that will be displayed on each screen; the navigation and interaction behaviours; specific programming requirements; and lists out required graphics. The more experienced the project's producer is in the field of app development, the more insightful this foundation document will be.

The most efficient method of learning to design apps is to seek out user interaction kits that are available online, and review the range of elements that are typically included. This is also a great way to familarise yourself with the specific terminology relating to device-specific elements, behaviours and features.

If you are designing a native app, it is strongly recommended that you go to the source and review a user interaction kit that has been produced by the device's manufacturer (Apple, Android, etc.). If you follow their well-documented guidelines, your design decisions should not negatively affect the app approval process.

## Modifying the user interface (UI)

Review the apps that you use most frequently and take note of design patterns for how you interact with the app. For example, where are the 'Cancel' and 'Done' buttons placed? If echoing the positioning of these items would lead to a more intuitive user experience, why break from standard conventions?

⊙ **Kew app**

The Kew Gardens app was developed to help visitors find their way around the 300-acre park. Visitors can use this educational app to see what's currently in bloom and dig deeper into Kew's scientific and horticultural endeavours.

**← Showcasing** Blogs are fantastic platforms for showcasing a wide variety of images, experiences and viewpoints. The Formlines blog cleverly hints at more posts by fading out posts on each side of the one selected.

**← Blurring the line** As websites and templates become more accessible, the boundary between a website and a blog is blurring. The travel blog Formlines is so professional and polished that it could be easily mistaken for a fully functional website.

**← Trending** Many platforms have a number of features built in, such as a trending posts feature. This allows viewers to jump straight to the most popular content and, in some cases, you the designer can choose/manipulate what these trending posters are.

**← Social media** Blogs are, in theory, a form of social media, so it is a great idea to link them to your other platforms. Instagram is a perfect visual example of how travel on a personal level ties into a blog hobby. However, be wary of your representation, since not everyone wants to see you drunk on a beach on holiday!

### Protect the site
When working with CMS projects, always assign complex passwords to the database and also for the admin access. This will help prevent attacks from hackers. Try using a random password generating service, such as www.random.org/passwords.

### Selecting themes
A theme is a collection of pre-designed web page layouts around a centralised concept, where the arrangement of the pages' structure has been specified by the theme's author. A theme may feature a series of page layouts for different content areas of the website, such as home page; about us page; blog page; contact page; gallery page; portfolio page; full-width layout; and two-column layout. Many commercially available themes are highly customisable, giving the designer the opportunity to make adjustments to ensure the resulting website is unique to the client. For larger projects, a designer might partner with a programmer to create their own theme, from the ground up, based on the project's exact requirements.

### Installing plugins
The functionality of the basic CMS structure can be enhanced by adding plugins, also referred to as widgets or modules. A plugin could be comprised of a contact form, a social media feed, banner ads, weather forecast, live chat, recent post summaries, dated post archive list, keyword-based tag cloud and testimonials, and may automatically add social media 'like' buttons to a web page's layout. Most CMS systems offer a wide range of plugins for free. Additional plugins may be available from commercial entities for a nominal fee.

### Visual customisations
While themes are highly customisable – allowing you to adjust logos, colours, background visuals, etc. – they are limited in some respects and a certain degree of flexibility is required. Most visual customisations can be specified via the theme option settings, and additional stylisations can be controlled by amending the CSS (Cascading Style Sheets) code. Although some CMS do not allow you to adjust the code.

### Integrating site content
Define the navigational structure of the site using the flow chart as a guide to the established taxonomy, then

create the required pages for the website, inserting the specified text and imagery. Crop/resize images as necessary. Define the categories for the news feed or blog posts – these dated entries are usually referred to as posts – and generate a range of initial posts, so as to populate the website with visual examples.

### Training

If your client will be editing their own site, it is reasonable to provide a certain level of training or orientation in working with the dashboard. Often, designers will create a customised user manual that identifies specific elements within the layout and the corresponding instructions on how to update the content, since the process can vary per theme. Many open source CMS's like WordPress have an online library of user manuals which can be useful to refer clients to for easy things like adding pages.

### Maintenance

CMS and plugins are routinely updated with security patches. You should be regularly processing these updates as you are notified by the system. Comments to blog or news items should always be moderated, to prevent comment-spam from appearing on your live site. Security plugins and/or site monitoring services should be utilised to prevent potential security attacks.

⊕ **SEE ALSO:** PROJECT DEVELOPMENT PROCESS OVERVIEW, P142
BANNER AD DESIGN, P176

## TIPS ON SELECTING THEMES

- **The newer the better** Updates to CMS systems usually feature new innovations, in addition to security patches. Themes released (or updated) within the last six months usually take advantage of current innovations.

- **Focus on functionality** Avoid selecting themes that have been created for different intended uses, because they may feature different navigational behaviours. For example, a 'portfolio' theme may be structured so that when you click on a thumbnail, a larger view is presented. Conversely, in a 'corporate' theme, clicking on a thumbnail would launch a new web page.

- **Note the widgetised areas** These spaces are designated locations within the structured layout of a theme. Typically located in the bottom portion of a website, widgets offer the ability to add one to four columns of useful information, ranging from contact details to spotlighted links and social media feeds. The narrow column of a two-column page layout is also typically a widgetised area, expanding in height to correspond with the number of elements you assign to the column widget area. Typically, side column widgets include subnavigation links, search box, archives list, banner ads, etc.

- **Review the customer** Reviews, documentation and message board comments, if available.

**Categories:** A taxonomy structure for designating dynamic content (posts) to appear in similar, or different, news feeds within a site. Can be used as search criteria for displaying similarly themed posts.

**CMS:** Content management system. The structured framework of a dynamically driven website.

**Dashboard:** The administrative back-end for a CMS.

**Plugin:** A WordPress term for an element that adds a functional enhancement to the basic CMS structure. Also referred to as widgets and modules.

**Tag cloud:** A keyword-based navigation element where keywords can be selected in order to refine search criteria to display similarly themed posts.

**Widget areas:** Locations within a CMS theme where plugins and widgets can be inserted into the physical layout. Typically, these are located within the side column and lower (footer) area of a web page.

---

### THEME AND PLUGIN RESELLERS

ThemeForest.net
WooThemes.com
Themezilla.com
ElegantThemes.com
GraphicPaperPress.com
WPMUdev.org
CodeCanyon.net

### WORDPRESS.ORG VS WORDPRESS.COM

**WordPress.org** is the open-source application that you install on your web server. It's yours to edit as you like. You have access to customised themes and plugins. However, you are responsible for processing occasional software and plugin upgrades.
**WordPress.com** is a commercial entity. It's free to start, but many enhancements are available via paid, 'premium upgrade', options. You are required to pay to have sponsored adverts removed, pay to be able to edit the visual styles, and pay to access 'premium themes'. Software updates are processed on your behalf.

### PAGES AND POSTS

At the most basic level, a page is considered to be an individual web page within the website's navigational structure. A post is an individual item (for example, a news announcement or blog entry) that is presented in linear, dated format within a page.

| PART 2 | PRACTICE |
|---|---|
| CHAPTER 7 | WEB DESIGN |
| MODULE 11 | **Banner ad design** |

Online advertising fuels the continued development of the Web. The revenue generated from placing banner ads on websites can be impressive. Equally impressive can be the number of sales leads generated by a successfully designed campaign. At some point, most web designers are called upon to design web layouts that incorporate banner ad placement, or to create designs for banner ad campaigns.

### Campaign models

In a website development project that features banner advertising, it is important to understand the differences in campaign models, because they can have an impact on the overall website layout. A web designer would consult with their client for specific instructions relating to the number of banners, the requested dimensions, and banner placement within the layout.

**Cost per M (CPM)** The 'M' stands for 1,000 impressions. In this model, advertisers pay based on how many times their ad has appeared to the viewing audience. Generally speaking, this option is the least expensive for advertisers and, therefore, quite popular. Sites that follow this model usually have a large number of banner ads placed within each layout, so they can maximise advertising revenue.

**Cost per click (CPC)** Cost per click allows advertisers to pay only for the targeted leads they receive from visitors who have clicked through their ad. For the designer, this means that there can be a fewer number of banners incorporated into the layout.

### Designing banner ad campaigns

As part of a banner campaign, a designer may be asked to adapt their design across a range of banner ad sizes. Additionally, they could be asked to create a series of different designs featuring different text content and/or visual imagery. This would allow the client to determine which designs work best, based on the statistics they receive on their campaign's activity.

---

TYPES OF BANNER ADS

Banner ads are traditionally broken down into the following categories:

• **Text-based** Simple text-based ads, typically connected to an online ad server such as Google Ads that dynamically inserts the content into your web page when it loads, based on selected keywords. While these ads are not designed, designers will allocate space within the layout and insert the related HTML code.
• **Static graphics** A single, still image, usually incorporating text. Static graphics can be created in Adobe Illustrator, Fireworks, or Photoshop. The artwork would be supplied in either PNG, JPEG, or GIF file formats.

• **Animated GIF** Created using a limited amount of animation, designed to catch the viewer's attention. This art can be created and easily animated in Adobe Photoshop by displaying a sequence of static images, or 'frames'. Timing can be adjusted to further control the presentation. Animated GIFs must comply with established standards relating to overall file size, limiting the number of animation slides – usually three, since any more would exceed maximum file size – and a number of controlled rotations – typically animations are set to loop three times and stop. The artwork would be supplied in the GIF file format, or Animated GIF file format, depending on which application you are using.

• **Flash banner ads** A banner ad created using Adobe Flash or Animate CC allows the user to interact with the ad – for example by rolling over the art to reveal more content. Because it is a Flash animation, it will run more smoothly than an Animated GIF and, therefore, be less intrusive. Run time is limited to 15 seconds at 24 frames per second. However, they are more expensive to develop and are not supported by some smartphone and tablet devices. The artwork would be supplied in the SWF file format.

600 x 400 pixel Panel

Center City District SIPS Happy
Hours Banner Ad Campaign
Summer 2009

160 x 600 pixel
Skyscraper

300 x 250 pixel Banner

468 x 60 pixel Banner

728 x 90 pixel Banner

## BANNER AD SIZES

Most websites that feature banner advertising
comply with the established, standard ad
options (defined by the Interactive Advertising
Bureau) and will provide specifications
relating to dimensions and file size limitations.
While the range of sizes continues to evolve
over time, these are the most common
formats. They are measured in pixels, at
screen resolution (72ppi), in RGB colour
mode, with the maximum file size indicated.

• **Leaderboard – 728 x 90 pixels (40kb)**
A larger, more eye-catching version of
the traditional full banner (see below).
Usually placed at the top or bottom of
a web page.
• **Wide skyscraper – 160 x 600 pixels
(40kb)** A tall, thin banner ad, designed
to remain in view as the reader scrolls
down. Usually appears in a side column,
next to the body copy.
• **Banner ad elements  – 300 x 250
pixels (40kb)** An increasingly popular
option because it is large and typically

placed within the body copy, with the
text content flowing around it.
• **Rectangle – 180 x 150 pixels
(40kb)** This smaller ad size is popular
with blogging sites, usually appearing
in the side column.
• **Full banner – 468 x 60 pixels
(40kb)** Traditionally placed at the top
or bottom of the web page. Officially,
this once popular banner size
has fallen out of favour and it is
increasingly less available as a
size option.

🔆 **Banner campaigns** One of
the unique challenges of designing
a banner ad campaign is to create a
great composition that translates
across the different formats
(rectangle, leaderboard, badge).
Start by designing for the ad that you
consider to have the most challenging
dimensions. Then move on to the
easier sizes, maintaining as much
visual consistency as possible.

⬇ **Banner ad elements**
Successful banner ads usually
contain each of the following
items: a bold graphic with
a main focal point; a short
amount of type; a logo/
branding element; and a
clear call to action.

⚙ **Useful link**
**Interactive Advertising
Bureau**
This professional association
for online advertising works
to define the standards for
the industry as it changes
over time. The website is a
great resource for locating
current ad standards and
creative guidelines.
www.iab.net/guidelines

➕ **SEE ALSO:**
WEB TOOLS, P150

| PART 2 | PRACTICE |
|---|---|
| CHAPTER 7 | WEB DESIGN |
| MODULE 12 | **Search engine optimisation (SEO)** |

As part of any website development project, it is the designer's role to organise and structure the website in a way that helps it to be indexed properly by search engines, such as Google, Bing, and Yahoo!. The goal is to achieve unpaid, or 'organic', search results.

### Landing page
The search engine will search the landing page for key terms first, so make sure your landing page is full of tags and links to the web's content. This should not only make it more accessible to find, but should bump its position on Google.

### Page title (meta tag)
Meta tags are elements within the HTML code, used by the search engines to properly index your website. Depending on the specific tag, it may or may not be visible when viewing the actual web page. A designer could develop a site without using any meta tags, but it would not perform well in the search engines.

### Keywords (meta tag)
Keywords are the word combinations that web surfers use when they're performing their search queries. An initial step is to define all words and word combinations that a visitor might use to search and locate your site. You can do this on your own (from the dialogue your client supplied) or you can get them involved and ask them to compile their own list.

### Page title
The page title is what appears at the top of your listing in the search results. This is also what appears in a bookmark list and at the top of the browser window/tab. It can be truncated, so arrange the important information first.

Bad: Your Site | Recipes
Great: Chilli: Award-Winning Recipe | Your Site

### Site description (meta tag)
A site description is a sentence of about 20 words that appears within the search results. It should clearly define what information viewers will encounter on your site, using as many keywords as naturally possible.

### Images
Often, viewers discover websites by performing image searches and clicking the link to view the full website. For your images to be properly indexed in the search engines, you should make some adjustments.
- **Retitle your images** Adjust the file name to incorporate keywords or relevant descriptive information. Remember never to use spaces. Use hyphens (-) or underscores (_) to separate words.

  Bad: img00123-23.jpg
  Great: recipe-wins-the-chili-cookoff.jpg

- **Include ALT tags for the images that you use on the website** Think of this as a caption that you add to each image, which appears in the HTML code. Spaces are fine between words.
- **Do not put important text inside images** The search engines can't read pictures of words.

### Page rank
The more links to a website from other relevant websites, the higher the page appears in search results (SEO). Reciprocal linking — you link to a company's website and they link to yours — such as between a web designer and web developer, can be a good way to do this. Make sure you only include links to reliable sites/businesses/individuals.

**⬆ Search page results**
In the search results, the designated page/site title is displayed first, followed by the complete URL, and then the site description.

**⬆ Image search results**
A growing number of web viewers rely on image searches to discover websites. Make sure your corresponding artwork is presented so that it can be indexed properly in the search engines. Title the image file's name using relevant keywords, ALT tags and descriptions (or captions).

## PUTTING KEYWORDS TO WORK

Create a list of keywords (and keyword combinations) that you think site visitors would be searching for in order to discover your website. Then incorporate these keywords into your site using the following strategies:

- **Use keywords to create descriptive, human-friendly URLs** Name your web page documents using the keywords that relate to the information found on that page. Avoid using general terms or insider lingo.
  Bad:   www.yoursite.com/recipe.html
  Great:  www.yoursite.com/award-winning-chilli-recipe.html
- **Use keywords in your headline and subhead text** Within an HTML structure, these elements are usually defined by <h> tags (heading tags). The search engines read the words stylised by these tags and assign them higher priority.
- **Infuse your dialogue to contain the appropriate keywords** Often clients will overlook using keywords within their site dialogue, in favour of using pronouns (he, us, it, they). Where naturally possible, keywords should be used instead. But don't go overboard. The search engines know all the tricks. Strings of random keywords within your dialogue will negatively affect your rankings.
- **Use the keyword meta tag** You can insert a string of chosen keywords into your document's keyword meta tag. However, more weight is assigned to keywords that appear naturally within your site dialogue.

## PRACTICAL SEO ADVICE

**For designers** Never promise your client that their new site will receive top ranking in the search engines. A web designer's role is to make sure that a site looks great and is organised so that it can be indexed properly. You have no control over how popular the site will be, nor how high it will rank compared with other sites that may be paying for placement.

To put it in perspective, legitimate SEO/SEM analytics agencies can be hired to increase website rankings. They offer a multi-pronged approach, following the guidelines established by the search engines, and charge up to £20,000 on retainer.

**For your clients** If the designer has followed the advice given above, they will have delivered a website that will be properly indexed. There are also things the client can do to ensure the site ranks highly in the search results.
- Be aware that it can take up to one month for a website to appear in the search engines.
- What keywords are they searching for? Perhaps they are too generic and yielding too many results. Have they tried searching for keyword combinations that feature the city/town where they are located?
- Keep the site updated regularly.
- Promote your website directly to your audience by including your web address on material that you distribute regularly, from business cards to brochures and your email auto-signature.
- Create a presence using social media that drives traffic back to your website. Use status updates to keep your audience informed about new content additions and special offers from your site.
- Have you tried becoming an active participant in online forums and discussion boards? Use your expertise to share tips and advice. Establish yourself as someone people will want to do business with and they will seek you out.
- Have you considered paid placement (sponsored listings) within the search engines? Or sponsored advertising in social media, such as Facebook ads?

| PART 2 | PRACTICE |
|---|---|
| CHAPTER 7 | WEB DESIGN |
| MODULE 13 | **Online portfolios** |

Any professional web designer needs a strong and well-conceived online portfolio and the growing list of 'low-tech' options for displaying work online means that even non-web designers have little excuse for not having their work available for review online.

A successful online portfolio is a snapshot of work that reflects your abilities as a graphic designer. As with other design projects, you are designing for your target audience and addressing their needs. In reviewing numerous candidate websites in a single setting, potential employers are seeking a clear listing of skills and work experience, in addition to a complementary stylistic match for the work they produce.

### Elements of an online portfolio
Your online portfolio should be clear, uncluttered, and easy to navigate. It should feature fundamental, descriptive information, including your name, field of practice, geographic area, and your current availability. You should also use it to present a summary of your professional biography, organised for easy visual scanning on screen. Include a link to download your CV in PDF format. Finally, invite interested parties to make contact with you by including a clear call to action.

### Prepare your images
Limit the number of visual examples you present in favour of providing a snapshot overview of your experiential range. You can present more examples during the in-person interview phase. Most new designers find it challenging to decide which images to include in their online portfolio. Focus on presenting work that represents a solid foundation of design – typography,

composition, colour – in addition to your own aesthetic style. Ideally, your selected examples will complement the scope of work that is being produced by the companies that interest you. If that is not the case, you should work on bolstering your portfolio with new projects.

Portfolio images should be consistent in size and visual presentation. A typical size for a detailed view would be 800 x 600 pixels, at screen resolution (72ppi) and optimised for online viewing. Smaller, thumbnail views can be presented as proportionately reduced artwork or as strategically cropped designs, intended to intrigue your audience into clicking to view in more detail. Website design examples typically feature a browser 'frame' and app designs usually feature the device screen view.

A subcategory navigation structure can be employed to help direct viewers through the project-type examples that relate to the work they are interested in viewing, such as publication design, identity, packaging, and advertising.

### Getting started
To set yourself apart from novices or design hobbyists, you'll need your own domain name and a web hosting account. A domain name (for example, www.yoursite. com) is like leasing a car. Web hosting is like renting a parking spot for your leased car. You need both in order

↑ **Slideshow feature**
To reduce the visitor's need to scroll, project examples are presented in a slideshow format. Whether they are solid block images or tinted panels of thumbnails, they serve as the navigational element for reviewing the additional detailed images.

⊕ **SEE ALSO:**
WORKING WITH CONTENT MANAGEMENT SYSTEMS, P173

## OPTIONAL PORTFOLIO ELEMENTS

- Images can be captioned with brief project summaries to spotlight details or your specific involvement within the project (for group work).
- Concept sketches and creative explorations can effectively provide a unique insight into your creative process. Select one project, present it as a case study, and use visuals to guide your audience through your process.
- Additional interests that reinforce your design skills (photography, illustration) can be included to demonstrate a broader range of skills and interests, but should be presented with reduced presence, so as not to deter from your focus on seeking employment as a graphic designer.
- Invite site visitors to connect with your professional presence across social media accounts (LinkedIn, Twitter, Facebook Fan Page, Flickr, Pinterest, etc.). But, avoid linking to accounts where you represent yourself informally. Social media links are usually located in the footer, and are particularly good for retaining a relationship with the user after they have left the website.
- Maintain a creative design blog (or Tumblr micro-blog) with shared insights on where you derive inspiration and comments on related design trends.

## SELECTING THE RIGHT DOMAIN NAME

Start by using your own name, as opposed to labouring to conceive a clever business alias. It's easier to associate you with a web address that features your actual name. Use a '.com' domain, because people instinctively type that suffix. Select a name that is easy to remember or difficult to misspell, or consider purchasing multiple names. You can always set your domain names to reroute site visitors to your main web address.

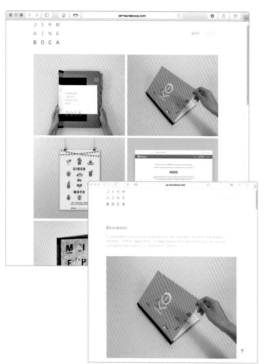

**First impressions** When a user visits a website, you have a split second to make a first impression, and around 15 seconds to persuade them to keep looking. When you design a portfolio, the work is the most important attribute of the site. Make it the first thing you see, and make it attention-grabbing. The use of interesting photographic angles or bright pops of colour on Jermaine Boca's landing page creates a strong impact and confidence in the work.

**Landing page** Similarly, with Theodor Swanson's portfolio site, first impressions are key. A landing page is the first page you 'land' on when clicking a link to the site. It is important that everything on this page is searchable, since search engines tend to quickly scan the landing page before anything else. Make sure all your portfolio images are named with searchable tags, e.g. theodor-swanson-graphic-design-portfolio-poster-typography-neon.jpg.

to establish your online presence. Both are renewed annually for a nominal fee. With a traditional web hosting account you also get email accounts for your domain, which you should use for professional correspondence.

Buy your domain name, even if you are not planning on having a website, simply so that no one else can. There are numerous warnings about individuals buying domains and selling them on at increased rates. Buy as many as you can afford, e.g. .co.uk, .com, .org, .me, .design, etc. There are so many options available, so it makes sense to own the obvious examples. However, some suffixes are not available in other countries, so it's worth doing some research into what you are buying. And finally, set yourself up a professional email address on the back of your domain, e.g. hello@joebloggs.co.uk.

### Low-tech online portfolios

Popular among non-web designers, there are a growing variety of online resources that provide designers with the ability to upload and share image examples from their portfolio. The utility-driven goal is to have the image examples available on demand, via hyperlink, as opposed to manually attaching images to email correspondence.

Your domain's settings can be adjusted to redirect your site viewers directly from your web address to a user profile on any of the following websites.

**Flickr.com** Although widely considered to be the most low-tech option, Flickr image galleries can be further subdivided into photo sets, based on related themes. This is more user-friendly than presenting a timeline-based photo stream.

**Tumblr.com** Tumblr is a micro-blogging platform, intended for sharing images, links, and short text-based posts. The traditional, linear timeline format of a Tumblr page design can be amended with the application of pre-styled 'portfolio theme' formatting. Typically, these commercially available theme styles focus on image-based posts, presented in a visual, grid-style format. Easy to update, each new post presents a new portfolio item. To revise the order of the presentation, you revise the date of the post.

**WordPress** Popular among creatives, the WordPress content management system (CMS) has a wide

⬆ **Thumbnails** This portfolio site contains a series of beautifully curated thumbnail images that when clicked will reveal more information and more in-depth photographs to explain the project. Thumbnails are a great way to condense and organise information, making your site clean and easy to navigate.

✱ **Self-promotion** Don't forget to include the address of your online portfolio on your CV, business cards, social-media account profiles, and your email account's auto-signature settings.

⬆ **Creative cropping** This example presents the artwork as both an angled perspective and a cropped view.

assortment of commercially available themes that have been specifically created for portfolio-style presentations. More complex than a post-driven Tumblr account, WordPress affords you the ability to add more functionality and styling enhancements.

## Traditional online portfolios

If you are seeking positions within the field of web design, the online portfolio serves as a perfect vehicle to demonstrate what you know, from HTML and CSS coding to crafting a memorable user experience. The level of design and coding should be representative of your level of technical expertise.

## Test your work

When you reach the point at which you think you have finished your project, take a break and return with a fresh pair of eyes. Click through all of your links to check that they are functioning properly. Check that your presentation is well organised and visually consistent. Review your grammar.

Conduct a 'beta test' within a small group of friends and/or family members and review their feedback. If your parents are having a challenging time navigating through your site, a potential employer may experience the same issue. Process all necessary adjustments before sharing your web address with a larger audience.

## EMAIL AND AUTO SIGNATURES

Regardless of which email system you use regularly (school, Gmail, Yahoo!, etc.), for professional correspondence you should set up and use an email account associated with your own domain name. Where a school email account communicates 'student' and a non-descript Gmail account may say 'hobbyist', your own domain serves as the foundation in creating a professional first impression.

Most email systems provide you with the ability to set up default auto signatures, where you can predefine a standardised closing signature for every email you distribute. Take advantage of this feature, envisioning it as if you are passing along a virtual business card to everyone you correspond with. Typical signature elements include name, desired contact details, and links to online portfolio and social media.

⬆ **Show off** If you are presenting yourself as a designer who can code HTML and CSS, your online portfolio is a fantastic opportunity to demonstrate your expertise. In this example, the designer is showcasing the website on both a screen and mobile, displaying responsive design skills.

⬅ **Establishing consistency** This portfolio presents thumbnails in a unified, greyscale appearance. When the visitor interacts with the thumbnail, the thumbnail is replaced with the colourised version of the graphic.

# CHAPTER 7: ASSIGNMENTS

## ⦿ FIRST IMPRESSIONS

In small groups, describe who you are in 15 seconds. 55% of visitors spend less than 15 seconds on a website. How can you make a good first impression in 15 seconds? Do it again, but this time plan what important traits you want to highlight. Spend a few minutes discussing how this can be applied to web design, bearing in mind that visual communication can happen much faster than verbal.

## ⦿ PAGE NAVIGATION

Select three simple websites you visit on a regular basis. Using a wireframe, draw up the navigation of these sites. Look for trends in how content is organised. Take note of sites that break from established trends. Identify which factors, unique to the website, benefitted from breaking from the trend. Measure the amount of white space – vertical and horizontal – that is used within layouts to separate content. Discuss in pairs why you think this website was designed in this way. Could you improve it?

## ⦿ CARD SORTING EXERCISE

Card sorting is commonly used in information architecture and can help web designers answer a variety of questions before the design phase even begins. Card sorting helps designers organise navigation, especially complex navigation, in the most efficient way possible.

Choose your favourite artist to draft a website for. For each page write a label on a card, e.g. Home, Work, Project 1, Contact, etc. and begin to lay them out flat in order of navigation. In a group discuss your choices and offer alternative solutions by physically moving the cards around. Pay specific attention to how links are named and how they are ordered. Remember to document the final decision(s) with a camera for reference. Once you are happy, digitally mock the navigation up in Illustrator.

## ⦿ CREATE A STYLE BOARD

A style board is a graphical representation of stylistic approaches that you would be proposing to your client. Designed elements are pulled out of the specific web layout so they can remain the focal point of the preliminary design consultations. Typically, designers present three style boards for a client to review: a conservative approach; a wild approach; and an approach that falls between the two extremes.

Select a website that you visit often and create three style boards. Start with the styles used in the current website. Then create two variations, one conservative, one wild.

**Identify:**
• Colour palette: dark, light, mid-tones, accent colours
• Typography: headline, subhead, body text, text links, quotes, captions, etc.
• Textures: background patterns, gradients, drop shadows, etc.
• Buttons: button size, shape, colour, corner radius, drop shadow, etc.

• Icons: icons as a button element, icons to define content, etc.
• Images: cropping (rectangle/square), border, padding/spacing, drop shadow, corner radius, etc.
• Adjectives: list four adjectives for each of your style boards. These adjectives set the tone for each approach and will be used to pitch your overall concept to your client.

## ⦿ WEB STANDARDS

Web standards are recommendations published by notable institutions associated with web design and development. Although very subjective, web standards aim to unite sites for ease and usability. Make a list of what you believe to be web standards and why. For example, a logo is always a clickable hyperlink back to the homepage. For more information visit www.evolutionoftheweb.com/ – a website that features a graphical timeline of innovations that have influenced the web over the past 20 years, from various web browsers, to code and functionality improvements, to presenting global web traffic numbers.

## ⦿ DREAMWEAVER SET-UP

In this assignment you will create a blank page with responsive settings. A site in Dreamweaver provides a centralised location for you to save and access the files that make your website work; this is called a root folder. Before you even open Dreamweaver you must save a folder, name it root, and keep all your website content here.

- Open Dreamweaver, if you see a welcome screen, you can close it now.
- Site > New Site.
- Name your site.
- Point to the root folder you will be working on from your computer and click choose.
- Set workspace to Beginner (top right drop-down menu).
- Open the Files panel and take a look at the files that make up your website so far (all project

files within your root folder). If you cannot see updated files, click the refresh icon.
- To create a home page: File > New.
- We are building an HTML page so select HTML as the document type.
- Select the Bootstrap tab (a framework that includes a set of prebuilt components that can save you a lot of time when creating a responsive website).
- Select Create New to create a bootstrap.css file. Dreamweaver will create this file based on some of the settings we select next.
- Since you are going to start with a blank page, make sure you uncheck the prebuilt layout option.
- Next, expand the customise settings – these settings define the default layout that will be created once the HTML file is saved.
- It's really helpful to design with a grid when making a website. Columns will help you organise and align components on the page. The column default is 12. Gutter refers to the space between each column and should be left at the 30px default.
- The screen sizes here refer to the different widths for small, medium and large screens. When you create your website, Dreamweaver makes it easy for you to switch between each of these screen sizes and customise the design for each one. (I would advise you to keep the default settings at this stage.)
- Click Create.
- The first thing we should do is save our new page: File > Save. Make sure you are saving to your root folder. Name the file index.html and then click Save.
- Notice the Files panel shows more files and folders. It now includes the index.html file we created as well as some folders that Dreamweaver automatically created for us. We won't be editing any of these default files and it's important to leave them intact to ensure our pages work correctly.

## ● ADD A PAGE TITLE AND CONTAINER

This assignment will help you to add the title that will display in the tab of the web browser and set your page apart in future search results, and add the container that will wrap the contents and make the design fit the width of the page.

- Click the Split View button in the document toolbar to see your live design and have access to the code simultaneously. By default the code sits below Live View, but you can move the code to sit vertically on the left. To do this go to View > Split Vertically, then View > Uncheck Live View on Left so the live view will appear on the right.
- To add a title to the page, click anywhere in Live View, then find the Properties panel below. Add your title to Document Title and it will appear between the title tags in the HTML.
- An asterisk (*) will appear on the file tab (index. html*). This indicates there are unsaved changes. Save your file using File > Save or Command + S on your keyboard.
- Select Preview in Browser (the small globe icon in the lower right). Select the browser you prefer. At this point the only content on the page is the title we just added; can you see it in the tab of the browser?
- Next we need to add an element called a container to hold all of our page's content. Select the Insert panel and go to the Bootstrap Components category. Bootstrap components are page elements that already have responsive behaviour built in.
- There are two options for empty containers that we can use to hold our page's content. The first is a container element and it allows us to define a fixed width for our web page. The container fluid component, however, allows the design to stretch the entire width of the page no matter what the screen size.
- Click anywhere in Live View and look for the word 'body' in the heads-up display, because we want to make sure we're about to add this element to the right area of the code, right after the body tag in the code window.
- Now click to add the Container Fluid element on the right-hand panel.

- Two things have now happened. We have a blue border in Live View, with a display that indicates the container we just added. It is an element called a div, and it's identified by a class name, which is container fluid.
- In Code View you can see the same thing written out in HTML: we have a div with a class name of container fluid <div class"container-fluid"></div>.
- A div is an empty container (HTML element). On its own it doesn't do much; however, we can tell this div to behave in certain ways using CSS, which is where this class name comes in.
- CSS is another web design language that tells HTML elements what to do and how to look. In order for the CSS to work correctly, however, it needs to know what element it will be styling, and that's why HTML elements are sometimes identified with class names. So when you add these Bootstrap components they come with class names, and some of their behaviour is predefined in the bootstrap.css document that was generated when we created the page.
- To reiterate and explain the difference between a regular container and a container fluid: they are both empty containers but they resize differently according to the different rules they were given in the Bootstrap CSS.

So far you have created a page, and set it up so that you can add content. At the moment there is nothing to see, as all the containers are empty.

# ASSIGNMENTS **7** CONTINUED

## ● ADD STRUCTURE AND CONTENT

In this assignment you will build the overall structure of the page by adding the HTML components to provide the framework for the page. Add placeholders for the main menu navigation, a slideshow, the main body of content, a thumbnail image and a footer.

### Navbar (Navigation Bar)

The first section we will add to the page is the main menu. Again you can use a Bootstrap component for this. Make sure the container fluid div is still selected – if not, you can click on the div node in the DOM panel; it will highlight in both Code View and Live View. The DOM is a really useful panel that allows you to see the entire structure of your web page in a visual and hierarchical way.

- In the Insert panel, under Bootstrap Components, find the Navbar component – it has a drop-down menu of various menu styles you can use. Click on Basic Navbar.
- Select the Nest option when prompted. This will place the Navbar inside the container we have selected. In this example the Navbar is a child element that lives inside the container, which is its parent element.
- As you can see from the DOM panel it is clear that the Navbar is nested inside the container fluid.
- We can now see the Navbar in the Live View. Dreamweaver also adds the necessary code in the Code View.
- To expand Live View, click the Live button, above the editing area. This will expand Live View and allow you to see more of what is going on.
- As you can see, the Navbar has some content that appears by default, Brand/Links/Search, etc.
- You can use the live menu scrubber to simulate how the Navbar will look across different screen sizes. (Pull right-hand bar across Live View.) Notice as the display size gets smaller, the menu collapses to a hamburger icon, which is a common interface for mobile device browsing.
- Click the Split button to go back to Split View, so we can add our next bit of content.

### Carousel

- Because we've been doing some clicking around we'll want to make sure we are about to add the next component in the right place. In the DOM find the node that says div > class="container-fluid", then select its child element, which is the node that says nav > class="navbar navbar-default". If you don't see the child element you might have to click on the div node to open up the stack.
- Now we want to add a Carousel element, which is basically a slideshow for images and text. Add this after the Navbar.
- In the Insert panel, select the Carousel element and select After when prompted. This adds the Carousel element after the Navbar element we have selected.
- Click Save. Dreamweaver presents a dialogue alerting you that the Carousel placeholder image is being added to the images folder in your site set-up/root folder. Click OK.
- In Live View you can interact with the slideshow (Carousel) and preview it at different sizes.

### Text

Next we are going to add some heading and paragraph text in the main body of this web page. To do this we need to first set up a container to add the text into. It's good practice to organise your sections in containers, and it will make it easier to style and restyle this section later.

- First, let's make sure we are in the right place in the code. Click div > id = "carousel1" class="carousel slide".
- In the Insert panel select the HTML category from the drop-down.
- Scroll down until you see the Article element. Select Article and select to place it after the Carousel when prompted.
- Now click the Heading: H1 button from the Insert panel. Choose to nest it inside the article when prompted.
- Finally, select the paragraph from the Insert panel. Choose to place it after the Heading: H1 when prompted.

### Thumbnail Images

- Click the article node in the DOM panel so we can add a thumbnail after the text we just created.
- In the Insert panel, select Bootstrap Components from the drop-down.
- Find and click the Thumbnails component.
- Choose to place it after the article when prompted.
- Click Save. Dreamweaver presents a dialogue alerting you that the thumbnail placeholder image is being added to the images folder in your site set-up/root folder. Click OK.
- In the DOM panel you can see that the thumbnail is built in an interesting way. First, Dreamweaver creates a row panel (div> class="row"), which spans the width of the page. Inside that row is a column (div> class=col-md-4"). This column contains the text and image that makes up the thumbnail.

### Footer

- Select the node with the class of row from the DOM panel.
- In the Insert panel, go back to the HTML category and select Footer.
- Choose to place the footer after the thumbnail row when prompted.
- Save the page and choose to preview it in the browser.
- It doesn't look like much yet, but we have our structure in place. The page is not styled at this point but it will be easier to change that now you have your foundation.

You have now made a basic template, which can be amended how you see fit. With a bit of research you now need to change the placeholder content that Dreamweaver adds when you use the predefined components from the Insert panel. Add your own labels to the menu navigation, and change the structure to match your final design. Replace the caption text for the slideshow and thumbnail sections to match the images. Finally, add text to the main heading and paragraph in the body of the page and replace the footer content with some copyright information.

Apply some style and layout to the text. Use the CSS Designer to add some colour and reposition the text in different sections of the page. Change the menu to give it a more modern look and blend it with the rest of the page design. Override the default styling of the menu to change the background colour, border and positioning of the menu within the page to get the look you want to achieve.

Finish the page by giving it a more polished look and change the default style of the images so they look effective on any device. Apply CSS to the slideshow images to make them stretch the width of the page/modify the thumbnail images to fit the width of their container.

## ● MOBILE APP ICON DESIGN

The app icon is the main branding element for a mobile app project. Select an existing app (or an app that you would like to create) and make or remake an icon. Successful app icons visually explain the utility of the app. Start by writing out a list of potential visual elements. Explore past the first visuals that come to mind and try to infuse a more unique perspective. Assemble your icon in Adobe Photoshop (72ppi, RGB). Resize your app icon design for use on an iPhone at the following dimensions (in pixels): 57 x 57, 72 x 72, 114 x 114, 512 x 512. Explore adjustments and modifications that may be required, so that your artwork can be presented clearly at the different display sizes.

If you are feeling particularly confident, there are many online resources to mock-up a live app to test on your phone with minimal coding required. Do a little bit of research and see if you can apply your design solutions for the app icon across the whole mobile platform.

## ● WEBSITE MAKEOVER

Most websites have a life span of only a few years, influenced by the refocusing of client goals or in response to revised trends in presentation or user experience. To have a look at what some notable sites actually all looked like in the past visit the Way Back Machine at http://archive.org/web/, a digital archive of the World Wide Web and other information on the Internet created by the Internet Archive.

Many web designers appreciate site revision projects for the simple fact that most of the content is readily available. Select a website that would benefit from a new approach. Start by defining the flowchart. Move on to exploring different content presentations in the wireframing phase. Finish by inserting actual content into your composition design.

## ● ONLINE PORTFOLIO

As a creative practitioner it is really important to be represented online. Using the questions below, create a proposal on what will be necessary for you to complete your own site and what you will need to organise before coding begins.

- What must the website do? What is the goal?
- How many levels will the site have? How will the content be organised?
- What navigation conventions will you need to ensure that the user can easily move between pages?
- What images and techniques will need to be generated?
- Consider domain registration and hosting of the site, since this may affect how you build it.
- Do you have access to all the relevant content to build your site?
- Who is the audience and on what size screen will the site need to be seen? Widescreen HD or mobile?
- Consider the target audience and the browsers from which they will most likely be visiting the site.

**Further Reading:**

Mike Monteiro, *Design is a Job,* Happy Cog/A Book Apart, 2012

Smashing Magazine, eBook, *Redesign The Web (The Smashing Book 3),* Smashing Media GmbH, 2012

Jeremy Keith, *HTML 5 for Web Designers,* Happy Cog/A Book Apart, 2010

Dan Cederholm, *CSS3 for Web Designers,* Happy Cog/A Book Apart, 2011

Jennifer Niederst Robbins, *Learning Web Design: A Beginner's Guide to HTML, CSS, JavaScript and Web Graphics,* O'Reilly Media; fourth edition, 2012

Patrick McNeil, *The Web Designer's Idea Book, Volume 3: Inspiration from Today's Best Web Design Trends, Themes and Styles,* HOW Books; third edition, 2013

Drew de Soto, *Know Your Onions Web Design,* Bis Publishers, 2014

# 8

# Expert Paths

By now you should have a good idea of which career path excites you, and will be interested in discovering what it might be like to work in a specific design field. Although expert knowledge in any one of the highlighted disciplines in this chapter will serve you well in the marketplace, remember that design is a collaborative field, and that it is becoming increasingly interdisciplinary. In fact, many of the skill sets in each path should be part of your repertoire. Build your expertise in the area that excites you the most, but find out enough about all of them to collaborate intelligently. Be aware that any job in the creativity industry will be quite fluid, and as a result you will be expected to work with tools that do not even exist yet. In this unit, each branch of a discipline is highlighted with the skills needed, the ups and downs you might encounter on the job, and some examples of the best in the business. It will provide you with resources and options to help you develop a career path that best suits your skills and aptitudes.

" Design is thinking made visual "
*Saul Bass*

## Logo design and brand identity

Based in the realm of symbology and sign, and originating in pre-Neolithic times, the logo, or ideogram, is no stranger to anyone these days. Instantly recognisable and distinctly memorable, a well-designed logo is versatile in multiple ways, but resilient enough to retain its identity instantly in the viewer's mind. It is both cornerstone and keystone for brand development. In logo creation, decisions on style, colour, aesthetics and typography set up a 'Rosetta Stone' upon which a client's whole branding and marketing strategy will be based. Designers must research, then refract, the essence of an idea into a system of elements showcasing a singular icon and idea, which in turn creates identity.

'Logo', 'corporate identity', 'brand', 'trademark'; no matter how you slice it, these terms all point to the creation of a cohesive defining symbol or set of rules that represents a client in every piece of communication. Easy and effective translation of goals, values and expertise is vital to build trust with potential customers and satisfy current ones. Business cards, letterheads, brochures, ads, websites, motion graphics and promotional items can all be used to create a public identity, and each element stems from the initial mark developed by the identity developer. The process can be a long one, often involving a committee with different opinions. By researching and collecting information from a client and their industry, the identity developer utilises their creativity and marketing savvy to generate several different ideas from multiple avenues of approach for a client to choose from.

Patience and understanding are then needed to survive the editing process, when a client mixes, changes and makes requests as you work with them to get their logo just right. As the process unfolds, keep in mind the alternatives for different contexts and consistency across a variety of media. An accomplished identity developer is a paragon of refinement and service that can keep the client happy and the brand beautiful.

### Identity, logo and corporate identity designers

A great identity developer should be detail-oriented, flexible and have well-developed design and problem-solving skills that employ clarity, simplicity and communication. Organisations spend hundreds of thousands of pounds annually to keep identity and branding fresh, current and innovative, and we know those clients are out there just waiting to find the right talent. Large companies employ in-house designers who develop and update their logos, but many turn to external graphic design firms, and individuals who specialise in this field, to develop their brand.

Whether you decide to work in an agency or a design studio, or go out on your own, you will run across a request for a logo every now and again. Sticking to the concepts of simplicity, clarity, scalability and innovation will provide a starting point for any successful logo.

### The exciting part...

- Opportunities for visual creativity and clever communication, especially for those designers interested in identity, marketing and sales.
- Accomplished identity developers are often independent freelancers who have spent many successful years in agencies and studios, making employment options versatile.
- Opportunities to engage interest in

marketing, strategy, psychology and business.
- It is always gratifying to see a brand you helped develop launch, expand and succeed.

### ... Not so much

- Many designers have created their 'perfect logo' only to have it modified beyond recognition, or trashed inadvertently by a visually uneducated client. Such is the life of a designer.
- Unless you are hired for a full branding development position with a company, you'll need to generate lots of clients who need logos and letterheads in order to pay the bills.
- Ultimately, the ability to be completely creatively present for the client, yet let go enough to meet their needs, regardless of all your training and better judgment, is a quality that is hard for some. Remember: you are creating their identity, not yours.

### Skills required

- A firm, creative understanding and love of typography, visual semiotics, symbolism, illustration, colour theory, brand design and marketing psychology.
- Knowledge of all pro-level software programs and printing systems, and familiarity with a variety of traditional and innovative marketing materials and campaign approaches.
- Great research skills.
- Great communication skills. Listening carefully to a client at the beginning and throughout the branding process is the only way to deliver the winning brand.

### ⊕ Best in the business

**Paul Rand,** Pratt Institute graduate, Yale University professor and American graphic designer who will go down in history for his groundbreaking work with some of the best-known corporate logo designs. A strong proponent of the Swiss style of design, Rand developed the foundation corporate identities for Apple, IBM, UPS, Westinghouse and ABC. He was touted as a consummate salesman who, through explaining the necessity of proper identity creation to clients and students, helped usher in a new era for marketing and design.

**Paula Scher,** Corcoran College of Art and Design doctorate graduate, began as a record cover art director at Atlantic and CBS Records and has developed a career and style that has won her many prestigious awards for her work and innovation in the field of design. Currently a partner at Pentagram in New York, she is best known for her identity and branding systems, promotional materials, packaging and publication designs for such clients as *The New York Times Magazine*, Perry Ellis, Bloomberg, Citibank, Tiffany & Co, Target, the New York Botanical Garden and *The Daily Show With Jon Stewart.*

**Ivan Chermayeff,** founding partner of Chermayeff & Geismar, a leading graphic design firm in the fields of corporate identity, brand development and logo design. Chermayeff studied at Harvard University, Illinois Institute of Technology and the Yale University School of Design. With partner Tom Geismar, whom he met at Yale, he has designed iconic marks for hundreds of companies, including Burlington Industries, Chase Manhattan Bank, Dictaphone, Mobil Corporation, Pan American Airlines, Xerox and the Museum of Modern Art.

**LloydNorthover,** one of Britain's most successful consultancies, working internationally in identity, branding and communication, prides itself on providing creative solutions to strategic problems. In giving companies a competitive market advantage by making them highly visible, clear and compelling, they have created many successful campaigns for Comet, De Beers, Elizabeth Arden, HSBC, Infiniti, Lexus, Mitsubishi, Morgan Stanley, Orange and Royal Mail.

## Career options

Logo and brand identity design is part of every designer's skill set, but if you specialise in corporate identity you can find a career in the following:
- In-house designer with a creative studio
- Ad agency brand development specialist
- Freelance designer
- Brand specialist for a web development firm
- Corporate in-house designer in any large company or institution

## Career path potential
- Junior and senior designer > creative director > partner in a firm

**See also:** Michael Beirut, Massimo Vignelli, Herb Lubalin, Armin Hofmann, Saul Bass, Gerard Huerta, Walter Landor

## Motion graphics

The field of motion graphics has transcended its early beginnings in film and TV opening titles and is now vital to the new media environment, interactive applications, post-production, advertising, animation and digital environments for the web and broadcast.

The emphasis in the motion graphics industry is on speed of communication – how quickly you can appeal to either a specialised demographic or a wide audience and communicate the product, proposal or information as clearly as possible. From corporations to production houses, web, digital and interactive media, music industry, television and film, this industry can be divided into three specialisations.

- Business-to-business (B2B) takes the form of idea proposals and pitches, training seminars and other info-graphics.
- Advertising encompasses everything from web banners and TV commercials to websites.
- Film/video specialisation covers music promotion, film/TV opening and closing credits and other animated visuals and effects.

As with many specialisations, you are likely to start in a long-established studio, under a creative director, art director or producer. Later you may freelance or set up a small studio of your own, although the brief structure remains the same. Occasionally, clients will give you the creative freedom to push boundaries; they will often have a specific aesthetic in mind. This industry demands a constant stream of new and fresh talent and ideas.

## Skills required

- Knowledge of communication strategies and rhetoric.
- Excellent grasp of typography, 2D and 3D composition, and colour.
- Good appreciation of pace, rhythm and storyboarding.
- Good spatial awareness and geometry.
- An ability to work comfortably with complexity and layering, both literal and metaphorical.
- Advanced and up-to-date knowledge of Flash, Animate, After Effects, Maya, Illustrator, Photoshop and some FinalCut.
- Diplomacy and a client-centred outlook.

## The exciting part...

- Working in a fast-paced, cutting-edge environment.
- If your work really communicates client concepts in an innovative way, it will be sought after.
- Motion graphics designers are multi-disciplinary and know how to collaborate. They are also masters of word and image and of many facets of design, versed in all the core skills.

## ... Not so much

- Much of the initial concept work will be time-consuming. Clients may not know exactly what they want, and you will probably have to develop many versions to actually pull it out of their heads.
- Turnaround speed can be crazy fast. Be realistic on what you can achieve in the time available to avoid missing your deadline.
- Motion graphics and animation can be labour intensive, and you can find yourself stuck in front of a screen for hours on end. It really is a labour of love!

## ✪ Best in the business

**Saul Bass** (1920–1996), the godfather of motion graphics, is best known for his iconic opening and closing credits on Hollywood films such as Alfred Hitchcock's *Psycho*, *North by Northwest* and *Vertigo*, and on *West Side Story*, *Broadcast News*, *Goodfellas* and *Big*. His animation styling set the standards for many who followed, and he was an accomplished poster and logo designer.

**Maurice Binder**, best known for his signature graphic work on the opening credits of 14 James Bond films, designed credits and animations for a wide variety of films from the 1950s to the 1990s.

**Kyle Cooper** studied graphic design under Paul Rand at Yale University. The multi-award winning Cooper has directed over 150 title sequences for film and television and has done much to have titling and motion graphics recognised as the art they surely are. He is the founder of Imaginary Forces and Prologue Films, and is best known for his work on the film *Se7en*, and most recent work includes *Argo*, *Sherlock Holmes*, *Mission Impossible*, *X-Men*, *Twilight: Breaking Dawn*, *Tree of Life*, *The Walking Dead*, *American Horror Story* and *Iron Man II*.

## Career options

- ✪ Film and special effects studios
- ✪ Broadcast stations and online content developers
- ✪ Advertising agencies and design firms
- ✪ Web development firm
- ✪ Promotion designer for a large company or institution

✚ **See also:** Angus Wall (Game of Thrones), Stephen Frankfurt (To Kill a Mockingbird), Garson Yu, R/GA Media Group Inc, www.momoco.co.uk, www.artofthetitle.com

## Web design

In the early days of the Web, the original designers who took the first stabs at web development were print-based graphic designers. Now, over a few short years, there are students graduating from colleges across the globe with concentrations focusing solely on web design and development, online communications, interactive media and web commerce. So, what does a career in web design and digital media have in store?

Companies and organisations hire hundreds of web designers annually to help them create and perfect their online presence and identity. For the more interactive designer with a penchant for heavier coding, design studios and advertising agencies have teams of web developers, coders and information architects to handle the contemporary online needs of their clients, such as interactive interfaces, e-commerce installations, content management systems and social networking platforms. No matter where your intrinsic skills lie, the field of web design has quickly become a rich tapestry of varying disciplines and skills in which any designer can match their talents and interests.

### Is it right for you?

Whether working freelance in a home studio or as an in-house developer at a creative firm, the current population of web professionals is made up of true devotees of emerging media. Countless personal hours are spent learning and mastering the latest HTML conventions, or JavaScript libraries, or CSS. Days are spent in a trial-and-error limbo as designers research and modify bits of coding to get the interface to react just as the client expects it to. During months of work, from initial thumbnails to final launch, developers and designers work together to create accessible sites that can be easily accessed and instantly understood by people all over the world. Millions of cups of coffee or tea are poured as these self-starters stay up into the wee hours learning digital languages that are never uttered nor seen, but experienced. All of this happens because there are always those who have the abilities and interests to see the possibilities in the enlarging world of the Web, and because they can see themselves within those possibilities.

### Hierarchy

Some web designers work successfully from home, conducting a large portion of their client contact by phone and email. Most of the time these solitary designers have a very good command of a wider array of web specialties, such as HTML/CSS coding, content management systems (PHP), Flash, Animate and Maya animation, as well as image correction and manipulation, and awareness of the user experience. In larger work environments, a web designer may collaborate with a team of professional code writers/developers/producers, content managers, marketers and executives. There may even be a variety of multi-disciplinary web designers and developers, or specialists that focus on one aspect of each project.

### Skills required

- Firm understanding of typography, composition, layout, balance, colour theory, imagery creation and manipulation.
- Understanding of the user experience (UX).
- Basic understanding of HTML and CSS.
- Growing familiarity with the usage of JavaScript, Ajax and PHP.

- Understanding of the concepts of user interaction and client goals, and their relationship to the interface.
- Desire to discover and stay current in the latest web languages and innovations.
- Understanding of such principles as web standards, web accessibility and search engine optimisation (SEO).
- Eye for detail, to the pixel level for the visual, and the ability to write clean code.
- Familiarity with how colour and devices work with regard to the Web and how that relates to the viewer.

### The exciting part...

- Involvement in a constantly evolving technology.
- Near-immediate edits and updates to a body of work with little fuss, as compared to print design.
- More opportunities for freelance and home-based work situations for web designers.
- The excitement of cross-platform and multi-device design.

### ... Not so much

- The proliferation of amateur work on the Web, and the disregard of good design in favour of speed and ease of format.
- Projects are ongoing, requiring regular upkeep.
- Technology updates are time-consuming, but you must stay current with revised standards in the industry.

### ✪ Best in the business

**Jeffrey Zeldman** is a lecturer and author on web design. He also runs his own web design studio, Happy Cog, which has created influential web work for clients such as AIGA, Amnesty International, Mozilla, Warner Bros. Films and Stanford University. His book *Designing With Web Standards* set the tone for modern-day semantic web design.

**Hillman Curtis** has spent a decade blending the Web, Adobe Flash and film through his company Hillmancurtis, Inc. to design digital media for such companies as Adobe, Hewlett-Packard, Intel, Yahoo!, Rolling Stone and MTV. Curtis and his company have been featured in many publications for their designs and have won many awards for their online work.

**Molly E. Holzschlag** is an award-winning lecturer and web designer, as well as author of over 35 books on web design and mark-up. She has worked with the W3C and WaSP, focusing on web standards, web accessibility, web sustainability and related topics.

### Career options

Here are the basic situations an emerging web designer may find when ready to enter the working world.

- ✪ Independent freelance web designer/developer
- ✪ Contract freelance web designer/developer
- ✪ Web designer/developer working with an agency
- ✪ Design, marketing or advertising for a variety of clients
- ✪ Web designer/developer working within a company. With a focus on the main site or sites for the company; often in charge of the office intranet, email, etc.

➕ **See also:** Chris Coyier, www.chriscoyier.net, who runs CSS-Tricks and writes the Shop Talk Show. He's more of the technical, front-end side of the web.

## Editorial design

Modern editorial design arguably originates from the 15th-century printing press of Gutenberg, when pages of type were manually set in movable metal type. Each page was set in relation to margins, gutters and borders, and printed in multiple copies – a huge leap from handwritten manuscripts. With evolutions in print-production methods and the influence of early 20th-century art and design schools such as the Bauhaus, the designer began to gain control over the page. Editorial designers now work in an unprecedented range of media and technologies. Many new forms of editorial design have been generated over time, and aesthetic considerations are wide ranging.

Editorial designers are key players in the production of books, print and virtual magazines, brochures and catalogues, with the task of aesthetically transforming raw text and image to maximise legibility, impact and communication.

Depending on the publication, there may be a need for flexibility in styling. In a publishing house a designer may work on a series of titles with different demographic target audiences: children, teen, young professional, special interest, parents or families are just a few of many possibilities. Each needs a different style, emphasis and direction. The aesthetic direction is generally agreed on by the upper production team, including the art director and design editor. It is the designer's role to implement these decisions, carry out instructions and respond to changes in the market.

Editorial designers also work on larger web-based publications, such as news websites, corporate web presence, and advertising and webzines. Smaller websites usually do not have a specialised designer. There are different design issues on the Internet, such as legibility of fonts, and other considerations such as type in motion for an editorial designer to take into account.

## Wide ranging

Editorial designers are driven by and focused on content, and usually work within teams in medium to large organisations; they are rarely freelancers. They are often the focal point for many streams of material, such as raw text from authors, images from photographers and illustrators, and overall concept styling from art directors and development teams. They are expected to consider and combine these assets to create the finished publication.

There are endless stylistic choices in editorial design, from minimalist problem-solving aesthetics to complex contemporary juxtapositions. As an emerging editorial designer, you need to be aware of design possibilities and design intelligently.

## Skills required

- Excellent appreciation and mastery of typography, hierarchy and grid systems.
- Good spatial awareness and compositional skills.
- Strong sense of design history.
- Ability to work well with complexity and layering.
- Accurate eye for content correction – whether it's grammar, colour or mood.
- Advanced and up-to-date knowledge of InDesign, Illustrator, Photoshop and, to a lesser extent, Quark.
- Team-focused attitude and diplomacy.
- Ability to negotiate extensive revisions to your designs, and to let your ego 'slide'.

## The exciting part...

- You are the designer for the layout and composition of pages/spreads of the publication.
- You see your work in the bookshop or on the Internet.
- You work on a wide variety of content (especially in book design).
- Your interpretation of content can set the mood of the piece.
- Your editorial visuals can be thought-provoking.

## ... Not so much

- As the focal point for many different information streams, co-ordination of deadlines and organisation of work can become tricky.
- As with many specialisations, design school rarely prepares you for the speed or amount of work involved in each project.
- There will inevitably be many corrections/revisions to the work on the way to the final product. You will need to be open to this process and respond well to feedback.

## ✪ Best in the business

**Alexey Brodovich, Neville Brody** and **Cipe Pineles,** known for their innovative magazine designs.

**Jost Hochuli** and **Jan Tschichold,** known for their book designs and contributions to modern typography.

**Bradbury Thompson** and **Piet Zwart,** known for their powerful and imaginative designs in many editorial contexts.

Also look at the work of **David Carson, Carin Goldberg, Herbert Bayer, Janet Froelich, Tibor Kalman** and **George Lois.**

## Career options

- ✪ Design assistant, junior designer
  Invaluable opportunity to learn the ropes by assisting on a wide variety of projects, but with limited room for creativity.
- ✪ Senior designer
  Greater opportunity to be creative, designing templates as well as working with them, and making image and direction choices.
- ✪ Art editor or creative director
  Managing the design of projects, overseeing freelance designers and working closely with editorial and production staff.

➕ **See also:** The Society of Publication Designers, www.spd.org, established in 1965 for international trade, corporate, institutional, newspaper and consumer editorial art directors.

## Environmental graphic design

Environmental graphic designers work with architects and interior designers to create distinctive design works that visually define the built environment. These projects can include exhibition design for museums, galleries and public art installations; wayfinding and architectural signage; pictogram design; mapping; complete branding and identity systems; and themed environments. Their work is in demand by the retail and entertainment industries, real-estate developers and city planners, and is a critical factor in public facilities and transportation where clear signage and efficient crowd circulation are essential.

Environmental graphic designers are among the most collaborative in the design disciplines, and will partner with experts in many areas to research, and then deliver, functional design in an informative, entertaining way. They combine their skills with those of digital media experts to create sophisticated interactive communications, work with product designers and industrial designers on fabrications, with landscape architects, and with individual clients in hospitals, schools and businesses. Large architecture firms may have environmental graphic design departments in house for signage, wayfinding, identity and supporting print materials. Others consult graphic design firms that offer environmental design services for big projects that require complicated information visualisation. Both types of firms may work with freelancers on a portion of or a complete project.

### In the thick of it

As with any graphic design project, in the first stage of development – the programming phase – the environmental graphic designer determines the client's objectives and researches the potential needs of the building/space, users or audience. This will enable the client and designer to determine the amount and location of signs and other fabrications for estimating. Then, the designer will begin the conceptual design process with a combination of sketches and 3D models or digital illustrations rendered in 2D or 3D. When the design is refined enough for estimates, the environmental graphic designer will supervise the bidding process for fabrication of the architectural elements, will work with the design team to select the fabricators, and is often on site for the actual installation of elements.

### Skills required

- Strong design skills in composition, form, colour, scale and texture.
- Good drawing skills.
- Ability to visualise three-dimensional space.
- Familiarity with the codes and regulations for signage.
- Understanding of human factors, including visual and lighting requirements, colour perception and behavioural psychology.
- Understanding of symbolism and multi-lingual needs.
- Strong interpersonal and communication skills.

### The exciting part...

- Your design work becomes a permanent installation.
- You will have a very hands-on research experience.
- You can see the effect your work has in public.

- You work with architects, structural engineers, industrial designers and fabricators.
- You get to work in 3D.

### ... Not so much

- The process is long and complicated.
- Mistakes can be expensive and time-consuming.
- Your deadlines are affected by the entire team and can make scheduling complex.

### ⊕ Best in the business

Look at:
**Ralph Appelbaum Associates**
**Pentagram Design Group** (especially the work of **Paula Scher** and **Andrew Freeman**)
**The Rockwell Group**
**Gensler**
**Local Projects**
**Deborah Sussman**

### Career options

Environmental design is collaborative and involves graphic designers, architects, interior designers, fabricators, and more. The designer should have excellent communication skills and the ability to work as part of a team. Areas of specialisation for environmental designers may include:

- ✪ Exhibition design
- ✪ Wayfinding systems
- ✪ Architectural signage
- ✪ Interactive visitor experience
- ✪ 3D visualisation

⊕ **See also:** www.thincdesign.com, www.segd.org, www.brandculture.com.au, www.p-06-atelier.pt

## Advertising

The designer whose strengths lie in developing innovative and convincing concepts can play a pivotal role in this high-energy, fast-paced industry. Advertising designers can sway the public consciousness not only through commercial advertising campaigns, but also as part of promoting social change, and raising awareness of local and global issues such as health, sustainability and politics.

Advertising is a very competitive field. Thoughtful, creative ads reach and influence more minds, attract more attention and generate more sales. With a team, the freelance or in-house advertising designer creates a campaign concept for a client to present to the public. As the visual arm of a marketing team, the designer must call upon psychology, marketing, communication and humour to create successful market penetration through media such as television, radio, newspapers, magazines, email, the Web and social media. The goal is to be more innovative, more thought-provoking and more memorable, so advertising designers keep ahead of the curve, are aware of emerging trends and are continually connected to current events and ideas.

### Advertising designers

Advertising probably still employs more talent to produce creative work than any other occupation, since everything is advertised in some way.

You can expect to work long, and sometimes inconvenient, hours, since the agency needs to meet the timing of clients who are often in other time zones. In a larger agency you're more likely to specialise in a certain area, such as pharmaceutical advertising, than in a small agency, where you're more likely to do a little (or a lot) of everything.

There are three main positions: graphic designers, art directors and creative directors. These roles can sometimes be filled by freelance and contract workers, or they may be full-time as part of a creative department. Regardless of the position you may take, a good advertising piece has a way of sticking with you – whether it's a memorable jingle, a clever catchphrase or a beautiful image. If you feel you have always had the eye for the perfect way to sell something to the world, advertising design provides a rewarding and exciting career for the up-and-coming graphic designer.

### Skills required

- Artistic ability and a knack for good, clever visual thinking.
- Being artistic and being a good designer are two different things; both are desirable. Being able to capture and communicate a client's message within the current cultural style, while keeping it clever, innovative and graphically sound, is a skill that will take you far.
- Research skills and knowledge of customer psychology and cultural tastes.
- Competitive edge – at times the advertising industry has been called cut-throat.
- The ability to work well to deadlines and under pressure.
- Knowledge of design and advertising history.
- Cultural currency.

### The exciting part...

- Upwards momentum and networking: great opportunities to meet other prospective employers and clients.
- You are involved in strategies to help clients make high-level business decisions.
- Great salaries if you move up.

### ... Not so much

- The larger the budget, the larger the possibility of failure.
- Advertising can create notoriously high-stress environments.

### ⊘ Best in the business

**Grey Advertising**, in all its forms, the giant ad agency that has been around for 95 years, and represents Volkswagen, 3M, Proctor and Gamble, Mars, Kraft, Marriot, Toshiba, E-Trade, Cannon, the NFL, among others.

**Wieden+Kennedy** has offices all over the world and has been at the top of their game for the last 30 years, with clients like Nike, Coca-Cola, Facebook, Converse, Kraft, Levi's and Sony.

**BBDO** employs 17,200 people in 287 offices in 77 countries worldwide, and is an award-winning agency network, headquartered in New York, that opened its doors in 1928. BBDO has been recognised for amazing work for high-profile clients such as Pepsi, Ikea, FedEx, BBC News, General Electric, Campbells, Gillette, Motorola, Chrysler, Pfizer, Wrigley, Mitsubishi and UNICEF.

**Ogilvy** was founded in 1948 as Ogilvy & Mather and is an international advertising, marketing and public relations firm that operates 497 offices in 125 countries around the world. Opened by David Ogilvy, the company quickly became a leading worldwide agency by the 1960s as it helped build brands for American Express, BP, Ford, Barbie, Maxwell House, IBM, Kodak, Nestlé, Pond's and Dove.

**Droga5** is one to watch, named 2012 Agency of the Year by Adweek, Creativity's 2011 Agency of the Year and number two on Advertising Age's 2011 Agency A-List.

**Leo Burnett** was opened in 1935, gained momentum in the 1950s and is still the ninth largest agency in the world. The agency has undergone many changes, but has garnered many big-name accounts along the way, such as McDonald's, Coca-Cola, Walt Disney, Marlboro, Maytag, Kellogg's, Tampax, Nintendo, U.S. Army, Philips, Samsung, Visa, Wrigley and Hallmark. Today the agency has 97 offices in 84 countries across the globe.

In addition to the agencies above, check out the work of these individuals: **George Lois, Joe Pytka, Lou Dorfsman, John C. Jay, David Droga**.

## Career options

- ✪ Working in advertising usually means at an agency, which provides great opportunities for teamwork, networking, higher budgets, broader-scoped campaigns, awards and unmatchable experience. Working for big-name clients is more common in bigger cities, and movement between agencies is an option for many designers as they graduate to head designers and art directors.
- ✪ Copywriter, marketer, account manager, production artist. The person who enters advertising design will often wear more than one hat.
- ✪ Interns and internships are in heavy rotation due to the fast-paced, low-attention-span nature of the public as it scans for the next big thing. Interns are temporary, like trends, and their work is creative, fresh and usually free. Being at an agency offers interns a lot of benefits – contacts, clients and projects – but teaches them only one thing they need to know about working in advertising: whether they love it or hate it.

➕ **See also:** Adweek, Advertising Age, The Clio Awards

## Information design and data visualisation

Information design, sometimes called information architecture, is a fast-growing and deeply rewarding profession for the right kind of person. Perfectionists and innately curious people are frequently attracted to information design, along with those who want to produce useful design that serves society rather than selling products. Information design is user-centred, and research and analysis heavy.

Signage, computer-generated information systems, graphs/charts, visualising scientific and technical data, digital control displays and computer interfaces, and the design of legal and technical documents are all part of information design, but the field is expanding. People drawn towards mathematics and science, but who are highly creative, are also drawn to information design. It requires all the skills of a designer, including problem-solving, the ability to communicate clearly, a high degree of typographic knowledge, image generation, and great research skills. However, the information designer must possess an additional level of rigour, be interested in resolving the tiniest details of a job, and be able to nail the relationship between form and content. Information designers frequently work with complex data, finding a way to visualise that information in the most direct and unambiguous way.

In addition to all the design skills mentioned, it's necessary for an information designer to understand how systems work and how they change in different environments (print/digital/3D/space). They need to have a strong grasp of how messages are perceived, how information is processed by readers/audiences (cognitive processing), and be prepared to spend many hours analysing and bringing beautiful order to chaos.

**Functional design**
Information design is important, meaningful, useful and functional. It is a powerful form of design that should speak to people in a clear, unambiguous language, putting the message first without sacrificing any of the innovation or beauty of design. If it works, it can illuminate a subject matter you previously thought nothing about. If it doesn't work, it can distort information, create confusion, or the information simply gets lost.

There's very little that's arbitrary or subjective in this profession, but the visualisations have become marvellously creative and are now in demand from every sector of the business world as full-page, or full-screen, illustrations.

## Skills required

- Great typography skills.
- Knowledge of image-making software.
- Ability to approach complex information logically and creatively.
- Understanding of systems and messages.
- Analytical mind.

## The exciting part...

- Rewarding (meaningful and useful).
- Serves society (potential for good).
- Working with multiple content(s) and complex data.
- Combines design and scientific rigour.
- Witnessing your design functioning in society.
- Working with interdisciplinary teams.
- Many different media and contexts for design.

## ... Not so much

- Detail oriented (not for everyone).
- Content driven.
- Involves complex problem solving.

## ⚙ Best in the business

**Eric Spiekermann** Information architect, font designer, and author of books and articles on type and typography. Founder of MetaDesign agency, Germany's largest design firm.

**Otto Neurath** (1882–1945), Austrian economist and sociologist whose work for the Social and Economic Museum of Vienna led to the development of the Vienna Method, or Isotype, to convey complicated information to the Viennese public. His use of iconic pictograms looks just as current today.

**Richard Saul Wurman**, architect and graphic designer, first coined the phrase 'information architecture' and is a pioneer in information design. Wurman has written and designed over 83 books, and is the creator of the TED conferences.

**Edward Tufte,** called 'the da Vinci of data' by *The New York Times*, the American statistician gained his reputation through his outstanding presentation of informational graphics.

## Career options

- ⊕ Designer in a company with a specialism in information design, systems design, user documentation or signage.
- ⊕ Web designer in a company dealing with information architecture.
- ⊕ Designer in government agencies that deal with delivering complex information to the public, such as health services, transportation and weather.

⊕ **See also:** Nicholas Felton (www.feltron.com), Toby Ng (www.toby-ng.com), Peter Grundy (www.grundini.com), and David McCandless (www.davidmccandless.com).

# Glossary

**AAs ('author's alterations'):** Edits made to the content of a file by the client. Usually handled before sent to press, if edits are made while the job is at the printer, AAs can prove very costly.

**Abstraction:** An aesthetic concept describing something that is drawn from the real, but has been 'distilled' to its barest minimum form, colour or tone, often removed from its original context.

**Ad server:** A web-based system for inserting advertising content dynamically into a web page.

**Additive colour:** System used on monitors and televisions, based on RGB (red, green, blue). When combined, these form white light.

**Adobe Acrobat:** The family of Adobe programs that create and manage PDFs.

**Advancing and receding colour:** Colours in the red spectrum appear to advance to the human eye, whereas those in the blue spectrum appear to recede.

**Alignment:** The setting of text relative to a column or page.

**Analogous:** Similar, comparable, alike; for example, two colours that are near to each other, such as grass green and leaf green, are analogous.

**Anchor link:** A navigational link that directs the user to a specific section of a web page.

**Anchor point:** In a design program, a point on or at the end of a curve or line that can be 'grabbed' by the cursor and moved around the canvas, either to change the curve shape or to move the entire curve.

**Artboard:** In Illustrator, the virtual 'ground' into which images are placed.

**Associations:** Connections between colours and emotions, culture, experience and memory.

**Asymmetry:** A composition where elements are juxtaposed and do not mirror the other forms on the page.

**Audience:** In its broadest sense, the consumers, voyeurs and occasionally participants of design work.

**Banding:** Series of lighter or darker bands running across an area of solid colour.

**Baseline:** The line on which the lowercase letters sit, and below which the descenders fall.

**Baseline grid:** Locks text onto consistent horizontal points.

**Bleed:** The overhang of content beyond the page tramline, so when trimmed this content runs straight to the edge.

**Book jacket:** Packaging that advertises both product and publisher.

**Brainstorming:** A visual aid to thinking laterally and exploring a problem, usually by stating the problem in the centre of a page and radiating outward spokes for components of the problem. Each component can then be considered separately with its own spokes, so that each point, thought or comment is recorded.

**Calibration:** Colour settings that should be set to show colour on screen as it will be in print.

**Canvas:** The virtual 'ground' that images are placed onto in Photoshop.

**Categories:** A taxonomy structure for designating dynamic content (posts) to appear in similar, or different, news feeds within a website. Can be used as a search criteria for displaying similarly themed posts.

**Centred:** Text that is aligned in the middle: symmetrical, with an even gap at the end of each line.

**Clip:** The name for a sequence of images or length of developed film or video.

**CMS (content management system):** The structured framework of a dynamically driven website.

**CMYK:** Cyan, magenta, yellow, key (black): the four colours that make up the full-colour printing process.

**CMYK break:** The computed percentages of C, M, Y and K ink that make up a colour.

**Coated:** A hard, waxy surface, either gloss or matt, and not porous (ink sits on the surface).

**Coated one side:** A paper that is coated on one side and matt on the other.

**Colorimeter:** Hardware that attaches to or hangs in front of your screen, allowing you to calibrate and profile your monitor.

**Colour modes:** The expression of colour in numerical values that enable us to mix them efficiently: CYMK, LAB, RGB.

**Column:** Vertical block of text.

**Complementary colour:** Colours, such as red and green, that lie opposite each other on the colour wheel.

**Composition:** The arrangement of elements or parts of a design (text, images) on the page.

**Comps:** Comprehensive sketch, a close approximation of the printed product.

**Concertina folds:** Folds in alternate directions.

**Connotations:** A colour's broader associations, for example: green – jealousy, naivety, illness, environment, nature.

**Consistency:** The considered selection of design elements that have similar attributes.

**Contextualisation:** The process of placing something within the interrelated systems of meaning that make up the world.

**Contrast:** Obvious differences in elements in a composition; size, form, colour and weight.

**Critical pathways:** Defining the desired route of a website's audience, as it relates to taking an action (purchasing, contacting, registering, etc.).

**Crop mark:** Vertical and horizontal lines at the corners of an image or page to indicate to a vendor where to trim off the bleed area.

**Customer profile/profiling:** The process of creating a series of parameters or set of information that defines the desires, trends or interests of a demographic so that designs can be pitched or marketed to them.

**Dashboard:** The administrative back-end for a content management system (CMS).

**Data:** Facts or pieces of information of any kind.

**Denotations:** What the colour means, or is; for example, a red rose is a green stem with red petals.

**Depth of field:** Distance between the object of focus and where the focus starts to blur.

**Diagram:** Drawing or plan that explains the parts of something, or how something works.

**Didactic:** A pragmatic and unambiguous method of giving clear information.

**Die cut:** A die that cuts predetermined shapes in different materials.

**Digital presses:** Automate direct image transfer from digital file to paper without the creation of plates.

**Digital printing:** Method of printing that uses a plateless computer-controlled press.

**Domain name:** The web address for a website. It is renewed annually by the site owner for a nominal fee.

**Dot gain:** A printed dot that becomes bigger than intended due to spreading, causing a darkening of screened images, mid-tones and textures. This varies with different paper stocks.

**Downsampling:** A form of compression that lowers the resolution of images by eliminating unnecessary pixel data.

**DPI (dots per inch):** Term to describe the resolution (sharpness) of an image.

**Drop-down (menu):** A navigational element that is revealed when a visitor clicks a main navigational link to reveal related links (subsections) that are displayed below.

**Dummy:** A prototype or mock-up of a final designed project, finished to a stage that it resembles the real thing for final proofing and client approval.

**Duotone:** A method of printing an image using only two colours, usually black and a spot colour.

**Earmark:** Identifying or distinguishing marks or characteristics of a typeface.

**Element:** One small part of a composition, such as a point or line, an image, a letter or a word.

**Email client:** An application used to review and compose emails.

**Embedding:** A PDF removes the need for multiple requisite files by including fonts and compressed imagery in one file.

**EPS (Encapsulated PostScript):** Graphics file format used to transfer PostScript documents that contain an image, within another PostScript document.

**Export:** To save a file in a format of your choice, such as a PDF, that is supported by other programs and can be viewed or printed without the use of your design software.

**F stop/focal length and aperture:** Size of aperture or 'iris' inside a camera, which controls the amount of light that hits the film or pixel sensor; the range on a general camera is f4 (large aperture) to f22 (small aperture).

**Favicon:** A small branded element that appears in the web browser's URL field, bookmark list or favourites list.

**Filter:** Plates of glass or plastic attached to the front of the lens in order to accentuate different qualities. For example, a polarising filter cuts down light glare; a colour filter enhances different colours.

**Flexography:** Method of printing that uses rubber relief plates.

**Fly-out (menu):** A navigational element that is revealed by extending out to the side of a main navigational element.

**Focal point:** The point where you want to draw the reader's or viewer's eye, which can be achieved with hierarchy and design solutions that make certain elements stand out.

**Font:** One size, weight and width of a typeface: Garamond Roman 12pt is a font.

**Footer:** The lower section of a web page layout, usually featuring navigation and copyright information.

**Four-colour process:** A standard, usually digital, printing technique, that creates all its colours by combining cyan, magenta, yellow and black (CMYK).

**FPO:** For position only; the use of a temporary placeholder or low-resolution image in place of the high-quality counterpart during the design process.

**Frames:** A frame is a single graphic in a collection of graphic images that when built up make a moving image. The speed of an animation is measured by the amount of frames per second.

**French folds:** Sheets of paper are folded in half, so that they are double thickness. The two folds are at right angles to each other, and then bound on the edge.

**Gamut:** The complete range of colours available within one system of reproduction, e.g., CMYK gamut or RGB gamut.

**Gang-run printing:** Printing many different jobs on one large sheet.

**Gatefold:** A way of folding paper so that the outer quarters of a page are folded to meet in the centre. The result works like symmetrical doors that open onto an inner page.

**Gestalt psychology:** A theory that suggests that the mind perceives and organises holistically and finds patterns in that which appears to be unconnected.

**GIF (Graphics Interchange Format):** A GIF is a compressed file format consisting of a number of frames that make up a (usually) short animation.

**Gravure:** Method of printing that uses plates with recessed cells of varying depths.

**Grid:** Series of horizontal and vertical lines on a page, used as a visual guide for lining up words and images.

**Ground:** The page, surface or area in which the design will be placed.

**GSM:** Grams per square metre, or g/m2.

**Gutter:** The gap between two text blocks or spreads on either side of the book fold or binding.

**Handle:** An anchor point in a design program connected to the main vector path by tangential lines that can be manipulated to change the shape of the curve.

**Header:** The top section of a web page layout, usually featuring branded elements and the main navigational structure.

**Hierarchy:** The different 'weight' or importance given to type or image.

**High-resolution image:** An image with an extreme level of sharpness achieved by a higher amount of dots per inch.

**HTML5:** The fifth version of the HTML standard mark-up language used for structuring and presenting content on the Internet.

**Hyperlink (navigational link):** A clickable navigational element that allows site visitors to navigate through the website.

**Hyphenation:** The point at which a word is broken at the end of a line in continuous text, and a hyphen is inserted.

**Identity:** A unified, identifiable look for a product or organisation.

**Image map:** An HTML document that contains clickable hyperlinks.

**Information Architecture (IA):** A balance of the intrinsic nature of a website and established user expectations, combined with your client's overall goals.

**Inline text link (navigational link):** Hyperlink within the body of a web page layout.

**The Interactive Advertising Bureau (IAB):** An organisation that documents and works to define the standards for online advertising.

**ISO (International Organisation for Standardisation):** Sets a standard range for virtual film speeds in digital cameras.

**JPEG (Joint Photographic Electronic Group):** File format used to compress digital images.

**Justified:** Lines or paragraphs of type aligned to both margins simultaneously, creating different spacing in between words.

**Juxtaposition:** The process of putting two or more unrelated or opposite elements or objects together to create different effects.

**Kerning:** Adjustments to the spaces between two letters (used extensively for capitals).

**Keyframe:** Either the frame of an animation at a key stage, or a frame in a clip where a transition is due to start.

**Laid:** A paper that has lines on its surface from its means of production. Often used for stationery.

**Lateral thinking:** A form of research where the emphasis is on indirect, creative forms of inquiry and thinking.

**Law of closure:** The mind creates a solid object on the page from suggestions of shapes and placement and proximity of elements.

**Layer Comps (Photoshop):** A feature that allows the user to record which items are viewable in a complex, multi-layer document.

**Layout:** Placement of words and images on a grid or document to organise information.

**Layout roughs:** Loose concept sketches for page design that organise space without showing detail.

**Leading:** The horizontal space between lines of type. Related to the historical use of strips of lead in letterpress.

**Letterpress:** A type of block printing using inked wooden or metal movable type and pressing it onto paper to create an impression.

**Letterspacing (tracking):** The space between letters, which can be adjusted.

**Ligatures:** Two or more letterforms joined to create a single character.

**Linear reasoning:** A form of thinking that implies strategic thought process, one in which step-by-step logic is employed.

**Linen:** Similar to laid, but finer lined.

**Linguistic:** Of, or relating to, language.

**Lists (unordered/ordered):** An unordered list is a bulleted list of similar concepts. An ordered list is grouped in order, by using an alphanumeric sequence.

**Lossy:** A compression format that removes or 'loses' certain areas to achieve a smaller file size, yet reopening the file causes the program to 'guess' at the missing data, possibly creating a lower-quality version.

**Low-resolution image:** A low-quality image with a low level of sharpness achieved by a lower amount of dots per inch. Used mainly for digital outcomes.

**LPI:** When printing halftones, such as in one-colour newspapers and reproductions, the lines per inch is the number of lines that compose the resolution of a halftone screen.

**Margin:** The usually blank space to the top, bottom and sides of a page between the trim and the live printing area. Headers, footers and page numbers are traditionally placed within this area.

**Market research:** The process of collecting and collating data from questionnaires, interviews and comments from the public regarding a concern, a problem or a possible solution.

**Matt:** A dull, non-shiny quality of paper, used for newspapers, for example.

**Measure:** The length of a line of text on a page, based on inches, centimetres, points or picas.

**Metaphor:** Word or image that sets up associations; for example, a 'piece of cake' is a metaphor for easy.

**META tags:** Elements within the HTML code, used by the search engines to properly index websites.

**Metrics:** The strategy for measuring the success – or failure – of a project's goals.

**Monetised:** Earned revenue from online marketing activities, such as banner ad placement.

**Navigation (breadcrumb):** A path-based navigation that identifies the user's location within the structure of a website.

**Navigation (drop-down):** A navigational element that is revealed when a visitor clicks a main navigational link to reveal related links (subsections) that are displayed below.

**Navigation (fly-out):** A navigational element that is revealed by extending out to the side of a main navigational element.

**Negative space:** The white or coloured area around an element, e.g. a margin of a page.

**Offset lithography:** The digitally produced printing plate is treated chemically so that the image will accept ink and reject water.

**Onomatopoeia:** In typography, the use of type to suggest the sounds of a spoken language, such as adding a large 'o' to the word 'open'.

**Opacity:** The transparency of a colour or tonal value measured in percent. The ability to edit the opacity of design elements means the designer can make images that can overlap and can be seen through.

**Optical adjustment:** Making adjustments to letterspacing by eye, not mechanically.

**Organic results:** Search engine results based on the natural appearance of keywords within a site dialogue.

**Ornaments:** Typed characters that embellish the page. Also known as flowers.

**Orphan:** The last line of a text paragraph appearing at the top of the next page.

**Overprint:** To print additional content or another colour over a previously printed image.

**Page plan/flatplan:** A document with a series of numbered thumbnails set out in an ordered grid that represents each page in a book.

**Panel:** Device used to highlight information. Also known as a sidebar.

**Pantone Matching System (PMS):** An international system to ensure reliable colour selection, specification and control.

**Paper grain:** The direction of wood fibres that make up a piece of paper.

**Patch:** The space on a bookshop's shelf occupied by spines of books from the same series.

**Path:** A drawn line in a design program, mathematically determined; also called a vector.

**PDF:** The Portable Document Format is a universal file format that can be viewed in a large amount of programs and browsers. Its reduced file size makes it useful for sending in emails and online.

**PEs:** 'Printers' errors' are mistakes and omissions found at the proofing stage by the designer or client that did not, for whatever reason, make it from the supplied file to the press. The cost of these errors is usually absorbed by the vendor as a matter of customer service.

**Perfect binding:** Method similar to paperback binding, where loose sheets are encased in a heavier paper cover, then glued to the book spine. Edges are trimmed to be flush with each other.

**Photomontage:** The assemblage of various fragments of photographs.

**Pixel:** Pixel images are made of small dots that are individually assigned a colour and that build up to make the bigger picture.

**Placeholder:** A temporary or low-resolution image in place of the high-quality counterpart during the design process.

**Plates:** Separate printing plates for separate colours that overprint to create colour images in four-colour offset printing.

**Plugin:** A WordPress term for an element that adds a functional enhancement to the basic CMS structure. Also referred to as widgets and modules.

**PNG:** A Portable Network Graphics format is used for lossless compression. The PNG format displays images without jagged edges while keeping file sizes rather small, making them popular on the web. PNG files are generally larger than GIF files.

**Poetic:** A style that is less clear, but more artistic, more open to interpretation.

**Point:** A dot on a page, such as a full-stop (.).

**Point size/pica:** The relative size of a font. There are 72 points in an inch.

**Positive space:** A form, image or word printed or formed on the page.

**PPI:** Pixels per inch or pixel density is interchangeable with DPI, but usually refers to the resolution of an unprinted image displayed on screen or captured by a scanner or digital camera.

**Primary colour:** Red, yellow or blue.

**Primary research:** Gathering material that does not pre-exist, such as photographing, drawing, making prototypes, interviewing people.

**Proof or prepress proof:** A complete mock-up using inks, overlays and other cheaper finishes to provide an idea of what the finished product should look like post-production.

**Proximity:** The relationship of one object to another.

**Quality control strip:** Usually incorporated in printed sheets outside the grid to monitor the quality of plate-making, inking and registration. Checking black sections helps point out colour casting.

**Quantitative:** Related to quantities of things, or measurements (numerical).

**Ragging:** When text is aligned left some words at the end of the lines might jut out further than the rest and cause uneven-looking paragraphs.

**Ranged (or ragged) left/ranged (or ragged) right:** Text that is aligned to a column or margin, either left or right.

**Raster:** Assemblages of pixels on a 2D grid system that can be viewed on computer screens or print media.

**Ream:** Standard quantity of paper; 500 sheets.

**Recto:** The right-hand page in a book.

**Registration marks:** Hairline marks at the corners of a printed page to help ensure plates are lined up correctly and designate what will be cropped off.

**Relief:** A printing process that uses a raised surface, such as letterpress.

**Repetition:** The repeated use of select design elements within the same composition.

**Repetition with variation:** The alteration of select aspects of a repeated element.

**Representation:** Something that looks like, resembles or stands in for something else. In drawing, this is also known as figurative, since it deliberately attempts to mimic the thing drawn.

**Resolution:** The clarity of a digital image. A low-resolution image (30dpi, for example) will have clearly visible pixels; a high-resolution image (300dpi, for example) will not.

**Responsive web design:** The content of a website layout is coded to reposition itself in response to the specific devices on which the website is being viewed.

**RGB (red, green, blue):** The colour system used to project colour on a computer screen. By combining these three colours a large percentage of the visible colour spectrum can be represented digitally.

**Rhetoric:** A style of arguing, persuading or engaging in dialogue. For a designer, it is a way of engaging the targeted audience.

**RODI:** Return on design investment indicates the success of a project in relation to the project's unique goals.

**Roll-over folds:** A way of folding a page so that successive folds turn in on themselves and the page is folded into a roll.

**Rotations:** The number of times that an animated GIF file will play, from the first frame to the last.

**Roughs:** Loose sketches for concept and compositional development that do not include fine detail.

**Saddle stitching:** Binding method where sheets of paper are folded in the centre, stitched together along the fold, then glued into the cover spine.

**Sans serif:** Without serif. Typefaces such as Univers, Helvetica, Aksidenz Grotesque and Futura, characterised by their lack of serifs. Predominantly associated with the 19th/20th centuries.

**Satin:** A form of paper between matt and gloss.

**Schematic:** Simplified diagram or plan related to a larger scheme or structure.

**Screen printing:** Method of printing that uses stencils.

**Screen resolution:** The resolution of a file that will be viewed on a screen is 72 pixels per inch (PPI). When designing for high-density displays, the document's dimensions should be doubled, not the resolution.

**Secondary colour:** A mix of any two primaries: orange, green or violet.

**Secondary research:** Gathering material that already exists, such as design work, colour samples, written texts, newspaper/magazine articles.

**Semantics:** The study of meaning in language and elsewhere.

**Semiotics:** A system that links objects, words and images to meanings through signs and signifiers.

**Serif:** Structural details at the ends of some strokes in old-style capital and lowercase letters.

**Shift-scheduling:** Allowing presses to run all day and night.

**Simultaneous contrast:** The human eye tends to differentiate between two neighbouring colours by emphasising their differences rather than their similarities – background colours affect foreground colours (the image).

**SLR:** Single lens reflex cameras use a viewfinder and mirrors so that the photographer's sightline goes through the main lens and results in a what-you-see-is-what-you-get image.

**Spot colour:** Any flat colour, like Pantone or Toyo colours, printed as a solid, and not made up of CMYK.

**Statistical:** Related to the collection, classification and organisation of (often numerical) information.

**Stock:** A generic form or type of paper, such as tracing paper or matt coated.

**Storyboard:** A document similar to a flatplan, but with a sequence of thumbnails that specifically lays out the narrative for a comic strip or film.

**Stress/axis:** The angle of the curved stroke weight change in a typeface. Seen clearly in letters such as 'o'.

**Style board:** A presentation of proposed website stylisations for review by a client, independent of the overall website structure.

**Subtractive colour:** System used in printing, based on CMYK colours.

**SVG:** Scalable Vector Graphics are vector image formats that provide support for interactivity and animation.

**SWF:** ShockWave Flash, the file extension format for displaying animated vector files on the web.

**Symbolism:** A way of representing an object or word through an image, sound or another word; for example, a crossed knife and fork on a road sign means a café is ahead.

**Symmetry:** A composition where elements are balanced or mirrored on a page.

**Syntax:** The study of the rules for the formation of grammatically correct sentences.

**Tag cloud:** A keyword-based navigation element on a website, where keywords can be selected in order to refine search criteria to display similarly themed posts.

**Taxonomy:** A way to group related content in a structural format.

**Theme:** A collection of predesigned web page layouts, designed around a centralised concept, where the arrangement of the page's structure has been specified by the theme's author.

**Thumbnail:** Small, rough visual representation of a bigger picture or final outcome.

**TIFF:** A Tagged Image File Format is a graphic file format used for storing images.

**Timeline:** The linear timeline in Animate and After Effects in which keyframes can be fixed in order to designate animated milestones in a production.

**Tool tips:** A message that displays when a user hovers with a mouse over a linked element.

**Type anatomy:** The language used to describe the various parts of letterforms.

**Typeface:** The set of visual attributes (design or style) of a particular group of letters: Garamond is a typeface.

**Typographic rules:** Printed lines that direct the reader's eye.

**Uniform Resource Locator (URL):** The address of a website.

**User interface (UI):** The space where humans interact with machines. It is a part of the larger user experience (UX) of a website or application.

**User experience (UX):** The experience a user has with a website.

**Varnish:** A liquid sprayed or spread onto paper to give it a hard-wearing surface so that printed ink stays intact.

**Vector graphics:** Shapes and lines built by algorithms, which will not reduce in quality when expanded or reduced in size.

**Verso:** The left-hand page in a book.

**Vibration:** Complementary colours of equal lightness and high saturation tend to make each other appear more brilliant, and cause the illusion of motion along the edges where they meet.

**WebGL:** Web Graphics Library uses JavaScript to render interactive graphics within any compatible web browser without the use of plugins.

**Web hosting:** A designated online storage space for hosting a website and related email accounts.

**Weight:** Colours differ in perceived 'weight'. It is generally assumed that blue-greens look lighter, whereas reds appear stronger, and therefore heavier.

**White space:** The open space surrounding a positive image that defines shape and directs hierarchy.

**Widgetised areas:** Locations within a CMS theme where plugins and widgets can be inserted into the physical layout. Typically, these are located within the side column and lower (footer) area of a web page.

**Wove/smooth:** A smooth, uncoated paper that is very porous (ink sits under the surface).

**x-height:** The height of a lowercase 'x' in any typeface.

**Zone Information Protocol (ZIP):** A means of compressing files into a smaller size, so they can be transferred digitally with ease.

# Bibliography

*Eye: The International Review of Graphic Design* (magazine)

J. Abbott Miller, Ellen Lupton, *Design Writing Research*, Phaidon Press Ltd

Philippe Apeloig, *Au Coeur du Mot (Inside the Word)*, Lars Müller

Phil Baines, *Type and Typography: Portfolio Series*, Laurence King

Gabriel Bauret, *Alexey Brodovitch*, Assouline

Russell Bestley, Ian Noble, *Visual Research: An Introduction to Research Methodologies in Graphic Design*, AVA Publishing

Michael Bierut, William Drenttel, Steven Heller, D. K. Holland *Looking Closer: Critical Writings on Graphic Design*, Allworth Press

Lewis Blackwell, *20th-Century Type: Remix*, Gingko Press

Robert Bringhurst, *The Elements of Typographic Style*, Hartley & Marks Publishers

Michael Burke, Peter Wilber, *Information Graphics: Innovative Solutions in Contemporary Design*, Thames & Hudson

Italo Calvino, *Invisible Cities*, Hyphen Press

Rob Carter, Ben Day, Philip Meggs, *Typographic Design: Form and Communication*, John Wiley & Sons

Stephen Coles, *The Geometry of Type: The Anatomy of 100 Essential Typefaces*, Thames & Hudson

David Crow, *Visible Signs*, AVA Publishing

Department of Typography, University of Reading, *Modern typography in Britain: graphic design, politics and society*, Hyphen Press

Geoffrey Dowding, *Finer Points in the Spacing and Arrangement of Type*, Hartley and Marks

Johanna Drucker, *Alphabetic Labyrinth: The Letters in History and Imagination*, Thames & Hudson

Johanna Drucker, *Figuring the Word: Essays on Books, Writing and Visual Poetics*, Granary Books

Johanna Drucker, *The Century Of Artists' Books*, Granary Books

Johanna Drucker, Emily McVarish, *Graphic Design History: A Critical Guide*, Prentice Hall

Kimberly Elam, *Grid Systems: Principles of Organising Type*, Princeton Architectural Press

Stephen J Eskilson, *Graphic Design: A New History*, Laurence King

Alan Fletcher, *The Art of Looking Sideways*, Phaidon Press Ltd

Friedrich Friedl, Nicolaus Ott, Bernard Stein, *Typography: An Encyclopedic Survey of Type Design and Techniques throughout History*, Black Dog & Leventhal Publishers Inc

E. M. Ginger, Erik Spiekermann, *Stop Stealing Sheep and Find Out How Type Works*, Adobe Press

Steven Heller, *Merz to Emigré and Beyond: Avant-Garde Magazine Design of the Twentieth Century*, Phaidon Press Ltd

Steven Heller, *Paul Rand*, Phaidon Press Ltd

Jost Hochuli, *Detail in Typography*, Hyphen Press

Jost Hochuli, Robert Kinross, *Designing Books: Practice and Theory*, Hyphen Press

Richard Hollis, *Graphic Design: A Concise History*, Thames & Hudson

Allen Hurlburt, *The Grid: A Modular System for the Design and Production of Newpapers, Magazines and Books*, John Wiley & Sons

David Jury, *Letterpress: The Allure of the Handmade*, Rotovision

Robin Kinross, *Modern Typography: An Essay in Critical History*, Hyphen Press

Robin Kinross, *Unjustified Texts: Perspectives on Typography*, Hyphen Press

Willi Kunz, *Typography: Macro and Microaesthetics, Fundamentals of Typographic Design*, Ram Publications

Ellen Lupton, *Thinking with Type: A Critical Guide for Designers, Writers, Editors and Students*, Princeton Architectural Press

Per Mollerup, *Marks of Excellence*, Phaidon Press Ltd

Lars Müller, *Josef Müller-Brockmann, Pioneer of Swiss Graphic Design*, Lars Müller Publishers

Joseph Müller-Brockmann, *Grid Systems in Graphic Design*, Niggli Verlag

Alan Pipes, *Production for Graphic Designers*, Laurence King

Norman Potter, *What Is a Designer: Things, Places, Messages*, Hyphen Press

Paul Rand, *A Designer's Art*, Yale University Press

Paul Rand, *Design, Form and Chaos*, Yale University Press

Paul Rand, *From Lascaux to Brooklyn*, Yale University Press

Ferdinand de Saussure, *Course in General Linguistics*, Books LLC

Adrian Shaughnessy, *How to be a Graphic Designer, Without Losing Your Soul*, Laurence King

Paula Scher, *Make It Bigger*, Princeton Architectural Press

Bradbury Thompson, *The Art of Graphic Design*, Yale University Press

Jan Tschichold, *The New Typography*, University of California Press

Jan Tschichold, *Asymmetric Typography*, Cooper & Beatty

Edward Tufte, *Envisioning Information*, Graphics Press

Edward Tufte, *The Visual Display of Quantitative Information*, Graphics Press

Edward Tufte, *Visual Explanations: Images and Quantities, Evidence and Narrative*, Graphics Press

Wolfgang Weingart, *My Way to Typography*, Lars Müller Publishers

## Online resources

http://www.aiga.org/
American Institute of Graphic Arts website, membership, programmes and events for graphic designers

http://www.baselinemagazine.com/
International typographics magazine, showcasing new typographic designs and opinions

http://www.coroflot.com/
Job searching and postings website for graphic designers

http://www.designobserver.com/
Online magazine dedicated to design and designers

http://www.eyemagazine.com/
Magazine blog exploring concepts and critique in visual communication

http://www.grainedit.com
Website focused on classic design work between the 50s and 70s, and contemporary designers who are inspired by that period

http://www.hyphenpress.co.uk/books
London publisher of design and typography books

http://www.istd.org.uk/
Society promoting typography and graphic design, annually holds student competitions

https://www.myfonts.com/WhatTheFont/
Online application to identify fonts

https://www.service-design-network.org
Platform for designers to connect and build contacts

http://www.spd.org/
The Society of Publication Designers

https://www.tdc.org/
Organisation promoting typography via competitions, events and membership

http://www.thedieline.com/
Website dedicated to package design

http://www.thersa.org/
Royal Society for the encouragement of Arts, Manufactures and Commerce website

http://www.typotheque.com/site/index.php
Large online collection of downloadable fonts

# Index

# Acknowledgments

© 2012 Johns Hopkins University, p.143c

© 2013 Apple Inc. All rights reserved, pp.21cr, 171cl

© 2013 Nike, Inc. All Rights Reserved, p.22tl

© 2013 The New York Times Company, p.149tr

© Christie's Images/Corbis, p.35t

© Design Bridge, www.designbridge.com, pp.7br, 9tc, 20cbl, 70b, 78t

© Frost* Collective, www.frostcollective.com.au, pp.6bmr, 20tr/cr/br, 44b, 46t/c/b, 47b, 56c/78, 128, 131cl/cr, 147br, 150, 164bl

Aloof, http://aloof.co, pp.48t, 79t, 167r

Bain, Kitch, Shutterstock.com, p.137bc

Beck, Krissy, Drexel University, pp.81bl, 95bl, 129tr

Bell, Vance, www.vancebell.com, p.177tl

Beltramo, Lauren, Drexel University, www.laurenbeltramo.com, p.85tl/tr, 129br

Bessermachen DesignStudio, design and packaging; Stiig Helgens Binggeli, Brandhouse, for archetypes and the idea, www.brandhouse.com, pp.100bl, 130t

Bloom, Jeremy, Drexel University, https://involvio.com, p.63t

Boca, Jermaine www.jermaineboca.com, p.181tc

Bowden, Amy, www.amybowdenportfolio.co.uk, p.57r

Bluehand, Shutterstock.com, pp.8br, 97cr

Brandient, www.brandient.com pp.92cl, 93bl, 100bc, 101br, 116tr, 117 , 154tl, 156, 164cl

Bridgeman Images, p.39b

Bright Pink Communication Design, p.160t/c

Bryant, Warren, www.wb94graphics.com, p.114

Carreras, Genis, www.studiocarreras.com, p.3bl

Chi, Jenny, Drexel University, pp.88cl/cr/bl/br

Chipp, Kidd, Knopf Publishing, pp.6bcl, 84

Coffey, Marcy Zuczek, www.wfgd.net, p.34c

Cohen, Shira, Drexel University, pp.44t, 95cr

Cook, Kyle, www.kyleacook.com, pp.9bl, 57bl

Courtesy of the Herb Lubalin Study Center at The Copper Union, p.178cr

Courtesy of The University of Michigan, Designer: Steif, Ariela, http://www.arielasteif.com, p.159t

Daredevil Creative, www.daredevil-creative.com, pp.115bc, 162, 164bcl, 166

Davies, Alice, www.alicedavi.es, p.47

DeMirjian, Brielle, Drexel University, p.129tl

Dickson, Oliver & Sølling, Kristoffer, www.oliverdickson.co.uk, www.kristoffersoelling.dk, p.59tl

Dillon, Hannah, Drexel University, www.hannahdillon.com, p.33

Dominiak, Katarzyna, www.katarzynadomiak.com, pp.101br, 151tl/cl

Edwards, Victoria, pp.63b, 83t, 85b

Elboreini, Engy, www.engyelboreini.com, p.115tc

Elliott, Steven, Drexel University, p.76b

Ellis, Hannah & Malfilatre, Stella Gelardi, www.hannahellis.co.uk, www.stellamalfilatre.com, p.104cl

Émigré, http://emigre.com, pp.7c, 39t, 69t/c

Evans, Sarah, www.sarahevansdesign.co.uk, p.183tr

Flynn, Megan, Drexel University, pp.50tr, 83cl

Foster, Rebecca, www.rebeccafosterdesign.co.uk, p.161t/c/b

Fox, Joseph, www.josephfox.co.uk, pp.103c/cr/bc, 105

Gallagher, Erika, Drexel University, www.impartcreative.com, www.erikagallagher.com, pp.71b, 95tr, 132-133t

Garrone, Pietro, www.pietrogarrone.com, p.135bc, br

Germano, Frank, Man on Fire Design, p.3l, 17tl/r/cr/bl/br, 37r

GINGERMONKEY, www.gingermonkeydesign.com, pp.9tl, 16t, 17tl, 55bl/br, 58b, 62t, 149tl

Goldberg, Carin, www.caringoldberg.com, pp.53bl/br, 68b

Graff, Jody, Jo to Go Design, p.94l

Grand Union Design, email: studio@grandu.co.uk, pp.28t, 29tl, 50tl, 51t

Graphic Evidence Ltd, www.graphicevidence.co.uk, pp.24tc/tr, 155tr

Greene, Rachael, Drexel University, p.71cr

Grundy, Peter, http://grundini.com/, pp.59tl, 85tr, 96tr

Gundelsberger, Caitlin, www.caitlin-g.com, Drexel University, pp.32t, 129bl

h2a s.a, www.h2a.lu, pp.43tl/r, 54bl/br, 59tr, 72t, 81t

Hale, Don, www.donhalephotos.com, p.149bl

Happy Cog, www.happycog.com, p.149cl

Haring Jr., Don, pp.18b-19b

Hart, Jennifer, Drexel University, www.jenniferhartdesign.com, p.97cl

Hince, Mike, www.mikehince.com, pp.7bl, 170b

Huerta, Gerard, www.gerardhuerta.com, p.69br

Huff, Priscilla, www.priscillahuff.com, pp.147t/cl/bl

HUGE, www.hugeinc.com, pp.58t/c/bc

Jaegal, Sun & Smith, Ryan www.hearthesun.com, www.ry-an.co.uk, p.104tc

Jia, Fan, Drexel University, p.91br

Langdon, John, www.johnlangdon.net, pp. 8tr, 36br, 38btr, 69bl

Lareau, Alexa, www.alexalareau.com, pp.8br, 25br

Laschenski, Caroline, www.carolinelaschenski.com, pp.6l, 42, 77t/b

LeBlanc, Miguel, www.wnartdesign.com, (Photos lesmaximes.ca), pp.2br, 182tr/cr

Leino, Jari, iStockphoto.com p.139tl

Lewandowski, Catherine, Drexel University, www.c-lewandowski.com, p.34tc

M.Gazarelli, Drexel University, p.68tr

Make Agency Limited Copyright 2016 ©, www.makeagency.co.uk, pp.3br, 167cl

Malfilatre, Stella Gelardi, www.stellamalfilatre.com, pp.101bc, 102tl/tr

Massarelli, Nicholas, Drexel University, p.116tl

Matter Strategic Design, www.matter.to, pp.131t/tcl/tcr/131b

Matthiesen, Kai Damian, www.kai-matthiesen.com, pp.2c, 116c/br

McCune, Sascha, Drexel University,www.sasha-em.com, p.83cr

McGhie, Helen www.helenmcghie.com (# 6 from the series Fitting Rooms, Helen McGhie, 2013), p.102

Moralba, April, Drexel University, p.95tr

Mortal Muses, www.mortalmuses.com, p.149cr

Morton, Katie, Drexel University, p.45tr/cr/br

Mortula, Luciano, Shutterstock.com, p.97br

Mousegraphics, www.mousegraphics.eu, pp.34tl/cl/bl/bcr/br, 39tl/cl/bl, 50b, 101cr, 133b, 134tr, 135t

Nicholson, Katie, http://katiedesign.wixsite.com/portfolio, p.111tc

Neumeister, http://neumeister.se, pp.52b, 56tl/tc/tr

Octavo Corp/Source Library, www.octavo.com, p.45b

OlegD, Shutterstock.com, p.136cl/br

Palmer Brewster, Toby, email: 1192tobybrewster@gmail.com, p.136cl/bl

Park, Ran, www.ran-park.com, pp.10t, 11tl/tc/tr/cl/r/bl/r

Patel, Chandni, www.chandnipatel.co.uk, pp.9bl, 13tl/tc/tr

Penmore, Rebecca, www.formlines.co.uk, p.174

Peric, Zak,https://www.behance.net/zakperic, https://vimeo.com/85708559, p.119tl/tr

Pestana, Joana, www.joanapestana.com, p.93bc/br

Potter, Kirsty, http://www.cargocollective.com/nogutsnoglory, p.13bl/br

Quevedo, Luis, http://www.behance.net/luiseq, pp.9br, 57br, 80c

Raisner, Evan, Drexel University, www.evanraisner.com, p.47tr/cr

Ray, Fever, p.63c

RedPoint Design Direction, Art Direction, Design & Illustration: Clark Most, Design: Joe Rivard, www.designdirection.com, p.6cr

Rhode, Mike, www.rohdesign.com, pp.144-145t

Rice Creative, Images shot by Arnaud De Harven, http://rice-creative.com, pp.6br, 9cr, 20tl/cl, 131cr

Robertson, Scott, p.146tl

Santos, Luis, Shutterstock.com, p.21tl

Sauvan, Vincent, www.vincentsauvan.co.uk pp.124tr, 163br

Scher, Paula, Pentagram Design, www.pentagram.com, pp.8bc, 69tr, 70t, 73t, 82b

SeanPavonePhoto, Shutterstock.com, p.97t

Segura, www.segura-inc.com, p.149br

Seimon, Holly, www.hollysiemon.com, p.15cr

Shine, Nyki, http://nykiforever.wix.com/portfolio, p.48bl/bc

Shutterstock, Inc p.177cr

SMACK | Creative Digital Studio, www.SMACKagency.com, p.49tl/cl/bl

Smith, Ryan, Design Museum, http://designmuseum.org, p.75cr

Soppelsa, Moreno, Shutterstock.com, pp.136tr, 137t

Stewart, Sandra, pp.3bc, 138

Summer Studio, www.summerstudio.co.uk, pp.135cr, 163tl/tc

Swanson, Theodor, www.theodorswanson.com, p.181bc

Todd, Sarah-Jayne, www.sarahjaynetodd.co.uk, pp.14bl/bc/br, 15bl/br

Vasily, Smirnov, iStockphoto.com, p.134bl

Vaughan, Alice p.173

Wan, Cheng, Drexel University, p.91bc

Warnham, Hayley, www.hayleywarnham.com, pp.22b, 112br

Website designed and built by The Web Kitchen, www.thewebkitchen.co.uk, p.180tc/tr

Weinstein, Brielle, Drexel University, p.80b

Willie, Mark, Mark Willie Design, www.markwilliegraphicdesign.com, p.82tl

Yee, Karen, Drexel University, http://karenlyee.tumblr.com, p.91bl

Yoon, Ted Hyunhak, hyunhakyoon.com (Photography by Hanggab Lee. Copyright © hyuhakyoon.com All Rights Reserved.hyunhak.yoon@gmail.com), p.92tc

All step-by-step and other images are the copyright of Quarto Publishing plc. While every effort has been made to credit contributors, Quarto would like to apologise should there have been any omissions or errors — and would be pleased to make the appropriate correction for future editions of the book.

With thanks to Zak Peric for his contribution to the article on Animate and After Effects, on pages 118–119, and for the assignment on page 123.